CALLAHAN LIBRARY
ST. JOSEPH'S COLLEGE
25 Audubon Avenue
Patchogue, NY 11772-2327

Teaching Ideas for 7–12 English Language Arts: What Really Works

Teaching Ideas for 7–12 English Language Arts: What Really Works

Patricia M. Gantt and Lynn Langer Meeks, Editors

Christopher-Gordon Publishers, Inc.
Norwood, Massachusetts

Credits

Every effort has been made to contact copyright holders for permission to reproduce borrowed material where necessary. We apologize for any oversights and would be happy to rectify them in future printings.

All student work used by permission.

Book Cover, *Wuthering Heights*, Bedford Critical Case Studies edition. Copyright ©1992 by Bedford/St. Martin's. Reprinted by permission of the publisher.

"Giving Voice to Middle School Writers" adapted from Hamblin, L. (September 2000). "Voices in the Junior High School Classroom: Lost and Found," *English Journal*, 90. Copyright © by the National Council of Teachers of English. Reprinted by permission.

Lourie, R. (1980). "What It's Like Living in Ithaca, New York," Anima. New York: Hanging Loose Press. Reprinted by permission.

Cruz, Victor Hernandez. "Problems With Hurricanes" from *Maraca: New and Selected Poems*. Copyright © 2001 by Victor Hernandez Cruz. Reprinted with the permission of Coffee House Press, Minneapolis, Minnesota.

Poem, "Bad Mother Blues" from *The God of Indeterminacy: Poems*. Copyright © 1993 by Sandra McPherson. Used with permission of the poet and the University of Illinois Press.

Poem. "We Real Cool" from *Selected Poems*. New York: HarperCollins. Copyright © 1999 by Gwendolyn Brooks. Reprinted by consent of Brooks Permissions.

Photograph of Ann Simpson, Retired Chairwoman, English Department, A. C. Reynolds High School, Asheville, NC. Reprinted in chapter, "Gatsby Galas and Elizabethan Extravaganzas: Cultivating Higher Order Learning and the Personal Intelligences," used with permission.

Copyright © 2004 by Christopher-Gordon Publishers, Inc.

All rights reserved. Except for review purposes, no part of this material protected by this copyright notice may be reproduced or utilized in any form or by any means, electronic or mechanical, including photocopying, recording, or in any information and retrieval system, without the express written permission of the publisher or copyright holder.

Christopher-Gordon Publishers, Inc.
1502 Providence Highway, Suite #12
Norwood, Massachusetts 02062
800-934-8322
781-762-5577

Printed in the United State of America
10 9 8 7 6 5 4 3 2 1   07 06 05 04

ISBN: 1-929024-71-1
Library of Congress Catalogue: 2003110767

To Tom and Norm

Contents

Acknowledgments xiii

Introduction xv

Part I. Prereading and Reading Approaches

Chapter 1. Cover Stories: Teaching the Material Book
    by Trish Travis 1
  Looking at the Covers 1
  Examining the Physical Text 2
  The Importance of Visual Analysis 2
  Pedagogy: From Concrete to Abstract 3
  Moving to Deduction 6
  Variations and Extensions 7
  Connections to Cultural Studies 12

Chapter 2. Prereading Strategies: Preparing Students for Difficult
    Texts and Concepts
    by Brian White 15
  The Importance of Prereading Preparation 16
  Why Prereading Activities Work 17
  Two Kinds of Prereading Preparation 17
  Prereading Opinionnaires 19
  Scenarios 21
  You Can't Be Serious 21

Chapter 3. Recipe for the Reluctant Reader: Add Reading
    Strategies to Young Adult Literature and Mix Well
    by Lu Ann Brobst Staheli 31
  A Discovery of No Surprise 31
  Variations on Successful Sustained Silent Reading Practices 32
  Read-Alouds 34
  Using Audio Books to Build Reading Skills 35
  The Advantages of Using Audio Books in the Classroom 35
  Literature Partners Increase Reading Engagement 37
  Literature Circles Give Reluctant Readers Support 37
  Schoolwide or Classroom Book Clubs Engage Reluctant Readers 38
  When Adults Model Reading, Reluctant Readers Take Notice 38
  Selecting Books for Reluctant Readers and for Avid Readers 39

Part II. Reading and Writing About Literature

Chapter 4. Flash Fiction and Luminous Pedagogy:
  Using Short-Short Stories to Teach Writing
    by Albert E. Wilhelm 45
  The Appeal of Short Fiction 46
  What Short Fiction Offers Teachers 46
  Using Flash Fiction to Write About Literature 47
  Working With a Specific Story 48
  Student Responses 49

Chapter 5. Using *The Bean Trees* to Develop an
  Engaged Community of Readers and Writers
    by Rebecca Woosley 51
  Developing Lifetime Readers 51
  Beginning *The Bean Trees* Reading Journals With a Twist 52
  Journal Entries as Formative Assessment 54
  Pigs in Heaven: The Prequel 55
  A Talk Show Provides Summative Assessment 55
  Why Use These Assignments? 57

Chapter 6. "You Would Pluck Out the Heart of My Mystery":
  A Close Reading of *Hamlet*
    by Paul Stein 59
  Narrowing the Focus 60
  The Assignment 60
  Possible Forms for the Report 61
  Specific Questions for Student Investigation 62
  Evaluations of Student Work 63
  Reflections and Benefits 64

Chapter 7. How to "Clone" a Poem
    by Agnes A. Cardoni 73
  Why Use Models to Teach Writing? 73
  The Assignment 74
  Reflections on the Advantages of the Clone-a-Poem Assignment 80

Chapter 8. Shakespeare Teaches Writing:
  Persuasive Speeches in *Henry V*
    by Brett C. McInelly 83
  The Rhetoric of Aristotle, the Rhetoric of Shakespeare 83
  Teaching Ethos, Pathos, and Logos Through *Henry V* 85
  The Dauphin's Insult 85
  The Scene at Harfleur 87

The Scene at Agincourt 89
What About Logical Appeal (Logos)? 91
Student Responses and Some Final Thoughts 92

Chapter 9. Giving Voice to Middle School Writers
    by Lynda Hamblin 95
Desperately Seeking a Definition 96
The Tribute Assignment 98
The Multigenre Research Paper Assignment 99
A Read and Retell Assignment 100
What I Think of This Class Right Now:
    An Audience-Voice Awareness Activity 101
Nature Observation and Poetry Assignment 102
Good News and Bad News 104

Chapter 10. "All Such Beautiful Sweet Things": An Expanded
    Definition of Literacy in the Poetry Writing Classroom
    by Scott Minar 107
Personal Definitions of Literacy 108
The Idea of Aesthetics 108
Understanding the Differences 109
How Aesthetics Affect Teaching 110
Bridging the Literacy Gaps 111
Techniques 111
Reflection 115

Chapter 11. Stokely Was Right: Writing August Wilson
    Into the High School Curriculum
    by Patricia M. Gantt 121
Introducing Writers Into the Curriculum 122
Overview of Research Findings 122
Solutions to Particular Issues 123
What We Learned 126

Chapter 12. Graduation Time for the
    Literary Analysis Paper
    by Danette DiMarco 131
A Real-World Assignment 132
Facilitating the Case (Materials and Methods) 132
Analysis of Key Subjects (Discussion of Data) 135
Analysis of Key Subjects (Reflections on Data) 140
Student Response 140

Part III. Projects and Pedagogy

Chapter 13. Gatsby Galas and Elizabethan Extravaganzas:
  Cultivating Higher Order Learning and the Personal Intelligences
  by Kimberly R. Myers 145
  Bloom and Gardner: A Pedagogical
    Rationale for the Gatsby Gala 146
  Demonstrating the Intelligences 147
  Emphasizing the Personal Intelligences 147
  How the Gatsby Gala Honors All Intelligences 148
  Students Laud the Gatsby Gala 149
  Extending the Project to Other Grades and Eras 150
  Benefits to School and Community 151

Chapter 14. The American Museum Project
  by Jeff House 163
  Coming Up With a New Teaching Plan 164
  Background for Student Work 164
  Project Structure: Our Six Stages of Learning 165
  Advantages of Project Learning:
    Student-Teacher Reflection 168

Chapter 15. Survivor, the Literary Edition: A Suggestion
  for Concluding a Literature Class
  by Elizabeth Teare 177
  Survivor: The Literary Edition 177
    Who Survives? 180
  Student Responses to Literary Survivor 180
  Variations on Survivor: The Literary Tradition 182
  Students Write Their Own Concluding Lectures 182
  Beyond Survivor: Practical Applications 183

Chapter 16. Empowering Students With Portfolios
  by Darren Perkes 185
  Resistance to Reading 185
  Effective Portfolio Criterion No. 1:
    Teaches and Assesses Learning Objectives 186
  Effective Portfolio Criterion No. 2:
    Demonstrates Student Voice 188
  Effective Portfolio Criterion No. 3: Archives Student Work 190
  Effective Portfolio Criterion No. 4: Organizational Strategy 191
  Effective Portfolio Criterion No. 5: Student Reflection 193
  Outcomes 195

Charter 17. Poetic Drama: Breathing Life Into Poems and Poets
   by Carol F. Bender 197
   Using Poetic Drama 197
   Revamping the Course 199
   Creative Student Performance 199
   Impact on the Course 200
   Grading Performance 201
   Benefits for Students 202

Chapter 18. Powerful Poetry: Team Teaching
      Across the Disciplines
      by Annette McGrew and Ginny Dochety 205
   Planning the Lesson 206
   Learning and Adjusting 206
   Reflections on Student Learning 207
   Authentic Assessment 208
   The Teamwork Aspect 208

Chapter 19. Collaborative Nonfiction Unit: *Freedom's
      Children* and the Civil Rights Movement
      by Terri Rodriguez 213
   Freedom's Children and the Civil Rights Movement 213
   Forced-Choice Activity 214
   Comparison-and-Contrast Activity 214
   Using Films and Documentaries 215
   Interview: Making the Past Real 215
   Choral Reading: "The Ballad of Birmingham" 216
   Reading *Freedom's Children* 216
   Final Project: Rationale and Assessment 217

Chapter 20. Challenging "Frontal Teaching":
      How to De-center the Classroom
      by Heidi Estrem 225
   Rethinking Classroom Space:
      A Reformed Conductor's View 225
   Teaching With My Mouth Shut 226
   Stations Defined 227
   Using All Four Walls: Station Work Works 228
   Stations for Prewriting 228
   Stations for Poetry 230
   Revision Invitation Stations 231
   "Tricking Me Into Writing":
      Students' Perspectives on Station Work 233

Traveling Within the Classroom:
   Geography and Location Revisited 234

Chapter 21. Using Technology to
   Handle the Paper Load
     by Christine A. Hult 239
The Paradigm Shift in Writing
   Assessment: A Brief Overview 239
Portfolio Assessment Meets Computers 240
Computers Help To Manage the Paper Load 240
Handling the Paper Load: Course Management
   and Word Processing Systems 243
Electronic Homework Manager 245
No More Handwritten Comments 246

Chapter 22. Carnival in the Classroom: Bakhtin
   and My Search for Democracy
     by Jonathan Segol 251
Classroom Democracy: Possibility or Failure? 251
What I Wanted for My Students 252
Tools for Synthesis: Mikhail Bakhtin 252
Critiquing the Teacher 254
Students As Teachers 254
Further Tools for Synthesis: Crazy Eddie 256
Violating Contracts as Carnivalized Moments 256
Positive Changes: Evaluating Student Outcomes 256

Index 263

Author Biographies 267

Acknowledgments

This book would not have been possible without the supportive work of several individuals: Sue Canavan and Jamie Gisonde, our editors at Christopher-Gordon; our reviewers, who were first to express their enthusiasm; Christine Hult, who steered us through the byways of book production; the Utah State University English Department, a supportive group of colleagues and friends; our many contributors and their students, who were patient and creative always; and our husbands, who are forever in our corner.

Introduction

When we were beginning teachers, we looked around at all our talented peers, so full of creativity and dynamism, and thought, "If only we could get this group of premier teachers together and start our own school. What collegiality! What a wonderful learning experience we could ensure for our students!" The exciting concept of classrooms where student successes come tumbling one over the next is a goal that we have worked hard to achieve throughout the 72 years of our combined teaching experience. If you are holding this book in your hands, that goal is probably one that you share.

This book and its companion volume, *Teaching Ideas for University English: What Really Works* (2004), began simply because we were looking for more ways to nurture student success in our classrooms. For us, any book that offered practical teaching innovations or methods for presenting standard works through new strategies was sure to find its way onto our bookshelves. Far too often, however, we used a book for three or four ideas—sometimes just one—dog-earing a single section while the rest of the text remained pristine.

Once again we thought of our dream schools of so long ago: What if all the ideas in a volume were those created by award-winning English teachers? What if each one were classroom tested rather than merely a philosophical concept created in a vacuum? Although there are numerous books available that offer teaching ideas, we could not find one that presented those strategies exclusively from teachers who had won awards—not for grants or publications or community service, but for their actual face-to-face instruction with students across a wide spectrum of grades and learning abilities.

This book is a collection of practical teaching ideas from such a winning group of master teachers. Although some of them are now working at the university level, where they are involved in secondary teacher education, they have drawn on present or past experience to share lessons that have repeatedly been successful with students in grades 7–12. In each chapter the author explains the impetus for instructional change or a rationale for a particular classroom practice, gives the context in which it has been taught, details procedures for teaching (including any appropriate charts or handouts), provides examples of student responses and—where appropriate—how their work was assessed, and concludes with reflection by teachers and students.

The sections of the book are anchored around three key ideas: prereading and reading strategies, writing about literature, and projects and pedagogy. It is difficult to separate out chapters about writing or literature into a neat focus on each, because—as every experienced teacher knows—the two are not distinct categories, but are systemically linked. Educators realize increasingly that the literature we require our students to read is inherently a model for the writing we ask them to do. Furthermore, there are few chapters on writing per se. We have found numerous helpful books that guide us in teaching writing, but not enough that help our students to develop the thinking and analysis that provide the foundation for writing. That is what we set out to do, and that, we believe, is what the majority of this book is about.

Part I, "Prereading and Reading Approaches," begins with Trysh Travis's techniques for teaching literature through a close reading of book covers, both for what they indicate about standard literary approaches and for what they reveal about ourselves as readers and holders of definite cultural expectations. Her first sentence is key to the practices detailed in the remainder of the book—"Like so many of my best ideas, this one actually came from my students." Brian White and Lu Ann Brobst Staheli give us prereading strategies and ways to engage reluctant readers, including the use of audio books.

Part II, "Reading and Writing About Literature," covers a wide range of teaching strategies, from Albert E. Wilhelm's demonstration of how a close reading of a brief piece of fiction provides tools for investigating longer works to Danette DiMarco's strategies for re-visioning the research paper as a correlative to a celebration of graduation. Additional chapters in this section illustrate methods for teaching classic works in new ways (Paul Stein and Brett C. McInelly), using poetry as a bridge to writing (Agnes A. Cardoni and Scott Minar), developing voice in middle school writers (Linda Hamblin), and using or introducing contemporary writers at the secondary level (Rebecca Woosley and Patricia M. Gantt).

Part III, "Projects and Pedagogy," encourages us to extend the ways in which we ask students to demonstrate their learning. It also invites us to think about our own pedagogy and how we might alter it for greater student learning. Whether we want to model a student project on Kimberly R. Myers's literary extravaganzas, on Jeff House's museum visits, or on Elizabeth Teare's modification of *Survivor*, there are many innovative strategies for us to duplicate or adapt for our classrooms. Both Darren Perkes's "Empowering Students With Portfolios" and Carol Bender's "Poetic Drama: Breathing Life Into Poems and Poets" suggest alternative ways of assessing student learning. Two chapters, those by Terri Rodriguez and Annette McGrew and Ginny Dochety, illustrate how we compound successes when we join with colleagues in other disciplines—in their cases, history and keyboarding—to integrate subject matter. Heidi Estrem gives a rationale and method for decentering the classroom with activity stations, a method secondary teachers can beneficially adapt from their elementary peers. Now that we have all these lesson ideas, Christine A. Hult shares a valuable method for keeping up with student work in the concluding chapter, "Using Technology to Handle the Paper Load." Jonathan Segol's concluding chapter leaves us with an application of literary theory to classroom pedagogy, one that promises higher levels of enfranchisement for all our students.

In *The Courage to Teach: Exploring the Inner Landscape of a Teacher's Life* (1998), Parker J. Palmer describes what teaching is like when palpable, dynamic learning takes place in the classroom:

> I am a teacher at heart, and there are moments in the classroom when I can hardly hold the joy. When my students and I discover uncharted territory to explore, when the pathway out of a thicket opens up before us, when our experience is illumined by the lightning-life of the mind—then teaching is the finest work I know. (p. 1)

As the combined creativity and wisdom of the teachers and students represented here demonstrate, teaching is and always will be fine work. We hope this volume will help other instructors to duplicate their levels of joyous success.

Part I

Prereading and Reading Approaches

1

Cover Stories: Teaching the Material Book

Trysh Travis

Like so many of my best ideas, this one actually came from my students. I stumbled on it quite by accident, early in my career. The year in question I was a very young high school teacher; on this specific day, my frustration level was unusually high. Over our recent break I had assigned my ninth graders the first chapter of *Native Son* by Richard Wright, and now, on the first day back from vacation, I could tell from ambient hallway chitchat that almost no one had read it.

The fact that I hadn't exactly devoted my break to preparing to teach it, as I had planned, only made me more exasperated. To add to my vexation, the bookstore was selling both paperback editions of the novel: the old Harper Perennial reprint of the 1940 edition, and the new Library of America version, newly printed from Wright's final typescript. While I was eager to talk about the textual variations between the two editions, I was frustrated by the considerable differences in layout and pagination, anticipating a chaotic chorus of "What page are you on?" every time I wanted to discuss a specific passage. My unrest only increased as I settled into my seat—the students, giddy after the holiday, seemed unusually committed to bluffing their way through the hour, mocking the cover art of one another's books and attempting to draw me into their amateur art history diatribes.

Looking at the Covers[1]

The difference between the covers was striking. The 1940 edition featured an impressionistic dark face in three-quarter profile against a dark background, with the author's name and the title in 1970s modern lettering, the writing underscored by slashes of green and orange. The new edition had a bright, bold cover, featuring a black line drawing of a man's face framed by panels of red and green and dappled here and there with red spots. The facial features were clearly African American, but the face itself was purple. The author and title appeared in a heavy, black, somewhat irregular font. I was intrigued enough by the differences between the images to be drawn into my students' debates.

It is likely that my own underpreparation made me a less rigid teacher that day, but perhaps those students were also unusually prescient. The boisterous fragments of "Your cover is wack!", "Well, yours is boring!", "That guy looks crazy!", and "Not crazy—just stupid!" precipitated "Cover Stories," a lesson that uses the visual, material object of the book itself as a way into discussing literature. Our conversation about the covers of *Native Son* gradually grew less rowdy, but it never lost any energy. The students' candid, animated commentary on the illustrations and design flowed easily and naturally, and by the end of the class period they all seemed genuinely interested in what kind of novel might in fact lie beneath the pictorial interpretations they had just discussed. I remember it as one of my best teaching days.

Examining the Physical Text

After that experience, I began regularly to incorporate an examination of the physical book into my lessons. When I entered graduate school a few years later, that goof-off day with my ninth graders flowered into a whole area of study as I encountered the field of book history, an interdisciplinary kind of scholarship that focuses not simply on a literary text but on historically situated readers, the material object of the book, and the political economy within which they encounter each other. Now, teaching at the university level, I build the insights of book history into my courses in a variety of ways.

"Cover Stories" remains one of the most discrete and focused strategies I have found for bringing historical and material questions to bear on the study of texts. I present it here as a class-period-long lesson—equally appropriate for high school or postsecondary learning—a good starting point for or corollary to traditional literary instruction. I go on to suggest a variety of ways to expand its method and insights into writing and research assignments that depart from a narrowly textual notion of "English" and thus suggest the richness and complexity of the literary culture within which texts are created, circulated, and interpreted. By giving students the tools to understand how literary value is constructed through social institutions, political hierarchy, and cultural power, we can turn what is often an aimless rhetorical gripe—the grudging "Why do we have to read this?"—into a serious intellectual inquiry.

The Importance of Visual Analysis

Students today live in a visual rather than a print culture. There are exceptions, of course, but for the most part, students seem more comfortable and fluent with images occurring in simultaneous time than with the linear unspooling of verbal information. An English class shouldn't cave into this fact; quite the contrary, I believe it's my duty to move students out of their comfort zone of advertisements, TV, and the Internet and into the orderly flow of narrative that unfolds in time. That said, I still try to take the visual orientation of students' lives seriously. "Cover Stories" is a way to do that, and it offers a segue into the print world from a place where the students are fluent and comfortable. In addition, it is a form of analysis that runs perfectly parallel to standard literary interpretation, and it can help to reinforce the basic analytical skills of close reading for students who are by nature visual learners. Attention to the visual elements of an assigned book can be a way for a wide range of students—English as a second language (ESL) students, nonmajors, and those whose skills are not yet strong—to shine; their success with the elements of cover design can invite them to succeed in similar, more traditional literary tasks.

This chapter breaks down and codifies the spontaneous intellectual exchange that took place over the *Native Son* covers. In it, I talk about how to get students to take their casual observations about a book's cover art and elaborate them into a serious critical rubric. This involves, first, identifying the individual visual elements in a piece of cover art, and, second, abstracting or extracting from those elements a larger, more complex meaning. The mental process by which we make sense out of pictures is usually unconscious, and we therefore pay little attention to it. It is worth drawing attention to, however, because it parallels the act of close reading and analyzing passages from literature, and thus reinforces the skill set in play in the average English class.

The basic version of "Cover Stories" focuses on cover illustrations, but it can be elaborated further to include the textual as well as the visual material present in a book's design: author and publisher names, critical blurbs, plot summaries, and pricing, publication, and ISBN information. These provide useful and almost universally overlooked ways into understanding the world within which literature—so often served up by English classes as an isolated, naturally occurring phenomenon—actually exists. Finally, I offer ways to take the observational habits developed by "Cover Stories" further, suggesting research assignments that send students back into history or forward into the commercial culture within which they live but which they rarely question.

A final caveat: In this chapter I talk frequently about students who do and don't do a variety of things; who possess, lack, and aspire to a variety of skills. I am generalizing here from my own experiences in the classroom, which may vary considerably from those of others. I have had students whose skills are weak, and others who seem infinitely more adept than I was at their age. Some are ambitious, others are complacent; some long for a life of the mind and delight in language, others want to have decent-paying jobs and never look at printed matter more complex than *TV Guide* again. I would be lying if I didn't admit that those who were interested in language and literature were somehow closer to my own heart, but I try to teach the whole range of abilities and ambitions, neither forcing an intellectual agenda on my students, nor pandering to them. "Cover Stories" is one attempt to do that.

Pedagogy: From Concrete to Abstract

Abstraction is a real challenge in most of my classes. The best students want to move immediately to it; the weakest students, too, feel that they are supposed to be thinking "deep" thoughts—this is an English class, after all. Big ideas, I try to convince them, are only as good as the foundation of the small details on which they rest. One of the most difficult aspects of teaching, I think, is making students slow their thought processes down sufficiently to realize that their most abstract ideas *come from* concrete facts. Another hard task is convincing them that if they want their big ideas to stay "big"—that is to say, interesting to the readers of their papers, original, and useful—they need to shore them up with carefully processed and articulated concrete facts.

In their daily lives, students—like all of us—perform this process of abstraction thousands of times a day, taking only microseconds to process information and arrive at judgments. Asking a group of heterosexual female students to explain why Matt Damon is "a hottie" will elicit a rush of fact statements about eyes, hair, smile, and fit of jeans. The same experiment can be performed on colleagues. The question "How was the department meeting?" will provoke a similar and equally animated gush of information and anecdote, which, when abstracted, produces the adjective *boring*.

When we ask students to do analytical work in class, we are asking them merely to formalize and record a process that they perform naturally and unconsciously every day. Why, then, does it seem so hard for them? A close reading assignment denaturalizes an artless process: Students are forced to slow down their thought processes and to record the details that usually swirl by in a gestalt of meaning. Not only does working at such a slow speed feel awkward, but the objects of close reading in an English class (unlike, for instance, Matt Damon) can be foreign and, in many ways, off-putting. The power dynamics of the classroom compound this; there must be right answers, students believe, and that makes things a little scary. As a result, retrieving the accumulated sensory details that naturally and inevitably precede the abstraction of judgment begins to seem difficult. Students get stuck at the level of meaning, and can't tell you how they got there. The last paragraphs of *The Great Gatsby*, for instance, seem sad because, as one of my students memorably said, "There's a feeling of sadness in the words."

I think I have pulled off a great teaching trick when I get students to realize that close reading is not some foreign voodoo but in fact just a ritualized, stylized, slightly more in-depth version of a kind of thinking that they unconsciously do every day. Even once they are convinced of this fact, however, close reading still remains very difficult. It involves slow, methodical, informed labor with *words*—work of a nature and kind that is foreign in the lives of many students today. I address this problem in my literature classes by assuming the persona of "The Modifier Police" (complete with hat) and roughing up students like the hapless *Gatsby* reader: "Tell me the nouns in the passage that suggest or connote 'sadness.'" "Show me every verb that indicates that Winterbourne's actions in pursuit of Daisy Miller are 'desperate.'" My good cop–bad cop routine forces students back into a text's language, where they have to reckon with the connotations and denotations of words—the basic but often overlooked building blocks of literary meaning.

Nevertheless, one can stomp around the room in a police captain's hat shouting, "Give me the nouns!" only so often without seeming insane. "Cover Stories" allows me to repeat the same fundamental skills lesson—moving back and forth along the continuum of abstract and concrete in order to emphasize the relationship between the two—in a completely different guise. Analyzing the visual material of a book's cover, students make the same moves, in the same sequence, that they do when close-reading a passage. First there's a rush to judgment; then, more reluctantly, a rounding up of details in support of that judgment, and, finally, an informed revision of the original judgment. Looking at the cover makes everything seem a little weird—they are not used to looking closely at pictures in an English class. Talking about pictures appears to be easy. There are no "right" answers about what the cover means because, after all, it's just the cover and the *real* book is inside. Therefore, they are more willing to slow down, to break down their own thought processes, and to be willing, as the math teachers say, to "show their work" as they backtrack from the meaning of the image. The basic structures, then, of reading a cover are the same as those employed in reading a passage; that is why "Cover Stories" is a useful lesson even in a very traditional English class.

If the structures of reading are the same for covers and texts, however, the units of meaning within those readings are different. In developing "Cover Stories," I have relied heavily on art historian Jules Prown's approach to the analysis of material culture (1982), synthesized in his article "Mind in Matter." Prown argues that "Objects made or modified by man reflect, consciously or unconsciously, directly or indirectly, the beliefs of individuals who made, commissioned, purchased, or used them" (pp. 1–2). Students rarely think of the host of individuals who lie behind the man-made object of the book; the author biography may receive their attention, but the work of editors, designers, reviewers, and marketers usually goes on below their radar.[2] Nevertheless, these workers play a significant role in making the book what it is. Their "beliefs" about a text's meaning and value, as Prown notes, are embodied in the material book. Those beliefs intersect with and influence our own interpretations of it.

Prown lays out a three-part structure for reading-material culture artifacts. First comes *observation*, the cataloguing of visual facts. This is followed by *deduction*, the intellectual and emotional interpretation of those facts. Finally comes *speculation*, the "creative imagining . . . that might explain the various effects observed and felt" (p. 10). Clearly, this process parallels that of literary close reading, working upwards and outwards from concrete details to abstract interpretations. I try to attend rigorously to this three-stage schema when reading covers in class. Doing so fosters participation—students who lack high conceptual knowledge or sophisticated English vocabulary can still confidently observe and name pictorial elements. More important, observing the differences among the three modes of thinking draws attention to the fact that they are not all of a muddled piece; they are discrete, specific mental activities that need to work in sequence, to build on one other. The quasi-Brechtian alienation effect brought on by looking at a picture in an English class seems to make this clear to students.

Periodically, as we work through Prown's stages, I will point out the similarity between what we're doing in a given moment and what we do when close-reading texts.

The observation stage involves noting and naming pictorial and design detail on the front cover of the book.[3] Prown espouses a strict order for treating the various elements of an artifact (e.g., type of paper, ink, bindings), but I have found that it is nearly impossible to do this and still keep the participatory energy of the class. I do, however, try and treat issues of illustration (the artwork) and of cover design (placement of title and author's name) separately, postponing for later consideration the relationship between the two elements.

First looking at artwork, then, I ask students to *look at the cover in terms of its shapes and figures*. Are they recognizable and pictorial, or abstractions? If recognizable, what are they? Things must be named in the simplest, most concrete, least evaluative terms. At this point, I begin to construct an ad hoc chart on the board and scribble down student responses—"a human figure," "a house," "an empty street"—as they are called out. (Once students have caught on to the act of stripping away judgments from details, they will correct each other—"How can you tell that's 'a house'? All you can really tell is that it's 'a building.'") From there we move to *questions about scale and position within the picture plane*. What are the relationships among the elements? What elements are foregrounded, backgrounded, cut off, or marginalized? What is detailed, and what is left blurry or shadowed? Questions of material are important, too. The cover image is, of course, a mass-produced print, but *what were the original materials in which it was rendered*? Is it painting, photography, collage, or a drawing? How were the materials used? How can you tell?

Moving to Deduction

This cataloguing process takes considerable time and, typically, a great deal of chalkboard space. Only when we have exhausted our cataloguing, however, can we move on to Prown's second stage, deduction, which "involves the empathetic linking of the object with the perceiver's world of existence and experience" (p. 8). Now students can begin to abstract from their observations to interpretations, or, to put it another way, to move from nouns to modifiers. Personal, subjective, emotional responses can now be usefully discussed because the hard evidence of what compels those responses has been named and noted. Students are justified in saying that the "empty street" is a "scary street" because on the board we have chronicled a host of pictorial facts that connote anxiety: grays and blacks predominate; there is much shadow and little light; buildings on each side rise up and close off the sight lines; garbage is strewn in the gutters, suggesting that the street is infrequently used; a hard vanishing point places the viewer within a constricted space.

Deduction is the beginning of interpretation, and because this is interpretation grounded in carefully accumulated fact, it is usually interesting. The conversation can become sophisticated quite rapidly. Working with the new edition of

Native Son, details like "fingerpainted—can see the paint blotches," "interior color overlaps thick outlines," "black borders with cutouts and notches," and "prominent African American features" yielded deductions like *primitive, harsh, childish, powerful,* and *Afrocentric*. In the deductions stage, students are still talking about the artwork, but they are beginning to imagine a reading of the text as well.

At this point I typically remind them that the cover represents the artist's and the designer's interpretations of the text, their expressions through images of what they think the book is about. This allows us to segue into the third level of Prown's analysis, speculation, and I invite the students to imagine, based on the artist's interpretation that they've just looked at, what they think the book will be about. Prown stresses that at the speculative stage "what is desired is as much creative imagining as possible, the free association of ideas and perceptions tempered only, and then not too quickly, but the analyst's common sense and judgment as to what is even vaguely possible" (p. 10). Accordingly, even the most off-the-wall and downright smart-aleck comments can become extremely useful here. In the *Native Son* class, one student shouted out that the book would be about a "primitive, harsh, childish, powerful, Afrocentric man!"—not an inaccurate assessment. Another student, whose major observation had been to point out that the face on the cover was purple, sarcastically suggested that the book would be about the importance of being the wrong color. A more thoughtful, imaginative comment on the *Native Son* cover built on the relationship among the pictorial elements, suggesting that the book might be about a big man who feels boxed in; another student elaborated on this reading to wonder if the red splotches in the box alongside the face might be blood.

When they read on their own, students—like almost everyone else in the world—typically read for the plot. To a certain extent, this focus disables their critical faculties; they are moved passively along by the momentum of the narrative. I typically conclude my "Cover Stories" class by asking the students to jot down on the inside covers of their books a brief speculation of what they think the text in question will be about, and urge them to keep that speculation in their minds as they read. This activates their reading, giving them specific issues, patterns, and images to look for as they are borne along by the current of plot. The gaps and overlaps between their initial speculations and their later readings can become fodder for papers or exam questions, as well as enrichment for further class discussion.

Variations and Extensions

What I've outlined above is my standard, basic version of "Cover Stories." While it relies heavily on Jules Prown's method, it in no way exhausts the potential for the study of the material book. In fact, in its exclusive attention to the pictorial element of cover design, it ignores many of the physical features that reveal the circumstances in which books are designed, constructed, and circulated. Later I will look briefly at these elements and suggest some ways to bring them up for discussion in class, and to evaluate and develop the ideas they spark.

First, however, I want to touch on some variations on the standard lesson I described above.

While the contemporary cover illustration—designed and executed by professional artists with a specific text in mind—is the type of cover that most easily prompts useful speculations about the text itself, classic covers are also interesting and fun to discuss. There are two types of classic covers, both common in reprint series designed for the classroom. The first relies on a nonpictorial design, whereas the second features well-known artwork of the same period, theme, and/or culture as the text it enfolds. Although both images can be technically rich, their nuances may be difficult to detect because they are small-scale reproductions. In addition, it can be difficult for students to feel confident drawing connections between the text and the cover image, because they are aware that the latter is "just" artwork, something that exists separately from and bears no necessary connection to the text onto which it has been placed.

I finesse this difficulty by assigning interpretive agency not to the artist but to the book designer (a task made easier when that person receives a credit somewhere in the jacket copy). Introducing the idea of conscious design and packaging allows students to think about other, nonpictorial elements of design that typically accompany classic covers. These include the ratio of art to wording on the cover; the relative sizes of author, editor, and publisher names as well as text and series titles; and the presence of uniform colors, motifs, and other design elements that repeat throughout a series, including colophons, border styles, and insignia. In addition, the back jacket copy of most classic covers prominently features not only an artist credit but also a museum credit. Like the image itself, these elements frame and interpret the book even though they aspire to transparency.

Students are ever attuned to power plays, however, and they will quickly pick up on the ways in which classic cover design is meant to convey a rarified notion of literary value, one distinct from the pleasures of mere "beach reading." Again, observation of concrete details leads to insightful critiques—if not of the text per se, then certainly of the literary apparatus that upholds it. The Bedford Critical Case Studies edition of *Wuthering Heights* (Figure 1-1) figures the title in white rather than black type, larger than any of the other words, and positioned above all the other cover elements. Noting these details, a student commented that the design suggested, "You're already supposed to have heard about this book and to kind of know what it's about. They don't need to be explaining or selling it."

Figure 1-1. *Wuthering Heights* Bedford Critical Case Studies Edition

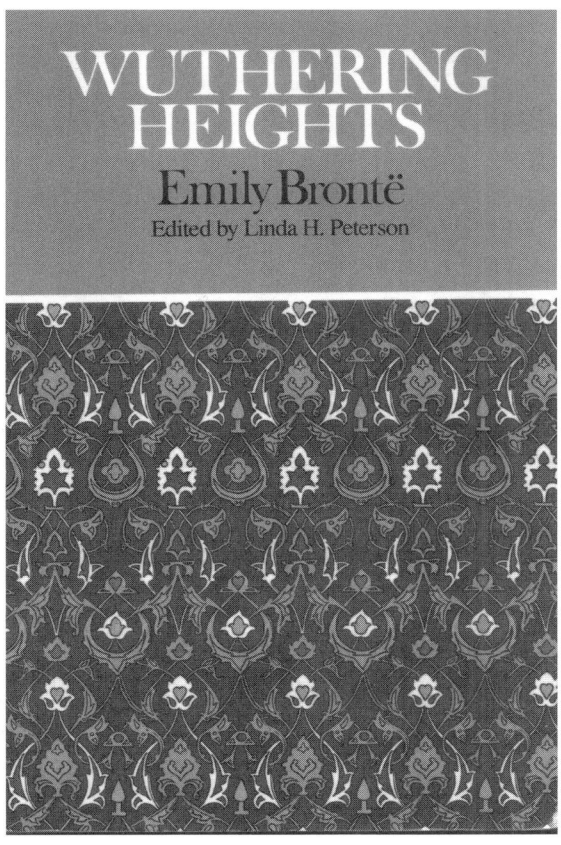

Similarly, in a discussion of the Collier trade edition of Edith Wharton's *The Age of Innocence*, which features a detail from James Whistler's *Symphony in White #2*, a student observed, "The lacy dress, tasteful jewelry, antiques, and fresh flowers suggest that the woman is rich. She's standing by a mirror, so maybe she's like a mirror of the characters in the book, or maybe [a mirror of how] the people who read it are, or want to be."

Another student wrote the following about the back cover of the Penguin Classics *Heart of Darkness* by Joseph Conrad:

> The plot description is in very small writing, with lots of long sentences, and compares the book to other books by "famous" authors. The word "classics" appears twice. Combined with the totally uninteresting picture of an old boat on the front [a detail from Hans' *The Steamer Stanley*], this tells the reader it's a book only for people who like reading.

Observations like these are excellent points for metatextual discussions or writing assignments. In a time when "the culture wars" have raged all over the media as well as in the classroom, students are keenly aware of the fact that institutional power dynamics shape what they will read in classes. They are also aware of, and often troubled by, the fact that their own reading pleasure tends to clash with what they are taught is "great" literature and "good" reading. Consideration of the extrapictorial elements of classic editions creates a way for them to begin to name and assess the literary-critical power structure that has shaped their lives as students, and invites them to consider critically their own relationship to it. One student of mine admitted that she liked the delicate colors and larger format of the Collier trade *Age of Innocence* by Edith Wharton, because it stood out from the "fat books" with "lots of gold and raised letters" that other young women read around the pool.

Similar questions about literary value, the hierarchy of taste, and the relationship of "great" literature to popular culture can be raised through an exploration of the movie tie-in cover. There is almost always an obliging highbrow in the class who will talk at length about how he or she went out of the way to buy any edition *but* the one graced by the movie still, so a comparison of different editions happens naturally. Unlike the floral-framed, contemplative portrait of the trade *Age of Innocence*, the Collier mass-market edition, released to coincide with the Martin Scorsese film, features a graphic clinch between stars Michelle Pfeiffer and Daniel Day-Lewis. A comparison of the two images—one "highbrow," one "popular"—raises useful questions about whether art has a life apart from the commodity realm of the popular.

What I have described thus far is, by and large, an approach to talking about the material book in the classroom. These insights can be taken further through research assignments that explore more fully both the history of book production, circulation, and consumption and the political economy of the contemporary literary scene. These two avenues of inquiry point generally, though not exclusively, to the library and the chain bookstore.

Work on the history of the material book can take many forms and is limited only by available library resources. Many canonical novels of the late 19th and early 20th centuries were originally serialized in upper middle-class magazines like *Scribner's*, *Harper's*, and *The Atlantic Monthly*. Even high school or small college libraries frequently hold these periodicals; it can be an eye-opening experience for students just to look at a novel in its original serial form. When they deduce the audience that a novel was intended to reach from a magazine's paper, typeface, illustrations, and editorial and advertising content, students come away with a far stronger sense of historical context than even my most skilled background lectures can impart.

Older covers, similarly, reveal a great deal about the fact that the status of both books and texts depend on historical context. The idea of the book as a status symbol suggested by the Collier trade edition of *The Age of Innocence* is reinforced by a look at a first edition of the novel. Variations in size, weight, materials, and construction complicate questions of value, and enrich any discussion of how canons are formed. Paperback and other cheap reprint edition covers can be used to convey this idea as well. The art of the Signet Classics cover illustration for *Heart of Darkness* (Figure 1-2) reflects and reinforces the prejudices of midcentury America, making blatant and heavy-handed Conrad's ambivalent attitude toward colonialism. When students look at an image like this, they immediately ask questions about the instability of texts and about the relationships among authors, audiences, and the business structures that mediate between the two. Awareness of the historical and material conditions within which books are produced makes even casual readers more critical and more careful with texts; because they tend to be curious about these issues, they become more conscious writers of criticism as well.

Figure 1-2. *Heart of Darkness* Signet Classics Edition, © 1955

Finally, investigating the material book can become a way into thinking about larger issues of cultural literacy and their relationship to the political economy of contemporary American culture. Close scrutiny of a book's cover can branch out into a material analysis of where and how it is sold and what those physical facts reveal about its value in the larger world outside the classroom. I have often assigned students to go to their local bookstore (usually a branch of a large chain) and work backwards from the assigned book's position on the shelf to understand how this mediating institution values it. What results, invariably, is a spatial map of a public space that dovetails almost perfectly with our current bifurcated, hierarchical literary culture. Positioning their books within the local Barnes & Noble, for instance, students raise questions like "What is the difference between *fiction* and *literature*?" "Why isn't 'African American Literature' just part of 'Literature'?" and "Why aren't the books we're assigned in class ever out on the tables at the front of the store?" Their experience working in the retail sales world means that many students are quite expert in issues of commodity categorization, placement, and promotion. The idea that literature might be trafficked in the same manner as jeans or sporting goods, however, is often new to them.

When they map the retail establishments where that trafficking takes place, they add a concrete dimension to the sometimes heady discussion of cultural capital that we have generated with our in-class attention to the book's cover. Some very ambitious students may even be prompted to work further outward, going from the spatial structure of the local bookstore to the larger (multi)national corporation behind it. This kind of work is a true exploration of the often overlooked material dimension of the cultural web within which literary texts take on meaning.

Connections to Cultural Studies

As a result of my predilections, "Cover Stories" raises a set of questions that are typically associated with cultural studies rather than with traditional literary scholarship. Questions about how power is exercised, how value is determined, and how public spaces and inanimate objects aid in that exercise and that determination may seem out of place in an English classroom. For classes that adhere closely to English as traditionally defined, "Cover Stories" may serve as an entertaining one-day diversion, a kind of close-reading practice that reinforces the attention to texts that rightly claims center stage. For courses that take a more culturalist approach to the discipline, however, "Cover Stories" can be a bridge to a more sustained, formal, and theoretical consideration of popular literature, multiculturalism, and canonicity. "Cover Stories" can add an element of historical materialism to a traditional New Critical syllabus, but it can also bring structured close-reading skills to a methodologically diverse Cultural Studies curriculum. It does not, I think, promote one version of English over the other; indeed, I think the lesson's greatest strength may be the degree to which it can promote dialogue across the theoretical and practical gulfs that divide many departments as well as the profession as a whole.

As I stated in my introduction to this chapter, I have found the material dimensions of book culture to be compelling enough to make it my area of scholarly specialization. I have not found a better way to understand how literature matters in the lives of everyday people than by explicating the political economy within which books circulate and assessing cultural capital's power to influence how books are consumed. Because the majority of my students are "everyday people," not professional or would-be professional readers, they also tend to find this approach compelling. It speaks to the reality in which they live, read, and write, and as such, gives them a stake in reading and writing more thoughtfully and critically. What more can we ask for?

Notes

1. Because book covers are complicated pastiches of images—original or reproduced artwork, typeface, copy, and trademarks—it is extremely difficult to obtain permission to reproduce them. I have relied on descriptions of cover images here except in those cases where permission was unnecessary because the material was in the public domain.

2. Bringing the work of these laborers to students' attention may interest those who have ambitions in the fields of marketing and public relations as well as in publishing, graphic design, or advertising.

3. Even my extended discussion will attend only to typographical elements. For an excellent treatment of how and why to teach not merely the surface aesthetics, but the deeper structures of book design and construction, See Groves (1996–1997).

References

Groves, J.D. (1996–1997). Dramatizing the familiar. *SHARP [Society for the History of Authorship, Readership, and Publishing] News* (Winter), 2–5.

Prown, J. (1982). Mind in matter: An introduction to material culture theory and method. *Winterthur portfolio*, 1–19.

2
Prereading Strategies: Preparing Students for Difficult Texts and Concepts

Brian White

When I started teaching, I *was* the English Department. The combined junior-senior high school hired me fresh out of graduate school to teach English to everyone in grades 7–12. Because I had learned so much about literature during my undergraduate years and in my master's program, I was confident that I'd be able to help my students enjoy literary texts. Since I had always loved to read, I wanted to share that love for great literature with my students. Nevertheless, like the new teachers Grossman describes in *The Making of a Teacher* (1990), I soon discovered that knowing a great deal about literature doesn't necessarily make a person a good teacher.

My 10th graders simply hated *Macbeth*, even after I explained it to them. A student named Kari told me in no uncertain terms that the play was stupid, especially the part where the sleepwalking Lady Macbeth tries to get invisible blood off her guilty hands. "Sure, Mr. White," she said. "How stupid. Some doctor who's not really a doctor says that she's asleep, but she obviously isn't asleep, and she's trying to get blood off her perfectly clean hands. Give me a break! This is so dumb." As a new teacher, I was not prepared for that reaction to the Bard.

Nor was I ready for what I believed were thoughtless and disrespectful attitudes toward great novels. My freshmen found Harper Lee's *To Kill a Mockingbird* boring. *To Kill a Mockingbird* boring? In fact, the first time I taught this novel, some of my students laughed when Tom Robinson was killed; they thought he was foolish to "try to escape." Similarly, my eighth graders laughed at Mafatu's exploits in Armstrong Sperry's *Call It Courage*; they thought the title was stupid in light of Mafatu's obvious cowardice. After I had explained how courageous Mafatu really was, they didn't laugh, but they still thought it was boring and they hated it. Things were not working out as I had planned.

The Importance of Prereading Preparation

After much exploration and experimentation, I realized that I was teaching my students as I had been taught—by assigning stories and poems for them to read. In class I desperately tried to get them to talk about the reading, but those discussions usually devolved into teacher-centered lectures. (Grossman, 1990; Hillocks, 1989; Marshall, Smagorinsky, & Smith, 1995; Nystrand & Gamoran, 1991). This technique had worked for graduate school professors, but it wasn't working for me and my students. Instead of developing their own interpretations, the kids were helping me to construct my interpretation (Marshall et al., 1995). Instead of arranging the environment so that the students could work together to create their own understandings, I was trying to transfuse my understandings into their minds, to transmit my knowledge to their blank slates (Freire, 1973; Hillocks, 1999; Smagorinsky, 2002). Instead of teaching students how to read and enjoy literature, I was teaching them how to reread by pointing out to them what I thought they should have seen the first time (Rabinowitz & Smith, 1998).

Perhaps the greatest revolution in my teaching occurred when I realized that I was doing almost all of the work of interpretation. I had been giving my students what I thought were important and interesting texts to read, but I hadn't been giving them the tools they needed to do the difficult, exciting, sometimes life-changing work of interpretation for themselves (Scholes, 1985; Wilhelm, Baker, & Dube, 2001). It was not sensible to hand them a difficult text with little or no preparation, hope that they would understand it, and then work hard to "remediate" their understandings *after* they have failed in their attempts.

Smagorinsky, McCann & Kern (1987) convinced me that appropriate introductory activities could "focus attention on key concepts in such a way that students can draw a clear correlation between their own experiences, values, and observations and those central to the [upcoming] text" (p. 2). When I began to use introductory activities in my literature classroom, I discovered to my delight that students who had considered key concepts and related personal experiences prior to reading *Macbeth* didn't find the play to be "stupid." In fact, they discovered fascinating connections between their lives and the lives of the characters in the play. For example, after thinking, writing, and talking about the effects that guilt can have on people, they found Lady Macbeth's handwashing to be rather extreme but not so very strange. When I prepared the next batch of freshmen for *To Kill a Mockingbird* by having them consider power relationships and individual differences, they didn't find the story boring or laughable; in fact, some of them cried in anger and frustration when Tom Robinson was killed. Subsequently, at every grade level from middle school through high school, I have found that when I design appropriate and engaging introductory activities to prepare my students for difficult texts and concepts, they are significantly more engaged and they read with considerably greater understanding (e.g., White, 1995).

Why Prereading Activities Work

Prereading activities allow and encourage students to remember and to apply previously acquired background knowledge and experiences when they encounter new learning. Schema theorists argue that new material cannot be understood in any meaningful way unless it can be related to existing knowledge. Ausubel (1967), for example, argues that meaningful verbal learning can take place only when the new material can find a home in previously acquired background knowledge and experience. If new material is not linked to previous learning, then the new learning is simply rote and meaningless and will soon be forgotten (Anderson & Pearson, 1984; Rumelhart & Norman, 1985).

Rosenblatt (1978) has argued consistently and convincingly that readers' personal experiences and responses are crucial to the understanding of texts. She emphasizes the importance of autobiographical experiences and personal understandings when she writes that "the reader's attention to the text activates certain elements in his past experience . . . that have become linked with verbal symbols" (p. 11). The act of reading, then, becomes a transaction. As the reader focuses on the text, the text stimulates the retrieval of what has been learned, experienced, and stored. Rosenblatt suggests that "one can think of this as an alerting of certain areas of memory, a stirring up of certain reservoirs of experience, knowledge, and feeling" (p. 54). Those fruits of previous learning are then available for students to apply to the text at hand.

Two Kinds of Prereading Preparation

In the remainder of this chapter, I'd like to introduce you to two specific kinds of prereading activities that I've used in grades 7–12: autobiographical writing before reading and small-group discussions of key concepts.

Autobiographical Writing Before Reading

Autobiographical writing before reading is an excellent way to help students make essential personal connections between their own lives and what they read. Students who have written before reading tend to be more on-task during discussion, to understand the text at more abstract levels, and to like the literature better (Hamann, Schultz, Smith, & White, 1991; White, 1995). Before my students and I begin reading a text—even before the students know what we're going to read next—I ask them to write and talk about their own lives in relation to some concept or event that is central to the upcoming text. For example, before beginning Jane Austen's *Pride and Prejudice*, I might ask students to write about their experiences with first impressions.

Table 2-1 shows a set of prompts I've used to prepare students for a literary unit on "growing up," or "coming of age." You may need to modify these to meet the reading abilities of your students.

Table 2-1. Autobiographical Writing Prompts for "Coming of Age" Unit

Directions: Please respond to one of the following prompts as specifically as you can. Write your answer on a separate sheet of paper. After 10 minutes or so, we'll be reading our essays to one another in small groups.

Choose either A, B, or C below. As you write, please remember to concentrate on experiences you have actually had. Discuss what happened, how you felt during and after the experience, and how the experience influenced your life. Please discuss in writing a time when the following occurred:

A. You knew for the first time that you were "grown up," mature, an adult. What happened that helped you to recognize your own maturity? Was it something you said or did? Or was it something that someone else said to you? Please describe the circumstances, and then go on to tell how you felt during and after the experience.

B. You tried to act grown up but really weren't. How old were you? What did you do? Why did you do it? How did you feel during and after the experience? Did trying to act grown up help you to grow up? Explain your answer.

C. You were with someone who was trying to act grown up. What did the person do and say that led you to believe that he or she was trying to act grown up? How did you feel about the person? How did observing this person's behavior influence your thinking about your own maturity or about maturity in general?

After writing, students share their essays in small groups. Listeners create two-column charts to record the characteristics of maturity and immaturity that each writer addresses. Next the group brainstorms a more complete list of characteristics in each column. The large-group report is almost always punctuated by important disagreements on the nature of maturity. Our goal during discussion is not to resolve these issues or to come to a shared fixed understanding, but to raise the issues so that we can use and modify our understandings as we read about literary characters in various stages of attaining maturity.

Here are some important points to remember when designing autobiographical writing prereading prompts. First, make the prompts autobiographical, not hypothetical. In my experience, a hypothetical question like "What would you do and how would you feel if you had lost a million dollars?" isn't as helpful as an autobiographical prompt like "Write about a time when you lost something that was very important to you." Second, don't make the prompts too personal. It's important to ask students to write about personal experience, but it's also important not to force students to write about things that they'd rather keep to themselves. One way to safeguard students' privacy is to give them a number of prompts to choose from (you'll see that all of my sample prompts give students choices). If a prompt raises issues that are too personal, students are free to choose a different one. You can also ask students to write on a topic but not require them to share it. If I ask students to write about a time in their lives when they felt very guilty, I do not ask them to read their essays or to share the specific circumstances that gave rise to the guilt. However, I do ask them to share how guilt feels, how they responded to the guilt, and how their experience might have changed them.

Small-Group Discussion of Key Concepts

On the other hand, personal connections are not always the answer. Sometimes, prior to reading a difficult text, students need to shore up their understanding of certain key concepts. For example, before (and while) reading *Romeo and Juliet*, students probably need to think carefully about the concept of love, what it is and what it isn't. However, high school freshmen might not have the kinds of personal experience with love and dating that would make autobiographical writing very fruitful. Similarly, before reading *To Kill a Mockingbird*, students might need to think and talk about what constitutes courageous action. In my experience, many high school students approach the novel with the belief that courage is a man with a gun in his hands. Sometimes we need activities that help students to consider their conceptual understandings prior to reading. Curry's (1987) research indicates that small-group discussions of key concepts, focusing on the data provided by instruments like opinionnaires and scenarios (Smagorinsky, 2002; Smagorinsky, et al., 1987; White & Johnson, 2001) can be very effective when students need more complete conceptual understanding prior to reading.

Prereading Opinionnaires

When students consider abstract concepts, they need to avoid discussions that are overly abstract or theoretical. For example, I never ask students to get into groups to "talk about *love*" or to "define *courage*." They need concrete data about which to argue. Prereading opinionnaires are helpful in this regard. Students respond to opinionnaires by agreeing or disagreeing with a number of statements focusing on an abstract concept. For example, an opinionnaire on the concept of courage might ask students to agree or disagree with the following statement: "Courageous people have learned not to feel afraid." After recording their own responses, the students discuss their opinions in groups. Table 2-2 is an opinionnaire I designed to prepare students for William Carlos Williams' short story "The Use of Force." It helps students to consider power relationships in doctor-patient interactions.

Table 2-2. Opinionnaire for "The Use of Force"

1. Most doctors kind of enjoy the power and prestige of their jobs.
   Strongly Agree   Agree   Disagree   Strongly Disagree
2. I feel kind of vulnerable when I have to see my doctor about something.
   Strongly Agree   Agree   Disagree   Strongly Disagree
3. Medical personnel should never force a patient to do anything.
   Strongly Agree   Agree   Disagree   Strongly Disagree
4. Sometimes, in order to help someone, whether medically or some other way, you have to be forceful.
   Strongly Agree   Agree   Disagree   Strongly Disagree
5. Medical patients should always have the right to a second opinion.
   Strongly Agree   Agree   Disagree   Strongly Disagree
6. Medical patients should always have the right to refuse to be examined by a doctor.
   Strongly Agree   Agree   Disagree   Strongly Disagree
7. Medical patients should always have the right to refuse treatment after diagnosis.
   Strongly Agree   Agree   Disagree   Strongly Disagree
8. Doctors really do know what's good for their patients.
   Strongly Agree   Agree   Disagree   Strongly Disagree
9. Most doctors genuinely have the good of their patients at heart.
   Strongly Agree   Agree   Disagree   Strongly Disagree
10. Sometimes, doctors have to do things that their patients don't understand and don't like.
    Strongly Agree   Agree   Disagree   Strongly Disagree

I've learned the following about designing opinionnaires:
- Focus the opinionnaire clearly on an abstract concept.
- Create statements that approach the concept from various perspectives.
- Word the items to provoke some disagreement.
- Ask students to take a stand on each item. (Note that I don't include a "Not Sure" or "Neither Agree nor Disagree" category.)
- Allow students to complete the opinionnaire individually before moving to groups for discussion.
- Ask students to share their responses and to identify the concepts that seem to have provoked the most disagreement.
- Ask students to attempt to achieve consensus on the most contentious concepts.
- Remind students that the goal of the discussion is increased understanding of various points of view, not increased agreement.
- As they try to achieve consensus, they will raise, defend, and attack various definitions and examples of the concept.

Scenarios

Like opinionnaires, scenarios give students data to focus on as they refine their understandings and definitions of key concepts. Students respond to scenarios by ranking conceptually focused vignettes from the best (or most acceptable) portrayal of the concept to the worst (or least acceptable) portrayal of the concept. For example, the vignettes might portray couples in various kinds of romantic relationships; the students would rank the vignettes from the best (most healthy) example of love to the worst (least healthy) example of love. Then they would discuss their rankings and their rationales in small groups. Appendix 2-A is a set of scenarios used to prepare high school students for a unit focusing on science and nature (including difficult texts like "The Birthmark," "Rappaccini's Daughter," and *Frankenstein*). Students rank the scenarios individually, then move to small groups to share their rankings and try to achieve consensus. For students who are less able readers, the scenarios can be read aloud.

The set of scenarios in Appendix 2-A gets students talking about the limits to which science can and ought to go in its interactions with nature. An additional set of scenarios (Appendix 2-B) focuses on the nature of courage. More prompt models are included in Appendix 2-C. The opinionnaire in Appendix 2-D prepares students for a unit on the American dream. Other examples of scenarios, including some courage scenarios, can be found in *Designing and Sequencing Prewriting Activities* (Johannessen, Kahn, & Walter, 1982) and *Explorations: Introductory Activities for Literature and Composition, 7–12* (Smagorinsky, at al., 1987; see also Smagorinsky, 2002).

You Can't Be Serious

Sometimes when I tell other teachers about how well prereading activities have worked in my classroom, they look a little annoyed or a little frightened. These naysayers usually focus on how much work it will take to develop autobiographical prompts, opinionnaires, and scenarios and how much time it will take to implement them. "I don't have time," they say to me. "I have too much to do and we have too many texts to cover." Let me respond to these very legitimate objections. First, I'd like to point out that when I didn't use prereading activities, I was working just as hard—but most of the work came *after* the students had read instead of *before*. More important, the before work gave me the results for which I had hoped. It does take work to develop these activities, but it's work worth doing: it's productive work, and it helps to alleviate the heavy burden of postreading remediation. I admit that it takes a fair bit of time to design and to implement these activities, to do the groundwork that Wilhelm et al. (2001) refer to as "frontloading," but if we teach thematically (e.g., Smagorinsky, 2002), one or two prereading activities can serve as preparation for a number of diverse but thematically related texts. I would add, however, that if the use of prereading activities means that we don't cover quite so many texts, so be it. To parade a long line of potentially meaningful texts past a room full of unengaged students is not a sensible choice. I'd rather cover fewer texts, knowing that my students are reading with greater engagement and understanding.

At every level, I have found that preparing students for difficult texts and concepts pays great dividends. Preparation is most successful when students are involved and engaged. It isn't something we can do for them or to them; it isn't something we can simply give them or tell them (Hillocks, 1999). Autobiographical writing before reading, opinionnaires, and scenarios have been tested by researchers and proven by classroom teachers. Simply put, carefully planned introductory activities help me to do my job as a teacher: to prepare students to succeed.

Appendix 2-A. Science and Nature Scenarios

Directions: Read each of the following scenarios carefully. Each scenario describes an incident in which science solves a problem. Please rank the scenarios from the most acceptable use of science (1) to the least acceptable use of science (4).

a. _____ The military dictator of an unstable, previously democratic nation has recently acquired nuclear and biological weapons. He has begun to use the biological weapons against his enemies within his borders, and he has threatened to use the nuclear weapons against any nation that tries to intervene. The dictator's enemies, including some members of his high command, have appealed to the United States for help; they want to restore democracy. Fearing a CIA assassination plot, the dictator has gone into hiding in a specially constructed, bomb-proof bunker and command center beneath the parliament building in the center of his densely populated capital city. He has publicly threatened the United States with nuclear holocaust if they attempt to kill him. CIA scientists have developed and tested a new smart missile that is guaranteed to penetrate the dictator's air defenses undetected, fly unerringly to the dictator's bunker, and kill all of its inhabitants upon impact. Tests of the smart missile have enabled the scientists to promise very little collateral damage. A spy within the dictator's high command has confirmed that the dictator is in his bunker and will remain there for at least 2 weeks. The president of the United States has authorized the use of the weapon and has ordered the production of five more missiles.

b. _____ Pleasant Valley is a town of 7,500 people in the midwestern United States. The largest employer in town is a factory that assembles widgets and supplies them to one of the big three automakers. In many ways, the life of the town revolves around the widget factory; nearly every family has at least one member employed directly by the factory, and most of the other businesses in town exist to do business with the factory and its employees (e.g., restaurants, office supply companies, trucking firms, clothiers). A recent headline in the *Pleasant Valley Gazette* sent shock waves through the community: "Widget Factory to Close December 21." The automaker's scientists and engineers have developed an automated widget assembly line consisting of a series of high-speed robots. Extensive testing has shown that the robots assemble the widgets much more quickly and accurately than the Pleasant Valley humans. Use of the robots will streamline the construction process, increase the automaker's profit margin, and eliminate the need for the Pleasant Valley factory. The automaker has ended its contract with Pleasant Valley and will begin automated widget production at a new, completely automated factory in Ohio starting the first of the year.

c._____ Proclaiming a "war on fear," a team of psychiatrists, psychologists, primary care physicians, and pharmacologists has developed a drug that they say will alleviate the mental suffering and emotional paralysis of millions of people. The medical scientists say that their new drug, Peligrogon, will enhance the average citizen's quality of life and the productivity of the nation's entrepreneurs and workers. A very low, daily dosage of Peligrogon can help a person to overcome chronic shyness, producing a feeling of greater comfort in social and business situations and allowing the overly self-conscious to take greater risks. At higher dosages, Peligrogon has proven to eliminate all consciousness of irrational fears. For example, people who were previously deathly afraid of heights have enjoyed the view from the observation deck at the top of the Sears Tower. The scientists predict that Peligrogon will stimulate the development of new businesses and the creation of new products as thousands of workers with good ideas begin to take risks to realize their dreams. After years of careful, clinical testing, the researchers have discovered no physical or emotional side effects; the drug is apparently not addictive. The FDA has approved the lowest dosage of Peligrogon for over-the-counter sale and the higher dosages for doctors' prescriptions.

d._____ Last month an Australian medical researcher who has been studying heart disease in pigs told his government that he has discovered a cure for heart disease. A technician in his laboratory made a mistake that caused a small explosion, sending fragments of decorative coral into the cages of several seriously ill pigs. After the pigs consumed the pieces of coral (which the scientist had gathered while exploring the Great Barrier Reef), their heart disease had completely disappeared. Upon reconstructing the events that led to the explosion, the scientist determined that the cure was wrought by the ingestion of coral coated with aspirin powder and iodine. In subsequent tests, pig after pig was cured by this strange accidental combination. Coral from other sources did not have the same effect—only coral from the Great Barrier Reef had the necessary qualities to effect the cure. The Australian government secretly approved human testing, and the coral, aspirin, and iodine combination worked in every case. The government began harvesting coral from the Reef for further testing and experimentation in spite of the objections of its own environmental scientists, who say that harvesting coral from the Reef will drastically alter the local ecosystem, lead to the extinction of several important and unique species of fish and crustaceans, and curtail tourism. The government, citing the deadly incidence of heart disease throughout the world, has continued harvesting coral.

Appendix 2-B. Scenarios for Courage Unit

Directions: Rank these scenarios from "most courageous action" (1) to "least courageous action" (4). Next to each scenario, jot a few notes to justify your choices. ("This is a 3 because . . .")

a. _____Max Nyfgut has been in and out of prison since he was 17 years old. He is now 40 years of age. Seven years ago, he attempted to rob the First National Bank and was severely wounded in a shootout with police in the bank's lobby. He was captured and, after recovering from his wound, was sent to prison. He was paroled 2 months ago and since that time he has been able to stay completely out of trouble. Because of his police record, however, Max has not been able to find work. He is broke. His girlfriend has threatened to break up with him if he doesn't get some money soon. This morning, Max returned to the First National Bank, produced a revolver, and made off with $30,000 in unmarked bills.

b. _____Clarence Peabody, 27, nearly drowned when he was 2 years old. Ever since that terrifying experience, Clarence has been deathly afraid of the water. Last week, as he was riding his moped along a lakeshore path, he heard a choking cry for help. Someone was drowning! He stopped his moped and shielded his eyes against the sun. Fear gripped him as he saw a hand sinking below the surface 30 yards from shore. Immediately, Clarence jumped into the shallow water near the shore and began dog-paddling to the drowning swimmer. "I'm coming!" he shouted, swallowing a huge gulp of water. "Don't give up!"

c. _____Clarissa Van Elp is a firefighter in New York City. Last night, at midnight, her company was called to a fire in a skyscraper. By the time they arrived, the fire had gutted the lower floors and was spreading quickly to the upper floors. A crowd of several hundred bystanders had gathered to observe the fire and the firefighters. Taking off her helmet and looking up through the smoke, Clarissa saw an elderly woman leaning out of a window high above the street. Quickly, she and another firefighter set up a ladder. Clarissa, oxygen mask in place, climbed the ladder and entered the smoky building 10 floors beneath the elderly woman. She ran up the stairs, searched frantically for the woman, found her, and carried her to safety.

d. _____Steven Supine desperately needs a new kidney or he will die. According to the doctors, he has only weeks to live unless a suitable donor can be found. Steven's brother, Brad, has been identified as a possible donor. The doctors have assured Brad that the transplant operation is nearly always successful and that he would be in very, very little danger. Brad knows the risks associated with a general anesthetic; he also knows that living with one kidney can be risky—he'd need a transplant himself if anything were to happen to his remaining kidney later on. Nevertheless, Brad decides to go through with the operation.

Appendix 2-C. Sample Autobiographical Writing Before Reading Prompt

1. For Armstrong Sperry's *Call It Courage* (or for any text with courage as a main theme), do the following:
   A. Think about a time in your life when you had to do something that you were afraid to do. What was it that you had to do? Why did you have to do it? Why were you afraid to do it? How did you know that you were afraid? Describe your feelings in detail. How did you feel during and after the experience?
   B. If you can't think of a time when you *had* to do something you were afraid to do, write about a time when you *chose* to do something you were afraid to do.
   C. Write about a time when you were afraid to do something and you chose not to do it because you were afraid.

2. For Jane Austen's *Pride and Prejudice*, I'd like you to do some writing about first impressions. Respond to one of the following prompts as specifically as you can, and pay special attention to your own actions and feelings.
   A. Think about a time when you met someone, formed an initial opinion, and later had to change that opinion as you got to know the person. Who is the person (no names)? How did you meet? What was your initial impression and what caused you to form that impression? What happened to change your first impression? If you're having trouble thinking of something to write about, consider your first impressions of certain teachers, neighborhood friends, cousins.
   B. Perhaps you'd like to "turn the tables" and write about a time when someone formed a first impression about *you* and later had to change his or her mind.

3. Prompt for Shakespeare's *Macbeth*. (Remember our discussions about appropriate subject matter for writing and sharing. We'll structure the sharing so that we can talk about guilt and our reactions to it without having to reveal the specific circumstances).
   A. Please write about a time in your life when you did something that you knew you shouldn't do. Be as specific as you can. What motivated you to do it? What influenced your decision? How did you feel before you did it? How did you feel after? Did you have to deal with guilt? What other consequences did you have to face? Describe the circumstances and your feelings as specifically as you can.
   B. If you prefer, you can write about a time when someone pressured (or tried to pressure) you to do something that you knew was wrong. What were the circumstances? Why did the person want to pressure you? How did you respond to the pressure? How did it feel to be pressured?

C. You could write about a time when you pressured someone to do something that you knew was wrong. Why did you do try to pressure that person? How did the person respond?
4. Prompt for Harper Lee's *To Kill a Mockingbird*:
   A. Think about a time when you met someone who was very different from you. Perhaps this person had a disability that you don't have. Or maybe this person was from a different culture, spoke a different language, or had a skin color different from your own. How did you feel while with that person? What sorts of things did you think about? Describe the "differences" involved and your feelings about them. Be as specific as possible.
   B. If you prefer, you could write about a time when you misjudged someone because you didn't know him or her well enough. When you finally got to know that person and "stand in his shoes" or see the world from his perspective, you had to change your original judgment.
5. For a unit focusing on money, possessions, and "the American Dream" (including *The Great Gatsby*, *Death of a Salesman*, and others). Respond in writing to one of the following prompts. We'll be sharing our responses in small groups in about 10 minutes. Please write for the entire time.
   A. Think and write about a time in your life when you really wanted something (an object, an experience, a relationship) because having that something would enhance your own status in the eyes of others. In other words, write about a time when you wanted something because it would make you look or feel more valuable. Maybe you wanted a car or a particular kind of car. Maybe you wanted to date a particular person or a person from a particular group. When did this happen in your life? What was the thing you really wanted? Why did you think it would enhance your own value? Did you finally obtain the object of your desire? If so, did obtaining your desire enhance your value? How did obtaining your desire make you feel about yourself? If you didn't obtain your desire, how did not obtaining your desire make you feel about yourself?
   B. Think and write about a time when you lost something that was very, very important to you. Perhaps someone stole a prize possession, or maybe an important object or ability was destroyed by accident or by a natural disaster. What was the important thing? Why was it so important to you? How was the important thing lost? How did you feel about the loss just after it happened? How do you feel about it now?
   C. Think and write about a time when you were envious of something someone else had. Who was the person you envied? What did that person have? Why did you want it so badly? Why couldn't you also have had it? Did you try to get it somehow? Were you successful?

D. Think and write about a time when you really needed something, but you couldn't afford it. What was it that you really needed? Why did you need it (not just *want* but need), and why couldn't you afford it? If you finally got it, how did you get it, and was it worth it? Did you really need it? If you never got it, how did you get along without it? What were the lasting effects of not being able to get what you needed?

E. Think and write about a time when you found yourself looking down on someone who had less (materially) than you had. What were the circumstances? How did you know that the person (or group) had less than you? How did you feel about him or her (or them)? Why do you think you felt that way? Did you express your feelings or keep them inside? As you reflect on this now, what are your thoughts and feelings? Would you still respond the same way in the same circumstances?

Appendix 2-D. "The American Dream" Opinionnaire

Directions: Please respond to the following statements by Strongly Agreeing (SA), Agreeing (A), Disagreeing (D), or Strongly Disagreeing (SD).

1. In the United States, you are what you own.
2. Equal opportunity for all is a reality in our nation.
3. People can be wealthy only at the expense of the poor.
4. Anyone can be successful in life if he or she is willing to work hard enough.
5. Sometimes success is based on nothing but luck.
6. People deserve whatever wealth they can accumulate.
7. It's OK to buy something you don't need if it will make you more popular or better accepted.
8. People should never buy things they don't really need.
9. Credit cards are a destructive force in society.
10. Rich and powerful people use entertainment (sports, movies, the music industry) to increase their own wealth and keep the rest of us down.
11. Most very poor people in the United States are just lazy.
12. I expect to be more successful in life than my parents.
13. Being poor means being powerless.
14. People on welfare shouldn't expect to receive the same kinds of medical and legal care that wealthier people can afford.
15. The acquisition of an expensive lifestyle for a few rests on the misery of many.
16. Social class (upper, middle, lower) isn't as important in the United States as it is in some other countries.

References

Anderson, R., & Pearson P. D. (1984). A schema-theoretic view of basic processes in reading comprehension." In P. D. Pearson (Ed.), *Handbook of reading research* (pp. 255–291). New York: Longman.

Ausubel, D. (1967). *Learning theory and classroom practice*. Toronto: Ontario Institute for Studies in Education.

Curry, J. (1987). Improving secondary school students' inferential responses to literature." Unpublished doctoral dissertation, University of Chicago.

Freire, P. (1973). *Pedagogy of the oppressed*. New York: Continuum.

Grossman, P. (1990). *The making of a teacher*. New York: Teachers College Press.

Hamann, L., Schultz, L., Smith, M. W., & White B. (1991). Making connections: The power of autobiographical writing before reading. *Journal of Reading, 35*, 24–29.

Hillocks, G., Jr. (1989). Literary texts in classrooms. In P. W. Jackson & S. Haroutunian-Gordon (Eds.), *From Socrates to software: Teachers as texts and texts as teachers* (pp. 135–158). Chicago: University of Chicago Press.

Hillocks, G., Jr. (1999). *Ways of thinking, ways of teaching*. New York: Teachers College Press.

Johannessen, L., Kahn, E., & Walter, C. C. (1982). *Designing and sequencing prewriting activities*. Urbana, IL: NCTE.

Kahn, E., Walter, C. C., & Johannessen, L. (1984). *Writing about literature*. Urbana, IL: NCTE.

Marshall, J., Smagorinsky, P., & Smith M. W. (1995). *The language of interpretation: Patterns of discourse in discussions of literature*. Urbana, IL: NCTE.

Nystrand, M., & Gamoran, A. (1991). Instructional discourse, student engagement, and literature achievement. *Research in the Teaching of English, 25* (3), 261–290.

Rabinowitz, P., & Smith, M. W. (1998). *Authorizing readers: Resistance and respect in the teaching of literature*. New York: Teachers College Press.

Rosenblatt, L. (1978). *The reader, the text, the poem: The transactional theory of the literary work*. Carbondale, IL: Southern Illinois University Press.

Rumelhart, D., & Norman, D. (1985). Analogical processes in learning. In J. R. Anderson (Ed.), *Cognitive skills and their acquisition* (pp. 335–359). Hillsdale, NJ: Erlbaum.

Scholes, R. (1985). *Textual power: Literary theory and the teaching of English*. New Haven, CT: Yale University Press.

Smagorinsky, P. (2002). *Teaching English through principled practice*. Columbus, OH: Merrill Prentice Hall.

Smagorinsky, P., McCann, T., & Kern, S. (1987). *Explorations: Introductory activities for literature and composition, 7–12*. Urbana, IL: NCTE.

Tyson, L. (1999). *Critical theory today: A user-friendly guide*. New York: Garland.

White, B. (1995). Effects of autobiographical writing before reading on students' responses to short stories. *Journal of Educational Research, 88* (3), 173–184.

White, B., & Johnson, T. S. (2001). We really do mean it: Implementing language arts standard #3 with opinionnaires. *Clearing House,* 74 (3), 119–123.

Wilhelm, J., Baker, T., & Dube, J. (2001). *Strategic reading: Guiding students to lifelong literacy, 6–12*. Portsmouth, NH: Heinemann Boynton Cook.

3

Recipe for the Reluctant Reader: Add Reading Strategies to Young Adult Literature and Mix Well

Lu Ann Brobst Staheli

Books are my passion, my life; therefore, some of my earliest memories center around books: I remember the Christmas Eves when my mother read *Rudolph the Red-Nosed Reindeer*, and her repeated bedtime readings of *Goldilocks and the Three Bears* and *The New Baby* from Golden Books. In grade school, we attended the book fairs. I brought home book order forms, and I was allowed to choose whatever books I wanted to buy. By the time I was in junior high school, I carried a book everywhere I went. In high school I always had two or more books with me during study hall "just in case." In college, I felt book withdrawal, even though I was an English major, because there was never time to read for pleasure. My typical relaxation before finals was to choose a novel and read.

Today I teach junior high English, but when I have time I do read mainstream adult fiction: mysteries and political, medical, and legal thrillers. I've even made it through a few of Oprah's selections, and I've always loved biography. Nevertheless, I'll give any of them up for the lure of a new title by a favorite author of young adult literature. Age makes no difference for the literary love of my heart. I will always be a young adult there. As a young adult I discovered books by Paul Zindel, Jean Craighead George, Lois Duncan, and S. E. Hinton. Today I recommend those same authors to reluctant readers, and they discover the magic I felt all those years ago. The number of quality authors and books for the young adult reader has greatly increased since my early reading years. Students deserve the chance to discover, explore, and enjoy them.

A Discovery of No Surprise

Although I teach in a rural area, my junior high school students come from a diverse background. Some are children of our local university's professors; some are from second-generation migrant worker families. Some students come to me passionate about reading, others passionate about avoiding reading. Most of my students are willing to read, but many do not have the strategies or skills to do much more than decode the words.

Several years ago, bored by repeated readings of the short stories and poems provided in the basal literature anthologies, I began reading contemporary young adult novels aloud to my students. Suddenly students were coming to class asking, "Are you going to read today?" "What did I miss yesterday?" "Can't you read to us the entire class period?"

Soon they began demanding that I read more books for longer periods of time. If it took me too long to get to the book they wanted to hear, they started reading it themselves and asked for time to read silently. They talked books to me and to each other. They read the novels other students recommended and constantly asked me to help them find a book they would like. I discovered what should come as no surprise: Kids like to read if the book is interesting and at a level they can understand. Now I rarely use the district-adopted anthology except for occasional modeling of how to read a short story. I've found other ways to include poetry in my curriculum, so nothing is lost, but everything is gained. Now even my reluctant readers are interested in what we are reading, and they select books to read on their own. The following are some of the most successful methods I've used to bring the text to the reader, both reluctant and motivated.

Variations on Successful Sustained Silent Reading Practices

Nancie Atwell maintains that "a reader's fluency is a function of sustained experiences with printed text" (1987, p. 156) and that "periods of silent, independent reading are perhaps the strongest experience [we] can provide students to demonstrate the value of literacy" (p. 157). Sustained Silent Reading (SSR) is a commonly used and effective strategy in many classrooms, but it doesn't work for all students. Those who struggle with reading problems, those who are not engaged in the selection of books, and those who do not have materials on hand will not efficiently use class time. These are not reasons to exclude SSR from the classroom, but they are reason enough to try some variations of SSR that I have found support reluctant readers.

Encourage Students to Read What They Want to Read

Just because I don't like R. L. Stine's *Goosebumps*, Stephen King, genre fiction, or Harry Potter doesn't mean that I shouldn't encourage students to read them. As a reminder, I ask myself: Am I more engaged in reading a book I select myself or one I've been assigned to read? Should I expect any different attitude from my students? I don't want students' experience with reading to be like Gregorio's, who told me, "The only book I ever read in school was Charles Dickens' *Great Expectations*; I didn't understand it, but my teacher assigned it."

Help Students to Love Reading Instead of Fearing It

I have stopped asking students to take a test, do a work sheet, or give a book report after every book they read. Students who are readers will talk about their books naturally. I use these discussions as a measure of achievement. My students write papers every other week to assess themselves as readers. In these papers they make connections, talk about language, or ask questions about the books they have been reading. I respond to these papers, not as a teacher correcting their work but as a friend ready to discuss the text. There is no right or wrong to these papers, simply a budding community of readers sharing their thoughts.

Lori's experience should help us all to reconsider how we ask students to report their reading. "Last year, I had to fill out a book report form on every book I read," she said. "I read a lot and got tired of filling them out, so I only did enough to get the points I needed. I like it a lot better this year. I feel like you really care about me as a reader, and you respect the number of books that I read."

Help Students to Avoid Boredom

My class is not biology. Therefore, I do not have to dissect every piece a student reads. Authors use plot, theme, characterization, simile, metaphor, irony, and many other devices. These are worthy of study and can be interesting reflections when discussing a work. Nevertheless, they are not a natural part of our engagement with literature, and it's less likely that most students will consciously use these devices outside the classroom. We should take our cue from Kathleen who said, "I like the fact that you just read some of the books to us, no tests or work sheets to do as we read it. It reminds me that reading can be fun and not just something we do for school."

Let Students Know It's Okay to Abandon a Book

Not every book is for every person. Not every book can sustain a reader's interest or support his or her reading ability. I let my students know that it is okay to stop reading a book that isn't interesting or accessible to them. I encourage them to decide quickly, then get on to the next selection and the next if that's what it takes. Students—reluctant readers, especially—who stop reading a "boring" book must be given the freedom to move on and start again until they find a book worth reading. Todd gave me a rare compliment: "This is the first time I've ever had a class where I could count parts of books that I read. I always did bad before in English because I had to finish a book. I never did."

Encourage Students to Listen

Use audio books and read-alouds. For some students their first positive contact with reading will be listening to an audio book. Of course, we eventually want students to read books independently, but listening to an audio book may demonstrate for them why we think reading is fun. In addition, listening to an audio book will give students the opportunity to take part in class discussions—a first for many reluctant readers or nonreaders. As Lars, one student, said, "I came into this class from resource and I was scared, but I can listen to a book on tape and it counts. I really like that."

Read Silently Yourself During Silent Sustained Reading Time

Linda Rief (1992) says, "All teachers *should* be readers and writers, but teachers of language arts *must* be writers and readers" (p. 10). If I read while students are engaged, they know that I value the time allowed for silent reading. "I thought the principal was gonna yell at Mrs. Staheli when he came into the room and saw her reading. Wasn't she supposed to be going around the room, making sure we were reading or something? He just smiled and left," Brigham said.

Read-Alouds

All students love to listen to a good book read aloud. If I choose an engaging (for young adults) book, practice my reading voice, and read long-enough chunks at a session, my students inevitably develop interest in the story. Even though I teach on an A/B schedule, which means 22 class days each term, I read a poem and use picture books nearly every day. I am able to read aloud four to seven novels each year in addition to the novels we study as a class. Thus, even my nonreaders are exposed to literature and see an expert reader modeling reading strategies. My goal is to develop lifelong readers. Here is how I accomplish that goal:

1. I dedicate enough time to read a poem or picture book in its entirety, or at least one full chapter of a novel. I often read two or more if they are short.

2. I choose a book to read aloud that is related to my teaching unit and that has characters who are exciting and memorable. Nonreader Jenna told me, "*Brian's Winter* [Paulsen, 1998] is one of the best books I've ever read," even though *I* had read the book aloud in class.

3. I'm not afraid to read a book that students have already read or heard even if I haven't. I encourage them to be the experts as I model using schema, predicting, connecting, and drawing inferences. I use questioning techniques to make meaning and clarify information. Leah's exuberant comment supports this strategy: "I couldn't believe Mrs. Staheli hadn't read Wilson Rawls's *Where the Red Fern Grows* before, but when she read it to us and showed us how to make predictions, she got some of the story wrong. That was cool. I thought teachers always knew the right answers." (See Keene & Zimmerman, 1997, for specific ideas.)

4. I use some books as entire class period read-alouds. This gives students a chance to engage in the story, listen to a good reader read, and use reading strategies themselves while the class discusses the story in progress. Sometimes, instead of reading aloud, I use a well-produced audio book. This saves my voice when we read J. K. Rowling's *Harry Potter and the Prisoner of Azkaban* (2000). The students have the additional advantage of listening to a professional actor re-create those marvelous English accents. For some nonreaders, this may be the only way for them to experience the excitement and satisfaction of a really good book. "I hate it when Mrs. Staheli stops reading *Stargirl* [Spinelli, 2000] just at the good parts," Kim said. "But I guess they are all good parts."

Using Audio Books to Build Reading Skills

Some teachers believe that listening to audio books instead of reading the text is cheating. This is wrong! Audio books can be a more efficient use of time for both adults and students. When I drive around town I listen to audio books. For me, it's better than listening to a "Golden Oldie" station or the often-mindless drivel of talk radio, and it also provides an educational opportunity. I recently learned of a truck driver who claimed that in one year, while she was on the road, she listened to enough audio books to give her the equivalent of a four-year college education. Although that might be a slight exaggeration, it is true that books on almost every topic are available, and many newer textbooks come with a CD of every selection in the text. When using an audio book in class, provide, when possible, hard copies of the text so interested students can follow along. Janet Allen and Kyle Gonzales (1998) claim the following:

> Recorded books allow students to experience the magic of a good book they are unable to read independently. Using unabridged recorded books as a form of assisted reading allows students simultaneously to see and hear both new words and commonly used words that may not have made it into their sight vocabulary. (p. 31)

The Advantages of Using Audio Books in the Classroom

Improve Scores on Reading Tests With Audio Books

I conduct an elective one-semester class called "Reading Is Fun." At the beginning of the term I give the students the Gates-MacGinitie Reading Test, which reveals a beginning score for both vocabulary and comprehension. At the end of the term, less than 40 class periods later, I give the test again. Almost without exception, the students who attended class regularly and spent their class time reading improved their scores from 5% to a whopping 75%! So did students who did no actual "reading" of printed texts but who listened diligently to books on tape in the classroom. Janet Allen (1999) cautions:

> So often our goals are true, but the furor of educational pressures makes us abandon the very things that would help us reach those goals. No strategies of teaching and learning new vocabulary will take the place of the wealth of words learned in a strong reading program that includes time for [the teacher] to read aloud to . . . students, time for [students} to read with [the teacher] and other students, and time for [students] to self-select books independently.

Audio Books Provide Access for All Learners

Some readers will come to middle school, junior high, and even high school still unable to read school-required texts. For these students, decoding individual words is tiresome, and those who struggle will soon give up and may in frustration act out. When these students listen to an audio book, they may for the first time engage in the text because they don't have to struggle to make meaning.

One young man who had never read a book on his own experienced success when I gave him an audio version of *Holes* by Louis Sacher (2000). Within days he was engaged, sharing with me both verbally and in halting written work how much he loved the book. It was exciting to hear him tell other class members, "You have to read this book," then see his classmates choose either the text or the audio version to followup on his recommendations. For the first time, he felt power in his new-found enjoyment, and he could share his expertise as a reader.

Students Show a Higher Interest Level With Audio Books

Many audio books are read by a professional actor who gives each character a dramatically different voice and personality. This automatically adds some excitement—even in texts that are not necessarily of high interest for that particular reader. Choose audio books that are already popular with students by taking a poll of titles they would like to have available in audio format. You can also purchase audio books you have used successfully as read-alouds. I also look for popular authors. At the end of each school year, I ask students to tell me the best book they have read in the past year. Students fill out a 4 x 6 card with the book title and author, then write a one- or two-sentence summary of the plot, why they liked the book, and why someone else should read it. I use these cards to help me decide what to purchase for my class library and what to read to prepare for book talks. Other students use these minireviews as a recommended reading list for summer or the next school year.

Audio Books Hook the Unhookable

One nonreader came to me from resource class and immediately declared, "I will not read. I hate reading!" The first day of class I gave him a tape player, headphones, and an audio book. Within a week, he was hooked. Class began at 8 a.m., but he arrived each day of the rest of the semester at 7:30, headphones on and audio book running.

Making Your Own Audio Books Saves Your Voice and Adds to Your Collection Inexpensively

Audio books will give your voice and eyes a rest. At one time or another all of us have decided to read aloud to our classes a short story or novel. The read aloud goes pretty well for one class period, and then my eyes start to ache or not focus properly. Next my throat starts to get scratchy, and I may lose my voice altogether. What I do now is record my own reading during the first class. Then I replay it for subsequent classes. This has two advantages: (a) During the first reading I can be very enthusiastic and dramatic, knowing that I don't have to save my energy, and (b) I automatically add to the class library, so the audio book becomes available for students who were absent. My students' favorite audio books include *Harry Potter and the Goblet of Fire* by J. K. Rowling (2002), *Touching Spirit Bear* by Ben Mikaelsen (2002), and *A Year Down Yonder* by Richard Peck (2002).

Literature Partners Increase Reading Engagement

Have you ever read a book and then immediately wanted to tell someone about it—somehow to engage beyond the text and discuss the fine points of the story or characters? Literature partners provide that opportunity. Books for literature partnerships are easy to acquire because two copies of any title are enough. To select titles for literature partnerships, I use a thematic approach such as "the effect of war on the lives of children," "survival," or "fantasy, mystery, and the unexplained."

To set up literature partners, I prepare students with an introduction to the theme and give a 30-second book talk on each title. Next I explain how to choose a book that looks interesting and is accessible in length and difficulty. I also encourage students to choose a partner of equal reading ability. Then students examine the books and make their choices. Inevitably some students will make poor choices. This past term two girls who were best friends wanted to work together even though their reading skills differed considerably. They quickly grabbed a book without thoroughly examining it or discussing their reading expertise. The next day the better reader of the two informed me that she didn't like the book and found some of the language offensive. I suggested they change books. She refused, saying that she had already read well over half and didn't want to start a new book. She finished the book by the next day and had to wait 2 full weeks for her much slower partner to catch up. Because of her poor choices, she spent nearly 3 weeks examining a book she really didn't like. I think she learned a great deal about herself through the experience.

Most partnerships, however, are successful. "My partner and I enjoyed reading [J. R. R. Tolkien's] *The Fellowship of the Ring*," Sarah said. "Preparing the movie trailer to share in class was a blast. It was great seeing the reaction of the other students. Maybe we will become movie producers some day."

Literature Circles Give Reluctant Readers Support

Literature circles involve small groups (3–10 students) reading and discussing the same novels. To facilitate discussion, I use job descriptions as adapted from Harvey Daniels (1994). The book selection process is the same as with literature partners, but students are able to read more challenging texts because larger discussion groups can help the weakest readers to understand the text. The books I have selected include classics, such as Mark Twain's *The Adventures of Huckleberry Finn*, four Shakespearean comedies, and an abridged version of Victor Hugo's *Les Miserables*, as well as contemporary novels such as *Homecoming* by Cynthia Voigt (2002) and *Walk Two Moons* by Sharon Creech (1991).

Within literature circles, students work together to prepare a class presentation that synthesizes their literary experiences. My students have produced a tremendous variety of presentations. However, the best projects are invariably the movies that students make based on the stories they have read. Students take these projects seriously and prepare costumes, set locations, and memorize scripts based on the text. The students demonstrate a sophisticated video and computer literacy as they add musical soundtracks, sound effects, and fades to their final product. These projects testify to the high level of engagement of these students with the novel. Best of all, students of differing abilities and language expertise can participate and contribute. "I never would have been able to read [Baroness Emmuska Orczy's] *The Scarlet Pimpernel* if it hadn't been for the other people in my circle," Ben said. "Then, when we acted it out for our movie, I really understood what the book was about. It was exciting, getting to wear all those costumes, and I got the girl in the end."

Schoolwide or Classroom Book Clubs Engage Reluctant Readers

For the past 3 years my junior high school has sponsored schoolwide book clubs and each year more students participate. This past year featured special visits from authors Carol Lynch Williams (*My Angelica*, 1995), Kristen D. Randle (*The Only Alien on the Planet*, 1996), and Sneed Collard (*A Whale Biologist at Work*, 2000) who taught writing strategies, answered and asked questions, and gave slide presentations about their work. The students were thrilled to meet these authors, learn about their writing process, and talk with them about the book they had read for book club. Louise said, "Carol Lynch Williams was so nice. I probably wouldn't have read her book on my own, but now that I've read one and liked it, I've invited her to come speak to my writers' critique group, and she said she would. A real live author!"

When Adults Model Reading, Reluctant Readers Take Notice

One of the most successful ways to show students the importance of reading is to let them see us read and to hear about the books we have read. This modeling should come not only from librarians and English teachers but also from all adults in the school. Several years ago a student came to me absolutely incredulous because he saw his history teacher reading a novel. The student told me that before then, he thought only English teachers read, so why would he want to read for himself?

Publishers try to tell us what books are targeted toward certain age groups, but how many adults do you know who read the Harry Potter books? The reading comprehension level for this series is appropriate for ages 9–12; however, Rowling would not have found her books at the top of *The New York Times* bestseller list for weeks on end without the adult fans who couldn't wait to read the next book. Teenagers love to read books they see their parents and friends reading. Personal recommendations will do more to promote a book than any advertising campaign. The resurgence of Tolkien's popularity among teens and adults serves as proof. Author Bob Mayer (2002) says, "There are no markets in fiction, no age limit on who can or should read it."

Book Talks

I keep 4 x 6 note cards handy so that when I finish reading a book I can jot down a few notes to share with my students. The school media specialist can assist with book talks on a particular theme or genre. Donald Graves (1991) encourages us to "Look for books which portray lifelike situations that parallel [students'] own experience or interests" (p. 78). Book talks can take many forms, even Power Point presentations. The importance of book talks is to let students know that there are great authors and books that can speak directly to them. I don't shy away from the tough topics. Favorite titles this year for my students included *Speak* by Laurie Halse Anderson (1999), *Choosing Up Sides* by John H. Ritter (2000), and *Cut* by Patricia McCormick (2002).

Selecting Books for Reluctant Readers and for Avid Readers

I've been using these methods now for 5 years. Of course, there have been some modifications and adaptations along the way, but what I have described in this chapter I have successfully used for at least 2 years. I have a few classic pieces of literature I use from year to year, like William Shakespeare's *Romeo & Juliet* and Jack London's *The Call of the Wild*. I also use more modern classics such as *The Cay* by Theodore Taylor (1969) and *Across Five Aprils* by Irene Hunt (1964), and more contemporary novels such as *Out of the Dust* by Karen Hesse (1989) and *Romiette and Julio* by Sharon M. Draper (1999). The freshness in my teaching comes each year as I continue to read and discover the newest novels, then share them with my students every way I possibly can. Table 3-1 gives a list of additional book titles.

You can tell what book is appropriate for your students to read the same way you select a book for yourself. Is the book entertaining? Is the subject interesting? Has the child seen a movie based on the story? Is the book at her independent reading level? Are there characters with whom the child can identify or sympathize? Are the language and situations appropriate to community values? Can the child make connections to the book and himself, another text, or the world? If you answer yes to any of these questions, the book might be one you should recommend. Remember: A good book is a good book, no matter what the age of the reader. My final piece of advice is allow your students to have success, no matter what, if you want them to become lifelong readers. Our world is in need of readers. Those who read, think; those who think, act; and those who act, change the world.

Table 3-1. Recommended Books for Read-Alouds, Reading Partners, or Book Clubs

> Over the past few years, I have had the luxury of buying and reading a number of young adult novels as a result of the Christa McAuliffe Fellowship I received. Many of these novels have rapidly worked their way into my classroom library and curriculum. I'm seeing reluctant readers and nonreaders come into my classroom and discover the joy of reading or listening to a good book, a book they can connect with through character, conflict, or theme. Although some of these novels become part of my formal curriculum, more often I simply share these books in one way or another.
>
> Draper, Sharon M. (2000). *Romiette and Julio.* New York: Putnam.
>
> Fletcher, Susan (1951). *Shadow Spinner.* New York: Atheneum Books.
>
> Gantos, Jack. (1998). *Joey Pigza Swallowed the Key.* New York: Farrar, Straus & Giroux.
>
> Haddix, Margaret Peterson. (2000). *Among the Hidden.* New York: Aladdin Library.
>
> Hobbs, Will. (1999). *The Maze.* New York: Camelot.
>
> Hobbs, Will. (2000). *Jason's Gold.* New York: Harper Trophy.
>
> Holt, Kimberly Willis. (2000). *My Louisiana Sky.* New York: Yearling Books.
>
> Myers, Walter Dean. (2001). *Monster.* New York: HarperCollins.
>
> Paulsen, Gary. (1998). *Soldier's Heart: Being the Story of the Enlistment and Due Service of the Boy Charley Goddard in the First Minnesota Volunteers.* New York: Delacourte Press.
>
> Paulsen, Gary. (2001). *Brian's Return.* New York: Dell Laurel-Leaf.
>
> Paulsen, Gary. (2001). *Guts.* New York: Delacourte Press.
>
> Peck, Richard. (1998). *A Long Way From Chicago.* New York: Dial Books.
>
> Pullman, Philip. (2000). *I Was a Rat.* New York: Knopf.
>
> Ritter, John H. (2000). *Choosing Up Sides.* New York: Puffin.
>
> Rowling, J. K. (1998). *Harry Potter and the Sorcerer's Stone.* New York: Scholastic.
>
> Sacher, Louis. (2000). *Holes.* New York: Yearling Books.
>
> Spinelli, Jerry. (2000). *Stargirl.* New York: Knopf.
>
> White, Robb. (1973). *Deathwatch.* New York: Dell.
>
> Williams, Carol Lynch. (2000). *My Angelica.* New York: Young Yearling.

References

Allen, J. (1999, November). *Saving our students through laughter.* Paper presented at the National Council of Teachers of English fall conference, Denver, CO.

Allen, J., & Gonzales, K. (1998). *There's room here for me: Literacy workshop in the middle school.* Portland, ME: Stenhouse.

Anderson, L. H. (1999). *Speak.* New York: Farrar, Straus & Giroux.

Atwell, N. (1987). *In the middle: Writing, reading, and learning with adolescents.* NH: Boynton/Cook.

Collard, S. (2000). *A whale biologist at work.* New York: Watts.

Creech, S. (1991). *Walk two moons.* New York: Harper Trophy.

Daniels, H. (1994). *Literature circles: voice and choice in the student-centered classroom.* Portland, ME: Stenhouse.

Draper, S. (1999). *Romiette and Julio.* New York: Scholastic.

Graves, D. H. (1991) *Build a literate classroom.* Portsmouth, NH: Heinemann.

Hesse, K. (1989). *Out of the dust.* New York: Scholastic.

Hugo, V. (1987). *Les Miserables.* New York: Signet.

Hunt, I. (1964). *Across five Aprils.* Chicago: Follet.

Keene, E. O., & Zimmerman, S. (1997). *Mosaic of thought: Teaching comprehension in a reader's workshop.* Portsmouth, NH: Heinemann.

London, J. (1993). *The call of the wild.* New York: Penguin.

Mayer, B. (2002, October). *The fiction writer's toolkit.* Paper presented at the League of Utah Writers Fall Round-Up, Salt Lake City.

McCormick, P. (2002). *Cut.* New York: Scholastic.

Mikaelsen, B. (2002). *Touching spirit bear.* New York: Harper Trophy.

Paulsen, G. (1998). *Brian's winter.* New York: Laureleaf.

Peck. R. (2002). *A year down yonder.* New York: Puffin.

Randle, K. D. (1996). *The only alien on the planet.* New York: Scholastic.

Rief, L. (1992). *Seeking diversity: Language arts with adolescents.* Portsmouth, NH: Heinemann.

Ritter, J. (2000). *Choosing up sides.* New York: Puffin.

Rowling, J. K. (2000). *Harry Potter and the prisoner of Azkaban.* New York: Bantam Books Audio.

Rowling, J. K. (2002). *Harry Potter and the goblet of fire.* New York: Scholastic.

Sacher, L. (2000). *Holes.* New York: Yearling Books.

Spinelli, J. (2000). *Stargirl.* New York: Knopf.

Taylor, T. (1969). *The cay.* New York: Doubleday.

Twain, M. (1986). *The adventures of Huckleberry Finn.* New York: Penguin.

Voigt, C. (2002). *Homecoming.* New York: Pocket Books.

Williams, C. L. (2000). *My Angelica.* New York: Young Yearling.

Part II

Reading and Writing About Literature

4

Flash Fiction and Luminous Pedagogy: Using Short-Short Stories to Teach Writing

Albert E. Wilhelm

Flash cards! Flash Gordon! Flash dancing! To this tradition of speed and spectacle, we now add flash fiction. This phrase provides the title for an anthology of very brief short stories edited by James and Denise Thomas and Tom Hazuka (1992). Along with Robert Shapard, James Thomas was also a compiler of two earlier collections entitled *Sudden Fiction* (1986) and *Sudden Fiction International* (1989). The stories in these two volumes range in length from 1,000 to 2,000 words. Those selected for *Flash Fiction* are considerably shorter—as few as 250 and never more than 750 words. In fact, Thomas et al. (1992) comment that their original plan was to print the complete text of each story on facing pages so that a reader could apprehend it "all at once" without even turning a page. Since this format would require "no enforced pause in the reader's attention, no break in the field of vision" (p. 12), they called the pieces *flash fiction*. I find these stories ideal for class analysis, not only from the standpoint of literature—with which students practice the analytical skills they will later transfer to longer works of fiction—but from a rhetorical approach that leads them to incorporate greater subtleties into their own writing.

Although the name *flash fiction* may be both inventive and apt, it has not been widely adopted. Instead, numerous other names have been offered for these very short stories and their slightly longer cousins. Depending upon length, such stories are called *mini-*, *micro-*, *quick*, or *skinny fiction*. Robert Coover's *TriQuarterly* has used the label *minute fiction* (as in *minute waltz*), and Philip F. O'Connor has suggested the name *sto*—a truncated version of the word *story* to denote (somewhat mimetically, one assumes) an abbreviated literary form (Shapard & Thomas, 1986, p. 243). Even more informal names like *snappers* and *blasters* have been used to describe some short-short stories (pp. xiv–xv).

The Appeal of Short Fiction

Such a wealth of nomenclature suggests a high degree of interest in this literary form by writers of fiction and critics alike. Philip Stevick has called very short stories "the ur-form of narration" (Shapard & Thomas, 1986, p. 242), and ancient fables and parables provide obvious evidence that the genre is indeed venerable. Even though the form may boast a long tradition, its current surge in popularity is still remarkable. In an age of capsule summaries, sound bites, and instant analysis, flash fiction could be no more than a superficial symptom of literary trendiness. On the other hand, it may be a more profound—and quite revealing—manifestation of the contemporary sensibility, which is becoming increasingly attuned to abbreviated reading, such as that seen on a Web site.

In his introduction to *Sudden Fiction International* (Shapard & Thomas, 1989), Charles Baxter attributes the broad appeal of short-short stories to the prevailing skepticism of modern times. "Explanations," he says, "don't seem to be explaining very much anymore. Authoritative accounts have a way of looking like official lies. [Hence,] If you don't know the whole truth, you might as well keep whatever you have to say short" (p. 22). In a similar vein, David Brooks comments that the very short story has emerged from a "structural/post-structural meltdown" in which the novel and the epic poem are "becoming unstuck" (Shapard & Thomas, 1989, p. 308). If one can discover, Brooks continues, "where the great omniscient narratives have gone" and be able to "explain where the glue went," then one may have "found the seedbed of the short-short story" (p. 308).

What Short Fiction Offers Teachers

Since sudden and flash fictions have captured the attention of writers and critics, perhaps these forms deserve more careful examination by teachers. Such stories may offer definite pedagogical value—especially in classes that use literary texts as the bases for writing assignments. Students who routinely receive much of their sensory stimuli from screens (televisions, video games, computer monitors) may have little patience with long reading assignments or even with the printed word in general. My students, especially the ones who might be categorized as "at risk," are often cowed by long selections. Fearing their own lack of capability, frequently they will genuinely protest that they "can't read all that" and throw up their hands in resignation. A lack of reading skill has reinforced an accompanying lack of confidence.

Trying to create lessons that will challenge such students while not undermining their confidence, I have looked beyond the usual textbooks and supplementary readings, searching for appropriate assignments that will engage but not intimidate. In today's market, we are very fortunate. The current abundance of high-quality short-short stories helps teachers to maintain high academic standards while using texts that students can and will read completely and perhaps even reread. My students' skills as readers and as writers have advanced dramatically using flash fiction, simply because, as they say, "Hey! I can handle this!"

Using Flash Fiction to Write About Literature

The use of sudden or flash fiction may be particularly advantageous in classes where students are learning to write about literature. In such classes teachers may sometimes be tempted to focus on literary analysis rather than writing skills, and students who are studying long texts may get bogged down in material they do not understand. The brevity and sharp focus of flash fiction allow appropriate exposure to literary techniques but conserve class time for judicious attention to writing strategies.

In her classic book on teaching writing, *Errors and Expectations*, Mina Shaughnessy (1977) notes that many kinds of reading assignments (e.g., literature, language, social studies) can provide "the base of information from which students draw their ideas" (p. 246). She believes, however, that in all cases students should be "led gradually and with awareness from relatively simple to more complex tasks of conceptualization, for it is largely by observing themselves 'get' ideas that students begin to understand the difference between facts and inferences, subordinate and superordinate statements" (p. 246). For several reasons, assignments of flash fiction can serve well in accomplishing this pedagogical task. The facts of a typical flash fiction are sparse but bristling with implication.

Given the paucity of events in most of these stories, a student should not be tempted to stick with the facts and merely write a plot summary. Instead, both the events and the obvious gaps in the narration can lead a student on to inferential leaps that may become the basis for informed and intelligent writing. Shaughnessy goes on to say that student writers should begin to develop "governing statements from small pools of data" (p. 246). Since very short stories limit the facts and sharpen the focus, they offer manageable pools of information on which good writing can be firmly grounded. With specific textual evidence readily at hand (not buried somewhere in the middle of a 400-page novel), the student may learn more easily to provide support for assertions and not descend to mushy generalizations.

Many examples of short-short stories suitable for class use are available in the three volumes named above. Some that I have found good for engaging students and stimulating good writing are "Any Minute Mom Should Come Blasting Through the Door" by David Ordan, "Reunion" by John Cheever, "Popular Mechanics" by Raymond Carver (all three from Shapard & Thomas, 1986), "Snow" by Ann Beattie (from Shapard & Thomas, 1986), and "232-9979" by Carol Edelstein (from Thomas et al., 1992). In addition, some standard textbooks include a few pieces of sudden or flash fiction. For example, *The Norton Anthology of Short Fiction* (Cassill, 1986) contains a fine story by Larry French. Entitled "Merry Christmas God," this piece contains fewer than 500 words but still provides a comprehensive study of the emotional dynamics of a failed marriage. It deals with a couple who are separated but get together briefly to decorate a Christmas tree and wrap presents for their small children.

Working With a Specific Story

French's story can serve as a good illustration of the pedagogical values of flash fiction. Since this piece is so economical in its use of detail, it permits the luxury of comprehensive analysis. I have sometimes introduced the story by asking students to consider a brief passage from Edgar Allan Poe's review of *Twice-Told Tales*. Here Poe asserts that in the entire text of a tale "there should be no word written, of which the tendency, direct or indirect, is not to the one pre-established design" (Hough, 1965, p. 136). Then, as a prewriting exercise, I ask students to produce an exhaustive anatomy of "Merry Christmas God"—to itemize details of setting, character, and plot and offer comments about how each detail contributes to the "design" of the story. We use a multitude of *why* questions, asking students for deep interpretations rather than shallow facts. For example:

- Why is the time of the story shortly before Christmas?
- Why does all the action occur around a partially decorated tree?
- Why do Christmas songs by Bing Crosby play in the background?
- Why does the hostile husband put tinsel on the tree "one strand at a time" (Cassill, 1986, p. 604)?
- Why does he suggest a Christmas gift of vitamins for his estranged wife?
- Why do the Christmas lights flash on and off?
- Why does the husband ultimately bite a flashing bulb until the glass shatters and he tastes blood?
- Why do tiny glass fragments fall on top of the children's gifts?
- Why is the title of the story appropriate?

Such specific questions, followed by detailed explanations, usually lead my students to significant insights. For example, one student commented on the ironic dissonance between the nostalgic background music and the harsh reality of the dysfunction depicted. The idyllic images of a white Christmas contrast sharply with actual scenes of holiday family combat. Another student saw the action of applying tinsel "one strand at a time" as evidence of the husband's "obsessive need for control—both of tree decorations and of people." Still another student interpreted glass fragments falling on the children's gifts as a suggestion that the unseen children are the real victims in this shattered family. After studying the story, many students reconsidered the meaning of its title and understood why French presents it without the usual punctuation. They saw it no longer as a cheerful greeting addressed to God but as a sarcastic indictment ending with an irreverent expletive.

Armed with a battery of specifics and some thoughts about how such specifics contribute to the overall effect of the story, students should be prepared for the next stage of writing. In Shaughnessy's (1977) terms, they can now progress from subordinate to superordinate statements. After this preliminary analysis they should be able to formulate arguments for papers and use appropriate specific evidence from their prewriting to support all assertions.

Student Responses

My students have found that working with flash fiction breaks down the real and imagined barriers they found in approaching the interpretation of literature, whether in their reading or in their writing. End-of-course evaluations invariably comment on how, when they entered the class, they thought they "would never be able" to read or write as literary critics with any feeling of authority. Now, they say, they can. Flash fiction proved to be a medium they could handle. In more recent years, I have used this form for classes of all ability levels, finding the same measure of success. Although some students may need to stay with flash fiction for a more extended time than others, every level finds short-short stories a most satisfactory beginning for the investigation of longer works as well.

In extolling the pedagogical virtues of short-short stories, I of course have no intention of devaluing those important literary works that are more expansive. My argument is simply that flash fiction may offer many advantages, both for the student and the teacher, in introductory writing and literature classes. Paul Theroux claims that in most cases a good short-short story "contains a novel" (Shapard & Thomas, 1986, p. 228). Surely, then, the student who learns to appreciate the craftsmanship of "Merry Christmas God" and to write intelligently about it can eventually do the same with longer and more formidable texts. Try it and you will be convinced.

References

Cassill, R. V. (Ed.). (1986). *The Norton anthology of short fiction* (3rd ed.). New York: Norton.

Hough, R. L. (Ed.). (1965). *Literary criticism of Edgar Allan Poe*. Lincoln, NE: University of Nebraska Press.

Shapard, R., & Thomas, J. (Eds.). (1986). *Sudden fiction: American short-short stories*. Salt Lake City: Gibbs Smith.

Shapard, R., & Thomas, J. (Eds.). (1989). *Sudden fiction international: Sixty short-short stories*. New York: Norton.

Shaughnessy, M. P. (1977). *Errors and expectations: A guide for the teacher of basic writing*. New York: Oxford University Press.

Thomas, J., Thomas, D., & Hazuka, T. (Eds.). (1992). *Flash fiction: Very short stories*. New York: Norton.

5

Using *The Bean Trees* to Develop an Engaged Community of Readers and Writers

Rebecca Woosley

After many years of teaching high school English, I am still surprised to discover that some of my seniors come with preconceived notions about reading assignments. These students assume that the assigned novels will be written in a style that they find difficult to read and understand. They also assume that the reading will bore them. It's no surprise, then, that these seniors are reluctant readers. Sadly, their previous experiences with assigned reading has taught them lessons their teachers never intended.

Developing Lifetime Readers

We all remember the book that turned us into a lifetime reader. It was so good, so interesting that we hated to finish reading it. Forever after, we've become readers in search of another book that will delight us as much as the first book. I wanted my seniors to have that same experience, but what book would work for them? As soon as I read Barbara Kingsolver's bestseller, *The Bean Trees* (1993), I knew I'd found *the* book. My instincts proved correct. When my students turned in their final response journals, I found that many chose to "assess" the novel, even though it was not required. One reluctant reader wrote, "I usually don't like to read, but I liked this book, because Taylor is a lot like me. She's struggling to be independent, but what she really needs is to *belong*."

Another student commented in his journal as follows:

> The first thing I noticed about this book was how Taylor thinks like I do. She tends to make obvious, simple statements, because she can't always express the complex ideas she has. Even though she is a girl, and I'm a guy, I understand her character. She often feels unsure of herself, and although she's deeply compassionate, she maintains a distant reserve with people until she knows them. What's more, had she been different, I'd probably have hated the book. Instead, it is the first

book I've "connected" with in a long time, and what's amazing—an *English teacher* assigned it!

When I read those responses, I knew we had struck "learning pay dirt"!

Like the students quoted above, most seniors accept *The Bean Trees* because they identify with Taylor Greer, the main character, whose predicament resembles their own. Like many high school seniors, Taylor comes from a nontraditional family, is anxious about her future, and struggles to define who she is. Most of all, she is eager to establish her independence. The special appeal of the novel lies in the perspective and the voice of a young adult. Besides capturing students' youthful imaginations, the novel challenges their preconceived notion about the kind of reading they will do in an English class. For many seniors, one of the novel's greatest values is the way it causes them to examine their own attitudes about social issues rather than simply accepting the attitudes expressed by others without question. This is critical, because my ultimate objective is to teach them *how* to think, not *what* to think.

Beginning *The Bean Trees*: Reading Journals With a Twist

Two of the assignments I designed for *The Bean Trees* study provide students with a focus and hopefully, invite insightful thinking about issues, such as gender, cultural stereotypes, and what constitutes a community.

Prereading With Journal Entries

Prior to beginning the novel, I provide students with a context for the novel to entice their curiosity. After 2 or 3 days of activities to develop context, I assign reader response prompts (Table 5-1). This initial assignment guides 15 of the 20 required entries, providing the foundation for all the activities and discussions that unfold during later study and discussion of the novel. These journal responses offer two advantages: (a) they provide even shy or reluctant participants with a "voice" during class discussions and group activities, and (b) they also become a place for students to express their thoughts in their natural "writers' voices."

In *The Bean Trees* journal requirement in Table 5-1, I define the number and minimum length of the journal entries and two due dates. I do this for several reasons. First, I want students to think, react, and/or respond to each of the issues I've included in the assignment. By designating a requirement for a specific number of responses, I can make sure that happens. Giving students the freedom to respond to the prompts in any order keeps the assignment from locking them into a rigid, artificially imposed order. Second, I ask students to write at least a half-page response each time to push their thinking. Often students who write only two or three sentences don't scratch the surface of their thoughts. The thoughts they express are superficial at best. Requiring that students add five additional topics gives them some flexibility. Often the topics of their choice are a pleasant surprise, like the ones mentioned earlier offering unsolicited praise of the novel.

Table 5-1: *The Bean Trees* Journal Requirement

> Due Date _____. Mid-Assignment Check Date _____.
>
> **Directions**: As you read Barbara Kingsolver's *The Bean Trees,* you will keep a reader response journal. Be sure you follow directions carefully to ensure full credit for the journal. It will count as much as a unit exam. Be sure to write at least a half page on each topic. Below are 17 journal topics. You may select any 15 on which to write. Add 5 of your own for the total required minimum of 20 entries. You may choose to write about these topics in any order. Make sure you include the letter of your choice of topics to identify it. Your entries *must* be responses to or discussions of key issues you encounter as you read *The Bean Trees.*
>
> A. Traits you share in common with Taylor or how you differ from her
> B. Character strengths and/or weaknesses of Taylor
> C. Gender roles
> D. Regional and/or social biases
> E. The significance of references to 1-800-THE-LORD
> F. The image the novel creates of life in Kentucky
> G. The treatment of refugees (immigrants)
> H. The ethics of choices made by Esteban and Esperanza
> I. Abandonment
> J. The meaning of *community*
> K. The significance of the rhizobia in *The Bean Trees* (discuss more than the superficial significance)
> L. The significance of all the emphasis on vegetables and plants
> M. The significance of the night-blooming Cereus in the context of the novel
> N. Taylor's name change
> O. Stereotypes
> P. Kingsolver's use of suspense
> Q. Good parenting skills

Journals give students a voice during class discussions by allowing them to write what they think, even if they lack the confidence or expertise to speak out in class. As students compare perspectives and share insights that they expressed earlier in their journals, they engage in an energetic, sometimes passionate, exchanges of ideas about issues like the treatment of immigrants. To stimulate their thinking, I bring in current articles representing both sides of the issues they discuss in class; I encourage students to do the same. Ethical issues, like Mattie's involvement with illegal immigrants or the circumstances of Turtle's illegal adoption, often draw the most insightful reflection and even provide the impetus for unassigned research. Stimulated by the need to support their arguments, previously unmotivated students voluntarily engage in purposeful research and return to class armed with credible evidence they can cite. The benefits of the initial response journal assignment make the time investment on the students' and my part worthwhile. Without my requiring it, students make relevant connections between *The Bean Trees* and their own lives. Those connections engage readers' thinking, fostering more effective reading skills. The real "icing on the cake" comes when students groan when class ends, and they even begin class discussion the next day without my direction!

Journal Entries As Formative Assessment

To ensure that all students make frequent, well-paced journal responses, I collect journals midway through the assignment period. Reading and responding to their entries at the midway point makes certain that students are keeping up with the assignment. It also reveals any confusion readers may have and prompts well-reasoned questions. More important, it gives me a window on their insights. I respond by writing notes in the margins of their journals offering encouragement to students who have expressed valuable insights, especially those students who were reluctant to participate in class discussions. Conversely, it allows me to push the thinking of a student who has missed the point.

The mid-assignment due date and a final due date for the response journals benefits the students. When responding to superficial early entries, I can encourage students to "revisit" the responses when they finish reading the novel. I ask writers to use a different color ink when they return to "finish their thinking" in an earlier entry. Frequently, when responding to a later prompt, after students have finished (or nearly finished) reading *The Bean Trees*, they will often refer to an earlier entry as they make a new connection or gain a deeper insight. For example, one student wrote the following:

> In an earlier entry I said I thought abandonment was a possible theme, because throughout the book I saw it happening repeatedly. Taylor, for instance, abandoned her Kentucky "roots," the Native American woman abandoned Turtle, Lou Ann's husband abandoned her and their baby, and both Esteban and Esperanza abandoned their daughter. Now that I'm finished reading the novel, I realize the book is more about "belonging." While Taylor did abandon her roots, in a sense, she was really looking for a place to belong—a support community. From the time she met Mattie, she became a part of an interdependent community of people supporting each other socially and emotionally. What's more, much like the rhizobia support the growth of plants, Taylor's community contributed to her growth as well.

To be certain I identify which topic students are writing about in each entry (because students may choose to write about the assigned topics in any order), I ask them to label each entry with the identifying letter of the prompt. If students identify their responses by letter, they are much easier for me to respond to and to grade.

The reflection journals receive the same point value I give an exam for several reasons. I want the students to know that I value the assignment and that I expect them to put some effort into writing their response journals. In addition, the journal can be a useful resource for students during class discussions. By giving them an incentive to invest in the journal and approach each response thoughtfully, I lay the foundation for their active participation in class and for their future success.

Pigs in Heaven: The Prequel

One way that I maintain student interest in their new reading connection is by sharing excerpts from Barbara Kingsolver's *Pigs in Heaven* (1994), a novel in which she explores the cultural controversy surrounding Turtle's adoption outside her Native American culture. Having already explored this issue during sometimes emotional discussions while reading *The Bean Trees,* the *Pigs in Heaven* excerpts I select now pique student interest, enticing them to read this second novel on their own. This, after all, is my goal. The "silver lining" is that my students become better readers, and, more significant, they become better thinkers because they engage directly with the book and with their peers whose opinions may differ.

A Talk Show Provides Summative Assessment

Using the response journal as a resource, we conclude *The Bean Trees* study with the culminating group activity (Table 5-2) in which all students participate. This activity, a summative assessment designed to evaluate students' understanding of characters and theme in the novel, establishes the framework and expectations for their group presentation. Group members have total ownership of how they satisfy the performance criteria. Before the group work begins, we view some prerecorded talk show video clips and analyze them. As the class discusses how real-world talk show formats vary from exaggerated, highly emotional productions to serious, fact-based scenarios, students gain a better understanding of what they are expected to do, and excitement mounts.

It is important that students know in advance what the teacher's expectations are and how they will be assessed. After reviewing the characteristics of the talk show format, the class examines the assignment in Table 5-2, giving group members the opportunity to clarify directions. I also emphasize the evaluation criteria I will use to assess each group. One advantage of this performance-based activity is that it offers students with different learning styles an opportunity to meet unit goals by demonstrating their insights and knowledge. By working together to plan their talk show, students share and clarify their ideas before presenting them.

Table 5-2: *The Bean Trees* Talk Show Requirements

Purpose: The purpose of this activity is to give you an opportunity to demonstrate your understanding of characters and theme in *The Bean Trees* using a talk show format. There will be four or five people in your group.

Directions:
1. All team members must take an active part in the talk show.
2. Each team member (except for the one who acts as host) will assume the personality and role of one of the eight characters listed below.
   - Taylor
   - Lou Ann
   - Taylor's mom
   - Mattie
   - Esteban
   - Esperanza
   - Edna Poppy
   - Virgie
   - Turtle
3. Your presentation will demonstrate:
   - The primary character traits of the characters you choose to portray
   - The influence of that character on other characters (Note: Consider this when selecting which characters your team will include in the talk show.)
   - How the characters need or support others
4. Your team will choose a creative title that "fits" the talk show.

Evaluation Criteria:
1. Logic of character choices
2. Quality of questions and responses
3. Depth and complexity of insights provided through the presentation
4. Accuracy of information (i.e., Was the information text-based or misrepresented?)
5. All team members involved
6. Creative show title

While all team members must participate by contributing to the script and by taking an active role in the presentation, they have control over deciding what that role will be. As a result, the artist and the literary analyst in the group make equally valuable contributions. These student presentations are always creative and engaging. The key value of this activity, however, is the insights that students reveal. That outcome often leads to more meaningful class discussions in later units of study.

Why Use These Assignments?

These two assignments accomplish several objectives at the same time. First, students read the novel—a unique experience for some—in order to complete the assigned tasks. Even reluctant readers ultimately read this book, because the issues in *The Bean Trees* are relevant to their world, making them want to participate in class discussions and even do purposeful research to support their positions. Then, as students share ideas and responsibilities, they develop their group social skills, and they better understand the social issues raised in the novel. The big advantage, however, is that their journal writings and their talk show presentations give them a better understanding of each other.

Always, when students write reflections about our year together, they praise these activities and encourage me to use them again next year. I not only engage my seniors in reading early in the semester but, best of all, I establish connections to good literature while laying the foundation for a community of thinking readers and writers. Through the nonthreatening journal format, I can assess students' written expression, their thinking abilities, and their study habits. By the end of our study, we all benefit from reading *The Bean Trees*. I know my students better. They know each other better and are now more receptive when I assign the next reading. Finally, they are willing to believe that not all assigned novels are difficult to read and understand.

References

Kingsolver, B. (1993). *The bean trees*. Boston: HarperCollins.
Kingsolver, B. (1994). *Pigs in heaven*. Boston: Harper Perennial.

6

"You Would Pluck Out the Heart of My Mystery": A Close Reading of Hamlet

Paul Stein

As a part of our senior curriculum, most students read the entire text of William Shakespeare's *Hamlet*; others read significant portions of the play. I teach *Hamlet* every year and have grown to love the drama in a way that I want desperately to engender in my students. Yet for some time I have had a nagging feeling that, in reading the play, many of my students were relying on me to do much of the work for them, rather than taking their own first steps in mastering the text. I began to look closely at the engagement displayed by my students, who are Honors English and Advanced Placement seniors. Even there, where we devote 5 or 6 weeks to the play, many students did not demonstrate what we might call "ownership" of the play. Since I had seen them become deeply involved in so many other works of similar difficulty, I knew it was up to me to devise a new approach. This idea sprang from that need and has served my students and me—and, I believe, Shakespeare's tragedy—very well.

It seemed to me that my students' lack of engagement was partly a problem of scale. How can they be kept individually focused and engaged while undertaking a task that can seem overwhelming: language, dramatic structure, complexity of characters, the necessity of spending so much class time explicating text, and the large number of themes? It seemed partly a problem of student competence. The difficulty of the reading makes it necessary to do a good deal of group work in dealing with the play. In the daily rhythm of class activity—watching video, discussing and explicating text, and dramatic reading—how does the teacher hold individual students accountable for their own struggles with the text?

It also seemed partly a problem of focus. In a play with such dramatic tension and powerful language, what stands out to students? How can students be taught to annotate text, assimilate information, and organize an interpretation when it seems to them that almost every line in the play could be highlighted? How can they escape the feeling that the play is a blur of landscape they are watching from a fast-moving train?

Narrowing the Focus

One answer seemed to me to be to narrow the focus of each student. In addition to responsibility for being on task during class and contributing to the discussion, each student is assigned a particular set of questions upon which to focus throughout the play. While students are reading, discussing, and thinking, they are also annotating the play for one topic, gathering evidence for a report to their peers.

In order to make the assignment more fun, students are told that, much like Hamlet's school chums (Rosencrantz and Guildenstern), they have been recruited by the king and queen of Denmark to spy upon Hamlet. Each spy (even if assigned to work in pairs or teams) must submit annotations, a report of findings supported by evidence from the text to the new king, Fortinbras, at the end of the play. In this chapter, all references to *Hamlet* are from standard editions that are out of copyright.

To add an element of authentic assessment, I ask my headmaster to play the role of Fortinbras, which, as a former English teacher, he does each year with great enjoyment, asking students clarifying questions after their presentations. Other knowledgeable people would do as well—a colleague on plan time, the district coordinator, or a professor from a local community college or university. The room is provided with a "throne" and His Majesty with a robe and crown, and students must demonstrate proper etiquette before the king. I collect and grade the annotations when we finish Act II, to see that students are on track, and again with the final reports. I give the report the weight of two regular essay assignments. Although I require each student to write a report, depending on class size, only one for each topic will be read.

The Assignment

"You would pluck out the heart of my mystery" (III, ii)

King Claudius and Queen Gertrude of Denmark have already sent for Hamlet's school chums, Rosencrantz and Guildenstern, to keep watch on Hamlet, as the king says,

> To draw him on to pleasures, and together
>
> So much as from occasion you may glean,
>
> Whether aught to us unknown afflicts him thus. (II, ii)

The problem is that Polonius, counselor to the king and father of the fair Ophelia, and Rosencrantz and Guildenstern are giving the royal couple contradictory readings of the situation. Polonius is convinced that Hamlet is mad. Yet what is madness? How is it defined, and by whom? How does one judge the sanity of another?

The king and queen have also sent for you, I tell the students, because of your unique opportunity to observe all that takes place in the play, and because, lacking full confidence in Rosencrantz and Guildenstern, they want other opinions from observers close to Hamlet's age. It could be well worth your while to be the ones who solve the deep mystery of Hamlet's odd behavior. Your task is to observe closely throughout the play and to take careful notes to present as evidence to the king and queen. Your annotations must note when and where the observations were made (act, scene, lines), and what the circumstances were.

The dilemma you face is that young Hamlet's behavior has not only been rude, strange, and inappropriate; it has also been inconsistent and somewhat contradictory. Not only that, but he has developed a fondness for speaking to others in riddles and for responding to complaints with further provocation. He appears to have become surly, resentful, and sarcastic toward his elders.

At other times he seems lucid, in command of himself and, indeed, quite cunning. Because they do not want Hamlet to know he is being watched, and because the task is complex and there are many of you, the king and queen have divided the assignment into a number of areas of responsibility. You have been asked to investigate the area of behavior assigned to you, make what sense you can of it, and report your findings to the king and queen.

By many twists of fate (and plot) the play has ended with Fortinbras of Norway's declaring himself king of Denmark, named by the dying Hamlet as heir to the throne and in satisfaction of ancestral rights.

Unfortunately, neither Claudius nor Gertrude has survived, and now the new king, Fortinbras, in consultation with Hamlet's friend Horatio, has determined to hear the reports ordered by Claudius and Gertrude, in order to satisfy both himself and the populace that all is now set right in the state of Denmark.

Possible Forms for the Report

Your report must take the following form, I tell the students:

1. Careful annotations concerning Hamlet's behavior, moods, and attitudes, bearing upon your assigned area, with notations of the place and circumstances of each observation. Each annotation must have proper textual reference (act, scene, lines), in case the king and queen wish to check the accuracy of your observations. Each spy must submit his or her own annotations, one to a note card.

2. A report to the king summarizing your findings. Your report should (a) emphasize the most important evidence to the king, explaining why it is significant, and (b) evaluate the evidence, taking into account and giving proper weight to its complexity and ambiguity and its somewhat contradictory nature. A simplistic reading that tells the new king nothing but what he already knows could result in the loss of your head. This evaluation should be supported by quotations and references to incidents.

3. A presentation of your findings at court before the king, the other spies, and assembled guests, should you be summoned, reading your report and making recommendations, should the king ask.

Specific Questions for Student Investigation

The following areas are to be investigated by the spies.

The effectiveness of Rosencrantz and Guildenstern in fulfilling their commission from the royal couple. What does their relationship to Hamlet seem to be? Have they betrayed him? What motives seem to be revealed by their speech and actions? Those in charge have sent you to spy on their spies. Observe and report on all aspects of their performance. How are they doing?

Various characters' opinions of Hamlet's sanity, including Claudius, Gertrude, Polonius, Ophelia, Laertes, and Hamlet himself. Is he mad or merely playing at madness? What bias does each have that might prevent an accurate assessment? An important consideration will be the opinion of the playwright, William Shakespeare, as it may be inferred from the evidence.

Hamlet's behavior and speech. What is he doing and saying, and why? Is there a pattern or is he truly unpredictable? Is he in control of himself? What are his ambitions? Does he have some sort of plan or goal in mind? Is he guilty of plotting against King Claudius?

Hamlet's relationship to his mother. How does he treat his mother? What does he seem to think of her? What are the conflicts between them? Do they have a strong bond? Are there hints of incestuous feeling between them? Is Hamlet right in regarding her as a weak woman led astray, or is she a shrewd woman who has moved to protect her position? Does she betray him?

Hamlet's obsession with death. For a young man especially, Hamlet seems obsessed with death. He broods on the death of his father at the beginning of the play and on the deaths of loved ones and friends. He seems preoccupied with his own death and speaks about it several times. What is the reason for this obsession? What is his attitude toward death? What does this say about his character? About his values and priorities? About his sanity?

Hamlet's fitness to be king. As the rightful heir of his father, and as the designated heir to Claudius, Hamlet is next in line for the throne. Is he fit to rule? Does he have the character? The temperament? The abilities? The sanity and clarity of mind necessary to be king? Would he be as competent a ruler as Claudius or Fortinbras?

Hamlet's many loyalties. Indecisiveness has been called Hamlet's tragic flaw. Yet he is drawn in many directions by his loyalties to country, king, father, mother, lover, the people of Denmark, and his own rights of succession and ambitions. How do these many loyalties play out? What are his priorities and strongest commitments? Does he make any attempt to balance these forces pulling at him and if so, how? Is he or is he not truly indecisive, or might he have other weaknesses that could account for his lack of action?

Hamlet's relationship with Ophelia. Does Hamlet love Ophelia? Does she love him? Have they slept together? Is she "honest"? How much of a role does disappointed love play in Hamlet's state of mind? Is she naive and innocent in complying with her father's wishes, or does she know what she is doing? What reason does Hamlet have for abusing her so brutally in the lobby scene (III, i)?

How is this treatment to be reconciled with his ostentatious grief at her funeral? Has she driven him mad?

Hamlet's feelings of being trapped. He tells Rosencrantz and Guildenstern that Denmark is a prison. Throughout the play, there are images of confinement and freedom. How does this imagery work? Is what holds him prisoner all in his head? What would it take for him to escape the bonds that hold him? Does he make any effort to free himself?

The supernatural. What is the role of the supernatural in this play? Who seems able to see and hear the ghost, and who cannot? Is Hamlet fated by some superior force to inevitably come to his end? How does religious belief, including a belief in life after death, affect Hamlet's behavior? The king's? The queen's? What sort of moral resolution is there at the end of the play?

Justice. What is the concept of justice in Elizabethan England? Does Hamlet receive justice? Do both the good and the bad get what they deserve? Is there a good that is greater than justice in the play? If so, is it achieved, and how? Is Hamlet's end tragic? Triumphant? Does he achieve justice or merely gain revenge?

Evaluations of Student Work

Rubric for Annotations

Excellent. A thorough job of taking notes on the topic: Quotations are marked with quotation marks and line breaks are indicated with slashes (/) when quoting verse. Quotations are of appropriate length, not exceeding five lines, and fully indicated. Incidents from the plot are recorded with notations of the circumstances. The act, scene, and line numbers are recorded for all evidence. An abundance of good evidence has been recorded, one annotation per note card.

Very good. Thorough notes, but with minor problems: There may be less judgment about the relevance of quotations. Some notes may be of questionable usefulness or length. Quotations are marked with quotation marks and line breaks are indicated when quoting verse. Act, scene and line numbers are recorded. Quotations are of appropriate length, not exceeding five lines, and fully indicated. An abundance of good evidence has been recorded. Most of the time, the circumstances have been noted.

Good. Thorough notes, but some may be of questionable quality: There may be some lapses in judgment in recording relevant and useful evidence, or in judging appropriate length. Line breaks; act, scene, and line numbers; and quotation marks are all in place. There is sufficient evidence to support all aspects of the paper. Circumstances may not always be noted.

Limited. There is not adequate evidence to support the paper, demonstrating lack of close reading or lack of understanding of the implications of the topic. There may be problems with the mechanics of presenting evidence. Circumstances may not be noted.

Rubric for Reports

Excellent. The report demonstrates a thorough understanding of the topic and clearly explains its importance in the play. The report is well organized, with a strong thesis that answers the prompt and with main points that advance the argument. Commentary is insightful and reflects the complexity and ambiguity of the play. Ideas are thoroughly developed. Abundant evidence has been marshaled to support the observations of the student, quotations are in the correct form, and references to the text are correctly attributed.

Very good. While sound in its assertions, the report may not demonstrate a thorough understanding of the topic or of its importance in the play. Observations are supported by evidence, but the evidence may be thin or not judiciously chosen in some cases. The report is well organized, with a strong thesis that answers the prompt and with main points that advance the argument. Commentary may be less insightful than in an excellent paper or may miss crucial complexity or ambiguity in the presentation of characters, themes, or language. Some ideas may not be thoroughly developed. Abundant evidence has been marshaled to support the observations of the student, quotations are in the correct form, and references to the text are correctly attributed.

Good. Paper may have flaws: Though mostly correct in its assertions, the report may not demonstrate a complete understanding of the topic or of its importance in the play. Observations are supported by evidence, but some evidence may be skimpy or not relevant. The report may have flaws in organization, a weak thesis, or weak main points. Commentary on the evidence may be lacking or may not account for the complexity or ambiguity of characters, themes, or language. Some ideas may not be thoroughly developed. There is adequate evidence to support the observations of the student; quotations are in the correct form; and references to the text are correctly attributed.

Limited. The report demonstrates a serious lack of understanding of the topic, or of its importance to the play. Evidence may be lacking or misused. Commentary does not adequately explain either the evidence or the argument put forth. The student may not have followed the correct form in presenting or attributing evidence.

Reflections and Benefits

Because of the lasting benefits of doing this assignment, I place it early in the year. The papers produced have demonstrated a growing ability of students to grapple with texts of various kinds: The project requires students to engage in close reading, collect and assimilate relevant evidence, and present a persuasive analysis in answer to the assigned questions. The same argument that can be made for "authentic" assignments in the teaching of science—that students should learn by "doing" real science—applies here. Students are in fact doing what professional literary critics do: constructing an interpretation by engaging the text.

The direct, lasting benefits of their work are many. First, students gain confidence in dealing with text, a necessary foundation for any successful analysis. The quality of their writing about literature improves because the process is in the correct order: rather than constructing a thesis and then searching the text for validation, students learn that a thesis evolves as a result of thoughtful reading and evidence-gathering, focused around a question. The central task over the weeks spanned by our study becomes thinking about the topic as a whole rather than looking for quotations. This difference, my students and I have found, changes their entire view of how to approach a text, regardless of genre.

In the papers produced as a result of this assignment (see Appendix 6-A and Appendix 6-B for samples), the most frequent faults of student writing are mitigated: skimpy theoretical constructs, lack of an established point of view, evidence loosely connected to thesis and main points, and the tendency to read literature as some read the Bible—searching for validation of a previously formulated thesis rather than examining the text to see what it actually says. The assignment is "student-centered" in the best sense, because it requires students to process information actively rather than merely take notes on a discussion guided by someone else.

There are at least two important indirect benefits as well. One is that the assignment improves class discussion, because students are thinking throughout the play about how new scenes, new insights into character, new developments, and new sections of the text relate to their question. They become much more aware of the context of the play in considering a specific passage that is discussed. They ask more purposeful questions and are proud to have an area of expertise to contribute. To my students' delight, I often defer questions to a student who has been assigned that subject area. Another is that although they have had a specific focus in reading the text, students seem to come away with a better overall understanding of the play. I believe that this is due to a closer attention to the language of the script.

By giving students a specific focus, I provide them with a perspective for approaching the text, at least partial freedom from being overwhelmed by the enormity of the task, and an experience in textual interpretation that is rooted in close examination of the script. Many have reported that their confidence in their ability to interpret literature has soared after this assignment. If they can deal with *Hamlet* on a sophisticated level, there is no work they need to fear.

Appendix 6-A. Student Sample 1

To Be or Not to Be: Hamlet's Divided Loyalties
Stephan Sosnicki

Hamlet is unable to reach a decision about avenging his father's murder because he is torn in many directions by his various loyalties. His loyalty to his father and to his own honor makes him want revenge on his uncle, Claudius. However, it also gives him a conflicted view of his mother. Overanalyzing his filial duties leads him to lose his courage many times and miss chances to get his revenge. Because he was so reluctant and indecisive, the issue is forced to a sudden and bloody end. Thus, Hamlet's indecision leads to his tragic demise.

When the play opens, Hamlet is the only one still in mourning for his lost father. Claudius has taken the throne and Hamlet's mother has hastily entered an incestuous relationship with the king. Claudius points out that even though others are celebrating his wedding, Hamlet still mourns. He says,

> That father lost, lost his, and the survivor bound
>
> In filial obligation for some term
>
> To do obsequious sorrow: but to persevere
>
> In obstinate condolement is a course
>
> Of impious stubbornness. (I, ii)

Claudius tells Hamlet to stop mourning, even though Hamlet is the only one showing his father the proper respect. When Hamlet is visited by his father's ghost, and he learns that he has been murdered, Hamlet responds, "Haste me to know't, that I, with wings as swift / As meditation or the thoughts of love, / May sweep to my revenge" (I, v).

Hamlet immediately demonstrates his unquestioned loyalty by asking who killed his father so that he can get his revenge immediately. His loyalty to his father also manifests itself in open resentment to the king. Even before he knows that Claudius was his father's murderer, Hamlet says to the king, "I am too much I' the sun" (I, ii). This pun blatantly tells Claudius that he resents being his son. His loyalty to his true father outweighs his loyalty to this impostor. When he does find out that Claudius killed his father, he says, "So, uncle, there you are. Now to my word; / It is 'Adieu, adieu, remember me'" (I, v). He has sworn to avenge his father, even if it means killing the king, his uncle. Hamlet lists his grievances, saying, "He that hath kill'd my king, and whored my mother; / Popped in between th' election and my hopes; / Thrown out his angle for my proper life" (V, ii). He means that Claudius has killed his father, married his mother, stolen his crown, and tried to kill him. So, he reasons, he can kill Claudius in perfect conscience. His other loyalties completely void any he has felt toward the king.

The ghost also tells Hamlet to take care of his mother, Gertrude. This causes a crisis for Hamlet. His loyalty to his father makes him hate Gertrude and want to take revenge on her, too, but his respect for his father's dying wishes and his natural love for his mother won't let him. Hamlet is openly bitter to her. She asks, "Have you forgot me?" He answers, "You are the queen, your husband's brother's wife, / And—would it were not so!—you are my mother" (III, iv). He points her sins out to her and then blatantly tells her that he wishes she wasn't his mother. Through all the bitterness, however, he still respects her as an authority figure. He says he "shall obey, were she ten times our mother" (III, ii). Because she is his mother, he would do her bidding even if she were ten times as evil as she is. Hamlet best shows his confusion when he says, "Let me be cruel, not unnatural: / I will speak daggers to her, but use none; / My tongue and soul in this be hypocrites" (III, ii). He is angry enough, and actually wants, to kill her, but he holds back out of respect for his father. He is so conflicted about his mother that he tries desperately to change her and balance some of his loyalties. In Act III, Gertrude tells Hamlet, "though hast thy father much offended," referring to Claudius. Hamlet replies, "Mother, you have my father much offended" (III, iv). He then goes on to accuse her of her sins and tell her, "You go not till I set you up a glass / Where you may see the inmost part of you" (III, iv). He wants her to see herself from the outside, take responsibility for her actions, and stop the offense against her former husband, thus reconciling some of Hamlet's conflicted loyalties.

Hamlet also finds conflict in his loyalty to the nation of Denmark. He says, "The time is out of joint. O cursed spite, / That ever I was born to set it right!" (I, v). Hamlet is a figure similar to Sophocles' Oedipus. He sees that crimes in his land have led to everyone's being punished and he must set it right for the good of the whole kingdom. However, whereas Oedipus jumps at the chance to save his city, Hamlet is reluctant. He says that he wishes he were never born into the dilemma, because he is afraid of the price he might have to pay. He doesn't want that responsibility. Hamlet also feels loyalty to the kingdom in that he resents Claudius stealing the throne. Hamlet says Claudius is

> A vice of kings;
>
> A cutpurse of the empire and the rule,
>
> That from a shelf the precious diadem stole
>
> And put it in his pocket. (III, iv)

Hamlet is calling Claudius a buffoon of a king and resents the fact that he stole the crown from its rightful line of descent. Hamlet does, however, make a wise choice in naming his successor. As he is dying, he says, "But I do prophesy the election lights / on Fortinbras: he has my dying voice" (V, ii). In naming Fortinbras as his heir, he is being responsible and leaving the kingdom in competent hands, even though his bloodline ends.

Hamlet's loyalty to the nation also manifests itself as loyalty to himself and his own rights of succession. When Claudius tells him he will be king someday, he answers, "I eat the air, promise-crammed; you cannot feed capons so" (III, ii). He means that he is fed up with promises of being the heir. He tells Rosencrantz that he "lacks advancement." Rosencrantz asks, "How can that be, when you have the voice of the king himself for your succession in Denmark?" Hamlet replies, "Ay, sir, but 'while the grass grows'" (III, ii). Hamlet is referring to the old saying, "While the grass grows, the horse starves." He means that he longs to be king and is not satisfied to be the heir. This resentment of the king does not come from love for his father, but only his own ambition. Hamlet's priorities are a little unclear when it comes to loyalty to his father and his own ambition. He certainly claims that avenging his father is his first concern, but he is cautious and worries about his safety. When Hamlet meets the ghost of his father, Horatio tells him that it could be an evil ghost and not to follow it. However, Hamlet makes a show of saying that he doesn't care about his own life. He says, "My fate cries out, / and makes each petty artery in this body / as hardy as the Nemean Lion's nerve" (I, iv). He says that the courage his father's memory gives him outweighs his fear for himself. However, in Act III, Scene i, in the famous "To be or not to be" soliloquy, Hamlet contemplates suicide, but he cannot kill himself because he fears death. Just as in this speech, he often says that he is not afraid to avenge his father, but his hesitation and lack of action prove otherwise.

Hamlet also feels his honor criticized by observing Fortinbras. When he hears that Fortinbras has gone to wage war over worthless land for no other reason than pride, he feels ashamed. He says, "How all occasions do inform against me, / And spur my dull revenge!" (IV, iv). He sees how, when honor is at stake, Fortinbras would risk the life of thousands, while he, who has been done incredible wrongs by Claudius, is doing nothing about it. Thus, feeling his honor at stake encourages Hamlet to get revenge.

However, Hamlet is never really able to reach a decision about killing his uncle. He often says that he trusts the ghost of his father. He states, "It is an honest ghost" (I, v). However, he waits and loses his nerve. To reassure himself, he stages a play that is a re-creation of his father's murder and watches his uncle's countenance. He once again says, "I'll take the ghost's word for a thousand pound" (III, ii). However, he still doesn't form a plan. He says, "Now I could drink hot blood / And do such bitter business as the day/ Would quake to look on" (III, ii). Once again he has resolved to do it, but when he gets the chance he backs down. He catches Claudius praying, and his first instinct is to kill, but then he hesitates and overanalyzes the situation. He says,

> A villain kills my father, and for that,
>
> I, his sole son, do this same villain send
>
> To heaven.
>
> O, this is base and silly, not revenge," (III, iii)

It is almost as if he is too loyal to his father, because his desire to be more hurtful to Claudius causes him to change his mind again. When he does finally kill his uncle, it is only after Claudius's poison has killed Gertrude, Laertes, and laid a death sentence on Hamlet himself. He never forms a plan; he gets his revenge only by accident when the opportunity is staring him in the face and he has nothing to lose.

Appendix 6-B. Student Sample 2

"Mad North-Northwest": Hamlet's Sanity
Lisa Gordon

Good King Fortinbras:

You are to be commended on your query. There were indeed many questions surrounding the sanity of the late Hamlet. Most believed him to be mad. Yet if there was madness, it was not constant. As Hamlet said himself, "I am but mad north-northwest: when the wind is southerly I know a hawk from a handsaw" (II, ii). As you have requested, I have outlined briefly below the opinions of several figures prominent in Hamlet's life.

The late king, Claudius, undeniably believed Hamlet to be dangerous. King Claudius and Queen Gertrude hired Rosencrantz and Guildenstern to spy on their son. However, as an objective observer I had also been keeping tabs on the situation. The king referred to Hamlet's state as his "transformation" (II, ii). Upon engaging Rosencrantz and Guildenstern, he remarked, "More than his father's death, that thus hath put him / So much from the understanding of himself" (II, ii).

It is important to remember as we consider the king's opinion that he had good motivation to doubt Hamlet. Claudius, as Old King Hamlet's brother, was not heir to the throne. When he claimed that seat, he usurped his nephew, a fact he knew well and that plagued him. Constant paranoia bothered the king. He worried, rightly, that Hamlet would react, both to claim the throne and avenge his father's death. The queen however, at this point disagreed with her husband, arguing that "His father's death and our o'erhasty Marriage" (II, ii) caused Hamlet to be too much changed. As of yet, she did not suspect that her son might be a threat to the king.

The king's chief advisor had still yet another opinion of Hamlet's sanity. Polonius found his own fair daughter, Ophelia, to be the main cause. He presented the matter to Hamlet's uncle thus: "I have found / the very cause of Hamlet's lunacy" (II, ii). He states:

> This is the very ecstasy of love;
>
> Whose violent property fordoes itself
>
> And leads the will to desperate undertakings
>
> As oft any passion under heaven
>
> That does afflict our natures. (II, i)

He reiterates this theme several times. After this discussion Polonius and the king proceeded to set Hamlet up for a "chance" interview with Ophelia. However, before that interview occurred, Hamlet and Polonius spoke. The nature of their conversation seemed to convince Polonius of Hamlet's fragile mental state.

However, upon closer examination, Hamlet's words are not mad, but rather cleverly disguised as such. It seems he has overheard much of Polonius and the king's conversation. Therefore, he mistakenly identifies Polonius as a fishmonger (II, ii). However, he is not addled. He is commenting on Polonius's treatment of his daughter. His replies throughout this conversation seem those of a crazed man to one such as Polonius, who already considers Hamlet mad. To our objective position, we can be assured that Hamlet still has control of his mind, as is proved by his cunningly disguised insults. However, we must again remember Polonius's position while we deliberate his opinion. As the king's advisor, Polonius obviously did not want to find himself on Claudius's bad side. He stood to gain from discovering the supposed solution to Hamlet's affliction.

In Hamlet's interview with Ophelia, we first noticed that perhaps Hamlet had lost control. The interview rapidly became a heated exchange of veiled insults and deception. Hamlet accuses Ophelia of base prostitution on her father's behalf. This meant, to Hamlet, that she has chosen her father over her lover. It is this desertion that drives him over the emotional edge. Here he launches into a tirade against women:

> I have heard of your paintings too, well enough. God hath given you one face, and you make yourselves another: you jig, you amble, you lisp, and nick-name God's creatures and make your wantonness your ignorance. Go to, I'll no more on 't; it hath made me mad. (III, i)

As Hamlet had overheard the previous conversation between the King and Polonius, he knew that they lurked nearby, overhearing every word. Yet he spoke unguardedly of what he felt at that moment. Even he himself claims this is madness. Yet it is the feeling of his heart. What is it that society defines as madness? Is only stoicism that which is sane? Do we not perhaps know ourselves best, as Hamlet does, when we loosen the strings of control over our actions? Perhaps this is what we are being asked to consider.

Ophelia is obviously convinced of Hamlet's addled state after the interview above. She cries out in anguish, "O, what a noble mind is here o'erthrown!" (III, i). Yet she failed to realize that it was because of her actions at that very moment, because of her lies and base deception, that Hamlet had lost his temper. From that point onward, Polonius is convinced that Hamlet is insane. Full of self-satisfaction, he continues to believe that his daughter is the cause. Yet the king, despite Hamlet's fiery tirades toward Ophelia, still feared something darker beneath:

> Love? His affections do not that way tend;
>
> Nor what he spake, though it lack'd form a little,
>
> Was not like madness. There's something in his soul
>
> O'er which his melancholy sits on brood. (II, i)

Claudius is not yet convinced of his stepson's insanity. Yet he still fears Hamlet's character. At this point, he resolves to send Hamlet packing to England, for a short (but permanent) exile (III, i).

As the play draws near, Hamlet works out the scheme whereby Horatio is to observe the king's expression during the play (III, ii). He also mentions to Horatio that he would act addled to further convince the others: "They are coming to the play: I must be idle" (III, ii). Obviously, Hamlet still considers himself sane.

However, we must remember that he is in both the worst and the best position to judge whether or not he is sane. Can one really determine one's own mental state? Or as madness invades, do the mad judge the world as wrong and themselves as true? Hamlet's behavior during the play certainly convinced many of his addled state. He seemed unable to control himself. His behavior was overtly sexual, which we know to be a sign, in Shakespeare's characters, of insanity. His jibes toward Ophelia become quite bawdy: "That's a fair thought to lie between maids' legs" (III, ii). He also seemed unable to keep track of time, commenting on how his father died not 2 hours past; when in reality it was some 4 months (III, ii). Hamlet did have motivation to want to convince others he was mad, but perhaps he carried it too far. By arranging the play as he did, he told the king of his intentions without being able to realize them. Was he in the best condition to judge his fitness for the task? The answer to that question will have to remain hidden, as none but Hamlet himself could provide the answer.

Hamlet's ravings throughout the play presented in Elsinore did much to convince the queen of his insanity, but what transpired next truly did. In her closet the two meet and speak at some length. In this interview Hamlet becomes demented. He strikes out angrily at Gertrude, at one point saying he wished she weren't his mother (III, iv). He clearly was not sane at this point. Hearing a noise, he kills the unfortunate Polonius, thinking it is the king, although he had just seen the king downstairs. He sees a ghost that Gertrude cannot see, though at the previous appearance of the ghost, all present observed it. Once Hamlet leaves his mother, she comments to her husband that Hamlet is "Mad as the sea and wind when both contend / Which is the mightier" (IV, i). The king, his fears now confirmed, is even more set in his mind to banish Hamlet to England.

Laertes, I believe, is the last character of whom Your Majesty asked. His attitude toward Hamlet was different from the others. After Polonius's death drove Ophelia to madness, Laertes' quest for vengeance against Hamlet is renewed. Claudius came to realize that banishing Hamlet had not worked. Thus, the duel between Laertes and Hamlet is hatched instead. Laertes, anxious for a chance to kill Hamlet, is easily manipulated by the king. I doubt if he was ever concerned with Hamlet's sanity. To him, Hamlet is one-dimensional, as the man responsible for the plight of his family.

I have quickly summarized the events of the past few months for Your Majesty. If I may, however, I would venture an interpretation that seems inherent in the evidence but undetected by the characters about whom you asked. Ophelia and Gertrude's treachery hardens Hamlet's heart against women. His uncle's sins enrage him. Yet his madness comes from within. It is only after he fails to achieve what he has undertaken that he loses control. As he watches the play, he sees that actors could play at what he should be doing but isn't. When faced with the chance to kill the king, he failed (III, iii). He observed the king defenseless and at his mercy, yet his indecision gripped him. He could not kill the king. That realization drives him mad. He doubts himself, and in the end that is his undoing.

As he himself said once to Rosencrantz and Guildenstern: "[T]here is nothing good or bad but thinking makes it so" (III, ii). He further remarked, "O God, I could be bounded in a nutshell and count myself a king of infinite space, were it not that I have bad dreams" (II, ii). This, that insanity comes from within, is perhaps what we should gather from this unfortunate event.

Good King Fortinbras, here is your report. I hope you will find it satisfactory. I also hope it answers your questions. We can, however, be assured the pleasure of discussing this topic for years, if we so desire, as there is much more that could be said.

7

How to "Clone" a Poem

Agnes A. Cardoni

Suppose you want to learn to dance, but you are shy. Dancing school is not an option, because you can't bear the thought of others watching as you stumble around the floor. Instead, you send for a kit with a compact disc, a booklet of directions, and some numbered yellow plastic feet. You practice in the privacy of your living room. Clumsy at first, you lumber from foot to foot trying to match *your* feet to the plastic ones beneath you. You keep at it, and gradually, even without a lot of talent or luck, you learn to dance. Now you can throw the plastic feet away and start trusting your own feet.

Why Use Models to Teach Writing?

Perhaps learning to write is like learning to dance. In both, following a model can be a great way to learn technique and understand style through imitation. Good dancers and good writers make their work seem effortless. They lead gently and surely, but they do not keep their yellow plastic feet or their 14-step writing process poster in plain view.

In discussing the value of models in writing, Gabriele Lusser Rico (1983) has this to say:

> Modeling . . . makes you aware of language rhythms and a spatial arrangement of words on which you will pattern your own writing. Modeling a professional piece of writing is simply one more way of contacting your inner writer to re-create your own unique inner world. It will also lead you to a better understanding of what a writer's 'voice' is—his or her unique style and content of expression—which in turn will help you become more conscious of the shape of your own writing and, ultimately, of your own emerging voice. (p. 44)

With modeling in mind, I have developed an approach to writing poetry that works with just about any students from remedial to Advanced Placement. I call it "cloning a poem."

In the past, when I explained that we were going to write some poems, I was met with the usual questions ("How long does it have to be?" "Does it have to rhyme?"). By switching to the cloning technique, I avoid the usual question *and* the usual results (rhymed couplets full of adolescent angst: "When he left me I did cry/ And sat home and wondered why").

"Cloning" a poem is little more than the strategy of closely reading a poem and then writing another one in the pattern of the first. Inviting students to follow a pattern, the "DNA" of the original poem, is a good way to help them relax and play with language. The questions of length and rhyme disappear because the objective is to follow the pattern of the original poem, which in this case is free verse of about 34 lines. The poem I love to work with is "What It's Like Living in Ithaca, New York," by Dick Lourie (1980). Not only is it in free verse, but it is chock-full of specific details. A simple clustering exercise in the prewriting phase gives students plenty of details for their own poems. Having used this strategy for more than 20 years, I can say with some certainty that it is nearly impossible to get a vacuous, boring, angst-ridden poem from this strategy. Here is the procedure for extracting the "DNA" from one poem to clone another.

The Assignment

Use Dick Lourie's poem, "What It's Like Living in Ithaca, New York," as a model for a poem about the place where you live:

What It's Like Living in Ithaca, New York
by Dick Lourie

here's what it's like: let's say you have just had
lunch someplace in Collegetown and you are
on your way to Karl Yentz's garage with
your VW because yesterday you noticed the brakes were beginning to
fade

you start down the Buffalo Street hill   it
looks like rain now after a sunny morning   :
when you slow down for the blinking yellow
light at Steward Avenue those brakes are
not good

and it gets worse   that huge old green
house on the corner of Fountain Place and
then the shiny face of Terrace Hill Apartments

flash by you like the past   you feel terror
in your wrists   your stomach   and you know
those brakes are gone and you won't be able
to stop at the red light on Aurora

where there are several people leisurely
crossing your path :   maybe on their way from
the Unitarian Church to Hal's
Delicatessen or they just left their
own apartment to go buy some flowers
or whatever errands we do all day —
in any case there they are and you can't stop

so this is what it's like :   as if your brakes
had failed and you couldn't avoid running
right through the crowd knocking them all apart—
panic   broken limbs   and screams   in the street

well the chances are that on any
given day at least one of these people
would be somebody you had quarreled with
last year and hadn't spoken to since   or
a friend you had visited only last week
or even the person you once were married to yourself
who would see   just before impact   that it was you
that's what it's like living in Ithaca

Preliminary Activity. Make certain that students understand the concept of clustering. You might begin by doing a clustering exercise with your class prior to beginning the poem. Write a common word on the board and circle it. Then, drawing lines from that circle, connect any ideas that come to mind associated with the word in the nucleus. Allow students to offer as many possibilities as they wish, for a collaborative cluster. At some point, the class will recognize that the cluster is complete (See Rico, 1983, for further samples). Figure 7-1 shows what one cluster might look like.

Figure 7-1: Preliminary Activity: A Model for a Collaborative Cluster

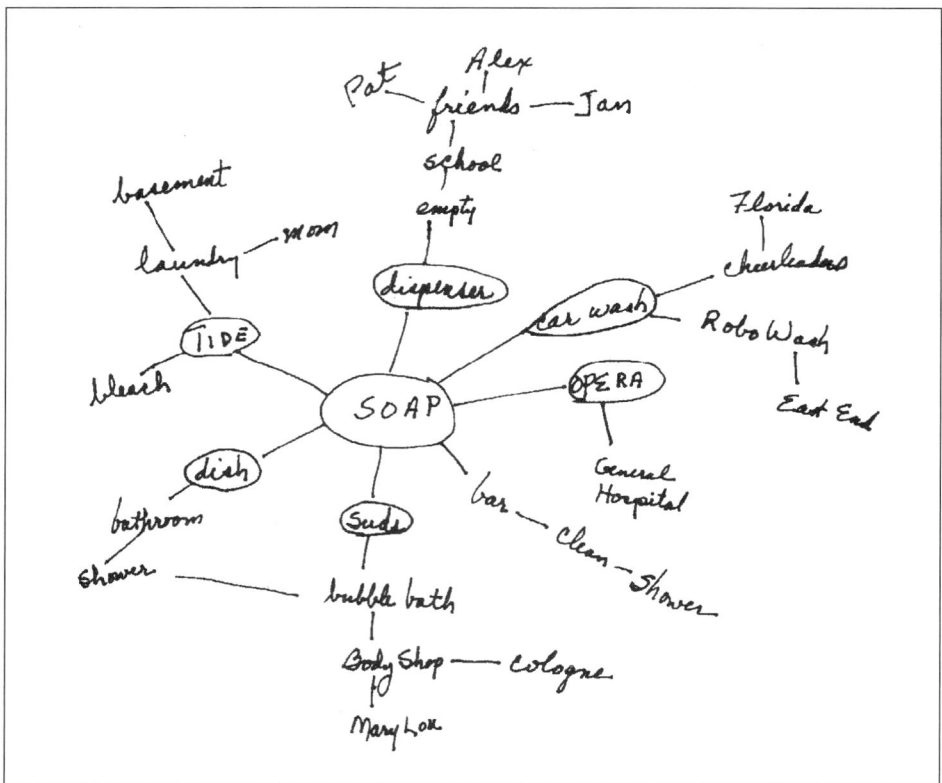

You might also ask your students to choose a second word and cluster in their notebooks, either in class or as a homework assignment, to help them get the feel of the technique.

The Clone-a-Poem Strategy: Directions for Teachers

1. Read Lourie's poem aloud and invite several different students to read it as expressively and creatively as they wish. This gets a sense of the poem out in the air, where it belongs. You may want to try choral reading or other techniques to reveal the many dimensions of syntax, imagery, and tone in Lourie's poem.

2. Direct students to underline or highlight the specific references to Ithaca, New York, contained in the poem. Ask them to point them out to the class.

3. Ask students to write the name of the place where they live in the center of a sheet of paper and circle it. Ask them to cluster anything that comes to mind about the place: landmarks, animals, interesting people, stores and businesses, restaurants, aromas, activities, attitudes, lines of songs, events, feelings, colloquialisms, and so forth.

4. Suggest to the students that they use the pattern Lourie sets up as the "DNA" for their poem, starting with "Here's what it's like . . ." Remind them to use ideas found in their clusters to give specificity to the poem.

5. Ask students to experiment with line lengths and word groupings in their poems, following Lourie's format, and to prepare a clean copy for next class.

6. "Publish" according to taste and custom. A celebratory reading of the poems makes an excellent Friday class activity. Opportunities also exist for publishing on the Internet. When their work is going "public," students often take greater care with an assignment than when they write just for the teacher.

Below is the "DNA" for Lourie's poem. I tell students to write their drafts on their own paper, and I remind them they want a poem about as long as the original. Simply filling in the blanks after the prompted lines of the "DNA" makes for a fill-in-the-blank effect and a very short poem.

The DNA of "What It's Like Living in Ithaca, New York"

What It's Like Living in _____

here's what it's like: let's say

and you are

because

you

and you

maybe

or

so this is what it's like:

well the chances are that

that's what it's like living in _____

Samples

The first sample, by Greg, followed the format diligently, and his poem conveys the ordinariness of life in Minot, Nevada, as he finds it.

What It's Like Living in Minot, Nevada

by Greg

here's what it's like: let's say you have just finished
lunch at the Longhorn Drive In. You are on your way
to the horse shoers to pick up your Dad's new horse
because he has to gather cattle tomorrow.

and you start up Main Street when it starts to thunder
and your Dad's new horse panics in the trailer
and it kicks the doors of the trailer open.

You stop but your Dad's horse jumps out of the trailer

and starts running down Main Street and it gets worse
a cattle truck full of steers on the way to the Saturday sale
turns left in front of the First Fidelity Bank as the horse
slides to a stop, barely missing the front bumper. You feel terror and
embarrassment as people you've known from childhood start

piling out of the Albertsons and McDougals Drug Store, laughing and
   pointing.
So this is what it's like: There's your grandmother with her hair in
curlers
followed by Emma, the owner of Cowgirl Curls Beauty Salon.

As you follow the horse, you catch sight of your
cousin, Paula, coming out of the Feed and Seed
with your Uncle Ken in one boot and one sock.
Well, chances are that before you catch the horse

you will see everyone you know or are related to.
And sure enough, there's your English teacher, Mr. Bennet,
in front of the Saddle and Tack shop.

Anyway, there they all are and you can't stop
because your Dad will either kill you if anything happens
to his new horse, or kill you for not
tying the horse in the trailer in the first place.
And that's what it's like living in Minot, Nevada.

   The second sample by Nicolette takes some liberties with the original format. You will see she has inserted some stream-of-consciousness techniques into her poem, and these add a poignancy and sophistication not found in the first sample.

1. You, the teacher, don't have to read a set of vacuous, self-involved poems devoid of images or specificity.
2. Your students can follow the "DNA" of an original piece of writing and yet produce something unique, vivid, and personal.
3. Reluctant writers, or ones who can't seem to compose poems without rhyme, find they can, and do, create another kind of poetry.
4. If you "publish" the cloned poems—in a celebratory reading, or in print or on the Web—listeners and readers will follow intently and respond with laughter and recognition, because the poems are about places they can see or have experienced themselves.

Whether we are learning to dance or learning to write, there is great benefit from following a model, from going through the motions over and over until they seem natural. Cloning poems from well-written originals can help students as they work toward mastering techniques that will serve them well as they develop their own style.

References

Lourie, R. (1980). "What it's like living in Ithaca, New York," *Anima*. New York: Hanging Loose Press.

Rico, G. L. (1983). *Writing the natural way: Using right-brain techniques to release your expressive powers*. Los Angeles: Tarcher.

8

Shakespeare Teaches Writing: Persuasive Speeches in Henry V

Brett C. McInelly

Like most English teachers, I regard William Shakespeare with a certain degree of reverence. Like those same teachers, I recognize that my students do not always share my regard for the master poet and his works. Students often cringe at the mere mention of Shakespeare's name, perhaps recalling their first tedious encounter with the archaic language of *Romeo and Juliet* in middle school.

Using Shakespeare to teach high school students rhetorical strategies for writing persuasive prose, then, might seem like an exercise in futility. Indeed, why bother with the complexities of a Shakespearean play when the teaching of writing comes preequipped with its own unique set of challenges, most notably student fears regarding writing? Students recoil at the thought of writing a research paper, and now I am going to add Shakespeare into the mix? Despite Shakespeare's skill in creating poetry, what can he teach students about writing persuasive prose?

Although there exists a variety of rationales for using literature to teach writing, I suspect that our passion for as well as our familiarity and experience with literature plays a determining role in our decision to bring it into the writing classroom. My efforts to use Shakespeare—specifically, *Henry V*—to teach persuasive writing, however, is motivated more by my passion for rhetoric than it is by my love of literature. To put it another way, I see *Henry V* not so much as a way of bringing literature into the classroom but as a way of bringing rhetoric into the classroom.

The Rhetoric of Aristotle, the Rhetoric of Shakespeare

In teaching my students both how to analyze and to write persuasive prose, I devote considerable class time introducing them to Aristotle's three modes of persuasion: ethos, pathos, and logos.[1] My aim in doing so is twofold: (a) I want my students to develop the capacity to critically assess the use and effectiveness of these modes of persuasion in a range of genres, and (b) I want them to learn how to deploy these modes effectively in their own written arguments.

Why use Shakespeare? Admittedly, there are many examples of persuasive writing from which teachers can draw to accomplish these goals, such as advertising media, political campaigns, and newspaper editorials. These examples certainly have more immediate appeal for today's students. Although I don't necessarily privilege Shakespeare over these other texts, which I also use in the classroom, *Henry V* is a particularly inviting text for rhetorical analysis. We recognize Shakespeare as a master poet, but he was also a master of argument. As was common in education during the Renaissance, Shakespeare's studies most likely consisted of the classical subjects of grammar, logic, and rhetoric (Baldwin, 1944). Shakespeare probably drew on rhetorical tradition[2] when he crafted *Henry V*, a play in which rhetoric assumes a prominent place. Shakespeare's protagonist, *Henry V*, effectively establishes his kingship, in large part, through his control over language. As the Archbishop of Canterbury coolly observes, the young king speaks in "sweet and honey'd sentences" (Brooke, Cunliffe, & McCracken, 1927, p. 332).

The play opens with Henry V's recently having come to the throne of England. A relatively young king and one who has spent his youth carousing with the likes of Falstaff, Henry begins his reign on tenuous grounds: The country's religious and political leaders, the general populace, and Henry's foreign adversaries all question the young king's ability to rule. Henry decides to assert his authority and establish his credibility as king by invading France (then a perfectly reasonable course of action for an English king). In leading his army, however, Henry's words—more so than his sword—prove his most formidable weapon, and his speeches effectively illustrate Aristotle's modes of persuasion. From Henry's rousing speech to his troops before the Battle of Agincourt to his wooing of Katherine, the French princess, Shakespeare masterfully adapts Henry's language to each specific audience and purpose. By examining these speeches, students see how credibility as well as emotional and logical appeals are created in an argument.

However, regardless of the grade level, using *Henry V* as a text for rhetorical analysis remains futile if Shakespeare's language intimidates students. For this reason, I generally do not require my students to read the entire play; rather, I focus on two or three contextualized scenes that best illustrate Henry's rhetorical prowess.[3] By focusing on relatively small parts of the text, my students are less likely to be overwhelmed by Shakespeare's language. Also, I supplement our reading of these scenes with clips from Kenneth Branagh's excellent film adaptation (1989), which makes the play even more accessible to students, allowing them to experience it visually, as was originally intended. These scenes are short enough that we can read, view, and discuss a single scene in 20–30 minutes. The focus on specific passages, coupled with Branagh's adaptation, allows our class time to discuss Henry's rhetorical expertise without reading the whole play.

Teaching Ethos, Pathos, and Logos Through *Henry V*

Before my students and I delve into *Henry V*, we briefly study the principles of Aristotle's rhetoric. Students learn that credibility and trustworthiness (ethos) as well as emotional (pathos) and logical (logos) appeals are not always self-evident but can be created through language, that is, by a speaker's or writer's word choice and delivery.

Once my students have a general sense of Aristotle's rhetorical concepts, we turn our attention to specific scenes from Branagh's film adaptation that help students contextualize Henry V's speeches. As Henry V speaks, students read the script version of the play. Three scenes in particular—Henry's response to the dauphin's insult in the play's opening act, his solicitation of the surrender of Harfleur, and his St. Crispin's Day speech—demonstrate the richness of *Henry V* as a text for rhetorical analysis.

The Dauphin's Insult

The key to introducing each scene is to establish Henry's rhetorical situation. Henry's reaction to the dauphin's insult represents, in some ways, the most complex rhetorical situation Henry faces. Responding to Henry's recent claim to "certain dukedoms" in France (Brooke et al., 1927, p. 55), the French prince sends a messenger with a gift of tennis balls, by which the dauphin suggests that Henry stay home and play games rather than lay claim to land in France. The dauphin's gift is an insult directed at Henry's previous unprincely behavior. In responding to the dauphin, Henry rejects his insult and establishes his own seriousness of purpose to the French as well as to his own advisors. Hence, Henry essentially addresses three audiences: the messenger, who has delivered the insult, the dauphin, and his own advisors[4] This is commonly known as "The Tennis Ball Speech":

> We are glad the Dauphin is so pleasant
>   with us;
> His present and your pains we thank you for.
> When we have match'd our rackets to these
>   balls,
> We will, in France, by God's grace, play a set
> Shall strike his father's crown into the hazard.
>   . . .
> And we understand him well,
> How he comes o'er us with our wilder days,
> Not measuring what use we made of them.
>   . . .

> But tell the Dauphin I will keep my state,
> Be like a king and show my sail of greatness,
> When I do rouse me in my throne of France:
> . . .
> And tell the pleasant prince this mock of his
> Hath turn'd his balls to gun-stones; and his soul
> Shall stand sore charged for the wasteful vengeance
> That shall fly with them: for many a thousand widows
> Shall this his mock mock out of their dear husbands;
> Mock mothers from their sons, mock castles down;
> And some are yet ungotten and unborn
> That shall have cause to curse the Dauphin's scorn.
> . . .
> So get you hence in peace; and tell the Dauphin
> His jest will savour but of shallow wit,
> When thousands weep more than did laugh at it.
> Convey them with safe conduct. Fare you well. (Act I, Scene ii)

Possible Discussion Topics

When Henry claims that he will use the tennis balls to "play a set" in France and "strike [the dauphin's] father's crown into the hazard," he is playing with the dual meaning of *crown* and *hazard*. On one level, the words refer directly to the game of tennis as it was played in the Middle Ages and the Renaissance: A crown was money that, in one sense, would have been a wager on the outcome of the game; a hazard was an opening in the walls of the court through which players would try hitting a ball, at which point the ball became "dead" and a point was scored. Henry plays off these more conventional meanings to suggest that the dauphin's father's "crown," or throne, is in peril ("hazard"). The opening lines of this speech, coupled with Henry's play on words, illustrate how irony can be deployed to achieve a persuasive effect. By saying one thing and meaning quite another, Henry shows his wit and indicates that he is a more formidable foe than the Dauphin realizes. Students generally suggest that such command of language effectively establishes Henry's intelligence, which Aristotle identifies as one quality (ethos) that will help sway an audience. Not only does the sophistication of Henry's language prove that he is not the immature boy the dauphin takes him for, but his cleverness far exceeds that of his antagonist. As Henry observes, the dauphin's "jest will savor but of shallow wit."

Students also consider the emotional impact (pathos) of Henry's words on the messenger and the dauphin as well as on Henry's advisors. Henry demonstrates Aristotle's notion of pathos: "[P]ersuasion is affected through the audience, when they are brought by the speech into a state of emotion; for we give very different decisions under the sway of pain or joy, and liking or hatred" (Cooper, 1960, p. 9). Henry's confidence—conveyed, in part, through the matter-of-fact language and unflinching tone of the speech—inspires fear on the one hand and courage on the other. Students frequently observe that rather than fly into a rage at the dauphin's insult—which they see as a less effective response and one we might expect if Henry were, in fact, immature and impulsive—Henry's calmness and calculated response projects confidence. This may unsettle a potential enemy while it encourages one's own troops. By studying this scene, students also learn how ethical, emotional, and logical appeals are not necessarily independent of each other, since Henry makes an emotional appeal, in part, by projecting a certain ethical stance.

The Scene at Harfleur

Henry's need for persuasion at Harfleur is more straightforward: He addresses the governor of the city in an effort to encourage the French surrender. Students should pay particular attention to the tone of Henry's speech as well as his use of imagery. The following questions are good discussion prompts: What images of war does Henry emphasize? What kind of self-image does Henry project through his language? What emotions does he attempt to stir in his audience? Why do these tactics prove effective? Following is Henry's speech at Harfleur:

> How yet resolves the governor of the
>   town?
> This is the latest parle we will admit:
> Therefore to our best mercy give yourselves;
> Or like to men proud of destruction
> Defy us to our worst: for, as I am a soldier,
>   . . .
> If I begin the battery once again,
> I will not leave the half-achieved Harfleur
> Till in her ashes she lie buried.

He that shall see this day, and live old age,
Will yearly on the vigil feast his neighbors
And say 'To-morrow is Saint Crispian.'
Then will he strip his sleeve and show his scars,
And say 'These wounds I had on Crispin's day.'
Old men forget; yet all shall be forgot,
But he'll remember with advantages
What feats he did that day. Then shall our names,
Familiar in his mouth as household words,
Harry the King, Bedford and Exeter,
Warwick and Talbot, Salisbury and Gloucester,
Be in their flowing cups freshly remember'd.
This story shall the good man teach his son:
And Crispin Crispian shall ne'er go by,
From this day to ending of the world,
But we in it shall be remembered;
We few, we happy few, we band of brothers.
For he to-day that sheds his blood with me
Shall be my brother; be he ne'er so vile,
This day shall gentle his condition:
And gentlemen in England now a-bed,
Shall think themselves accurs'd they were not here,
And hold their manhoods cheap whiles any
   speaks
That fought with us upon Saint Crispin's Day.

Possible Discussion Topics

A good starting point in analyzing this speech is to review Henry's relation to his troops: he is the king; most of his troops are mere peasants. If the English defeat the French, Henry stands to gain France; his troops, by comparison, will make no significant material gains. At best, Henry's troops will escape with their lives and compensation for their service. If defeated, Henry will likely be spared and ransomed back to England; his men will most likely die. Given their circumstances, it is easy to see why Henry's troops don't relish a fight. Henry thus faces a notable challenge: How does he establish a sense of goodwill toward his audience when they feel alienated from him and his world?

Aristotle claims that creating an ethical appeal (ethos) involves establishing an appropriate relationship to one's audience: the audience "should conceive [the speaker] to be disposed towards them in a certain way" (Cooper, 1960, p. 91). In Henry's case, creating a sense of goodwill involves connecting with his troops in a more personal and intimate way than was typical between king and subject. How does he do this? My students typically note Henry's choice of pronouns—*we* and *us*—and suggest that such words create a sense of camaraderie among individuals from very different social classes. They likewise observe that Henry further levels the playing field by using the more personal *Harry* to refer to himself. Such tactics help to create a sense of brotherhood—or "band of brothers"—among Henry's troops. Membership in such a brotherhood means fellowship with a king, which certainly appeals to a peasant soldier. Henry indicates throughout the speech that he will share with his men in both the fighting and the triumph; throughout, he presents himself as "one of the guys." Certainly Henry's men will be more willing to fight and perhaps die for a man with whom they identify than they would for a king with whom they feel no personal association.

Aristotle also teaches that establishing trust and credibility involves identifying with the values esteemed by one's audience: "The hearer is always receptive when a speech is adapted to his own character and reflects it" (p. 136). Henry reflects the values most esteemed by his audience—honor and manhood. Since Henry's troops will not gain materially by fighting, their gains will be intangible—namely, heroism and a heightened sense of what it means to be a man. To be viewed by others as a hero—particularly by one's own son, as Henry intimates in his speech—appeals to men who otherwise lead relatively uneventful lives. Henry thus instills in his troops a sense of pride that he likewise shares. In doing so he proclaims his goodwill toward his audience and further establishes his credibility as a military leader.

As he does in other speeches, Henry here shows a clear understanding of human emotion while addressing his men. At the outset of the speech, Henry's soldiers are scared stiff, and rightfully so. Most of his men undoubtedly wish they were back in England. However, through his rhetorical prowess, Henry lifts his troops' spirits by elevating them to the status of mythical heroes before the fighting even begins. Curiously, he makes no mention of how dangerous and intense the battle will likely be; instead he concentrates on the years afterwards, when his men, having not only survived but performed heroically, will talk of their glorious deeds with family and friends. Caught up in the emotion of such thoughts, his troops lose sight of the impending danger and their previous fears, and they are eager to fight, counting themselves lucky to be part of an elite group of soldiers who will be so celebrated. In short, Henry enlists the emotions of his audience by asking them to "imagine"—a fairly common and effective means of making an emotional appeal, which students can use in constructing their own arguments.

What About Logical Appeal (Logos)?

Admittedly, Henry's St. Crispin's Day speech seems to lack rational appeal. In general, Henry's persuasive speeches better illustrate ethical and emotional appeals, but this last speech does provide a good opportunity to discuss logos. Even while Henry appeals predominantly to his audience's emotions, an underlying logic permeates the line of his argument. Henry provides his logical claim early in the speech: "If we are mark'd to die, we are enow / To do our country loss; and if to live, / The fewer men, the greater share of honor." Henry persuades his men that honor is achieved by overcoming overwhelming odds, and he supports his claim anecdotally by asking his audience to imagine themselves as heroes who face and defeat a superior army. Though not the most logical of arguments, it is a line of reasoning that his audience accepts; that is, Henry's troops agree with the underlying logic of the speech and are consequently persuaded to meet the French army courageously and confidently.

Student Responses and Some Final Thoughts

Although I still eagerly await the day when my students will climb upon the tops of their desks, draw imaginary swords from their belts, and let go with a warrior's cry after viewing the St. Crispin's Day speech, I have nevertheless been deeply satisfied with the enthusiastic reception of this activity. More important, my students come away from our study of these scenes with a clear sense of Aristotle's persuasive techniques, and many students incorporate Henry's rhetorical strategies into their own persuasive essays. For example, they use personal pronouns like *us* and *we* to create a sense of goodwill between them and their audience; they make emotional appeals by involving their audience in hypothetical anecdotes; they tend to be more calculating in their use of language in general.

The *Henry V* examples recently made a student's list of "cool things we did in class" (I was flattered that there were enough things to constitute a list), and students frequently mention these activities on course evaluations. On one occasion, one student, a military history enthusiast, eagerly rose and described for the class the actual Battle of Agincourt, going so far as to diagram on the chalkboard the French offensive and English defense. One class was so captivated by the scenes we studied that they asked to see the entire play. Frequently students rent and view the video on their own as a result of their experience in class. Although fostering student interest in Shakespeare is, as I have mentioned, not among my primary goal for using *Henry V* in class, such a repercussion certainly cannot hurt. This enthusiasm makes teaching and learning more productive and enjoyable; moreover, students who view the entire play on their own generally pay particular attention to Henry's rhetorical strategies as a result of their analysis of the scenes in class. On one occasion as part of a journalism assignment, a student wrote a short rhetorical analysis of a scene she viewed on her own.

Interestingly, some of my biggest skeptics of this activity have been colleagues and not students. I once taught the St. Crispin's Day speech to a group of academically challenged students while being observed by a supervisor. Prior to the class in a preobservation interview, my supervisor questioned my use of *Henry V* in a class primarily composed of underprepared students. She wondered how this particular group of students would respond to it. To her surprise, the students were attentive and genuinely interested. This happened to be the same class in which my student rose and explained the Battle of Agincourt. The class was equally attentive to this student's minilecture. As we shifted our discussion from Shakespeare's play to Martin Luther King's "Letter from a Birmingham Jail," a text the students had been assigned to read and would later write about, my supervisor was impressed by their ability to transfer to King's letter the analytical skills they acquired through their study of Henry V's major speeches.

When bringing any literary text into the writing classroom, teachers can easily allow the complexities of such texts to overtake writing discussion. This is particularly true when dealing with both the thematic and the linguistic complexities of a Shakespearean play. Although we English teachers enjoy these kinds of discussions, such conversations in the writing classroom may compromise other and more important pedagogical aims. Hence, a larger rhetorical goal, not the literary text, should determine and control class discussion; that is, we need to consider the literary text primarily as a model for writing. I bring *Henry V* into the class because the play allows me to teach Aristotle's modes of persuasion. If students become more adept at reading and interpreting Shakespeare, great! However, such an outcome is merely incidental in light of my primary objective: that students develop an understanding of Aristotle's persuasive rhetoric and appreciate Shakespeare as a master rhetorician. This is why I think I have experienced success with this activity from one class to another.

Notes

1. *Ethos* refers to a speaker or writer's credibility, trustworthiness, and goodwill toward the audience. *Pathos* is an emotional appeal, and *logos* is a logical appeal.

2. Although Shakespeare probably did not possess a firsthand knowledge of Aristotle's *Rhetoric*, he certainly was familiar with the rhetorical principles I discuss in this chapter, as they were transmitted through the Roman tradition and the Renaissance.

3. I have assigned the entire text in some courses, and students can certainly benefit from a full-length study of Henry V's rhetorical prowess. I have found, however, that most curriculums do not allow for a full-length study. Nonetheless, two to three well-chosen scenes are enough to draw attention to how a speaker or writer can adapt his or her language to a particular audience to achieve a specific end. When time is especially short, I frequently teach just Henry's St. Crispin's Day speech, the best in the play and the one that generates, in my experience, the most discussion. In courses in which argumentation represents one unit or a relatively minor component in the curriculum, the St. Crispin's Day speech is an effective way to introduce Aristotle's principles of rhetoric and requires no more than about 30–50 minutes of class time.

4. All quotes are edited to appear as they do in Kenneth Branagh's film adaptation.

References

Cooper, L. (1960). *The rhetoric of Aristotle*. Englewood Cliffs, NJ: Prentice-Hall.

Baldwin, T. W. (1944). *William Shakespeare's small Latin & less Greeke*. Urbana: University of Illinois Press.

Brooke, T., Cunliffe, J. W., & MacCracken, H. N. (Eds.). (1927). *Shakespeare's principal plays*. (3rd ed.). New York: Appleton-Century-Crofts.

9

Giving Voice to Middle School Writers

Lynda Hamblin

As an eighth-grade writing teacher, I feel a strong sense of responsibility to prepare my young writers to meet the challenges of our state's writing assessment. The 6-week essay-writing unit that I teach gives the students a strong sense of audience, purpose, and development. Likewise, the ongoing instruction they receive in usage, mechanics, and sentence structure is adequate. However, the category of *"voice/style/tone/mood/persona"* (found on so many writing assessment scoring standards) has always troubled me. I have a hard time defining each of these terms myself and worry that I can't teach those terms to my students. I was sure that my students could not recognize subtle differences among voice, style, tone, mood, persona in professional writing or in their own writing. The State of Idaho's (1995) writing assessment makes this statement about the assessment category of voice/style/tone/mood/persona:

> These features often determine the readability of a piece of writing. Even though the purpose and the audience are clear, and the development (form) is appropriate to the purpose and audience, when these features are not present to some degree, the writing will not hold the reader's attention. These features may include appropriate vocabulary choice, figurative language, rhythm, alliteration, parallelism – any of the literary and stylistic devices that make a piece of writing powerful, engaging, and unique. (p. 29)

The assessment document goes on to explain that a 5 paper, the top score, "uses a strong, effective, vibrant, and consistent voice." The writer's voice in a 4 paper "may be lively and creative—effectively accomplishes the writer's purpose with the intended audience." A proficient, or 3 paper "contains a voice which is consistent and appropriate to the subject, audience, and purpose." A 2 paper, which is not considered a passing grade, "indicates the writer's voice may not be consistent to the subject, audience, and purpose." Finally, a paper scored as a 1 suggests that the writer's voice is ill-defined" (pp. 30–34).

Much of the writing that my students do—what Donald Murray (1996) refers to as "reflective narratives" (39)—is full of voice/style/tone/mood/persona. Their reflective narratives are snippets of minor tragedies from young lives, glimpses into an adolescent world through the death of a grandparent or the loss of a beloved pet, humorous anecdotes detailing a practical joke gone awry, and so on. There is a sparkle in the eye, a tone of the unmistakable uniqueness of each piece, a lift and fall of each voice as they relate their stories to me during conferences. Occasionally many of the students are able to transfer that voice into their personal narratives, but little transfer occurs when they are required to write an essay for the state writing assessment. How could I help the students to understand the category of voice/style/tone/mood/persona well enough to succeed on our state's eighth-grade direct writing assessment?

Desperately Seeking a Definition

My first task was to define each of the terms for myself. Pouring over scholarly journals and various writing texts, I discovered that very often the definitions for *voice, style, tone, mood,* and *persona* are interchangeable. For example in the index of Bogel and Gottschalk's *Teaching Prose: A Guide for Writing Instructors* (1994), a reference to tone refers the reader back to voice, and the notation for voice encompasses *persona*, as well (p. 423).

Confused, I turned to another authority, Purves's *Encyclopedia of English Studies and Language Arts* (1994). This work defines *tone* as the attitude of the writer toward the reader, the subject matter, and the self. "Tone is expressed primarily through style. Mood is best defined as the feeling the writer creates for the reader; therefore it is nearly indistinguishable from tone" (p. 1217). It says that *style* refers to the ways in which particular uses of language deliver meaning and effects to the reader. Style contains the kind of diction, the length of sentences, the variety of sentence patterns, and the use of figures of speech (p. 1130). Another source links the definition of *persona* point of view: "Point of view often gives birth to an identifiable *persona* (or speaker) with particular attributes in particular surroundings" (Burke & Tinsley 1993, p. 99).

As if these definitions weren't bewildering enough, the definition of *voice* appears to be the most elusive of all. The sheer difficulty in defining the term voice—especially for 12- and 13-year olds—is overwhelming. Randall Albers (1998) cautions that writing teachers should be careful when defining voice with metaphors like "juice" and the qualities of "magic potion, mother's milk, and electricity." This is understandable, as the students barely understand the term *metaphor* let alone the terms as we are trying to define here. My experience is that teachers of writing must also be careful not to characterize voice as another device in the long list of criteria that makes writing "good." Those students who already feel that they don't have what it takes to be a writer will interpret this as another reason to shut down. Voice in writing is much like a fingerprint—different and unique to each writer. Voice cannot be wrong or inferior. Donald Graves (1994) writes in the following:

> Voice is the imprint of ourselves on our writing. It is the part of the self that pushes the writing ahead, the dynamo in the process. The voice shows how I choose information, organize it, select the words, all in relation to what I want to say and how I want to say it. The reader says, "Someone is here. I know that person. I've been there too." (p, 81)

Murray (1996) defines voice as the writer revealed. He contends that "all of who you are goes into what you put down on paper. When we read your piece, we can tell who you are, what you are all about . . . you are there, on the page" (p. 39).

I was more frustrated than ever. The definitions seemed only to cross-reference each other. If I wanted to help students put voice into their writing, I was terribly underprepared and outwitted. I felt helpless and powerless. So I decided to turn my energies toward an area over which I did have control. My focus became the strategies and philosophies that I thought would help my students to improve their writing, period. Moreover, I thought, with any luck their voices would fall into place as we worked.

After careful consideration, I decided that style, tone, mood, and persona are driven by voice. Therefore, if I could teach my students to write with voice in their essays, they would have a better chance of doing well on our state's writing assessment. However, this revelation was not in the least helpful to me. After all the reading and studying I had done, I still was not sure that there was a definition of voice simple enough to share with my students. I was comforted by Frank Smith's (1990) comment that "Everyone is born equipped and ready to think and learn, as part of the continual exercise of the imagination that enables us to make sense of our world" (pp. 124–125).

However, my initial experiences teaching voice echoed those of Barry Lane (1993), who worked as part of a benchmark team for Vermont's portfolio assessment project. Lane found that it is sometimes easier to find voice in the writing of fourth graders than it is in eighth-grade work. He believes that too often middle school students are asked to conform their writing to their teacher's assignment, and therefore students say what the teacher wants to hear in easy academic formulas. Lane fears that middle school students don't write about what they know, but what they believe the teacher wants to hear.

Furthermore, Lane claims that students with the strongest voices are those who have learned that their experiences and perceptions are valuable. These students translate their thoughts into words without letting the audience get in the way. My theory and practice echo Lane's findings. I believe that the writing environment that best nurtures voice in young writers is a classroom in which students do the following:

- Write on topics of their choice
- Take ownership of their writing
- Talk about their writing before and during the process
- Have the time they need to formulate their ideas and to practice their writing
- Become immersed in models of good writing

- See an author's techniques repeatedly demonstrated
- "Try it out" on their peers and teacher in a risk-free environment

The Tribute Assignment

This assignment invites students to write a tribute to someone important in their lives, either living or dead. After I have introduced students to the tribute assignment, we spend several class periods reading tributes written by professional writers and by former students. Then I ask students to choose the person to whom they will write a tribute. The students have 2 minutes to share with their small group a story about the person they have chosen. As soon as they have exchanged stories, they take 5 to 7 minutes for freewriting on exactly the same story they just shared. Channing (a pseudonym, as are the names of all students here) received encouragement and acceptance from his classmates from the beginning when he shared his story. The students at his table were genuinely interested in what he had to say, but they had questions about the gaps in his story. As he answered those questions for his classmates, he found that he had much more to say than he thought he did.

I have observed that it is the talking that "frees up" the writing block students sometimes experience. I know that it is what helped Channing to transfer his feelings about his grandfather from his heart to the page. Here is what he wrote:

> When I was about four years old my grampy died. I was so sad because when I was little I used to help him feed calves, he would fill the bottle with warm milk and then he would hand me the bottle and let me hold it while the calves drank. The steaming milk would make little rivers on their fuzzy chins.
>
> And in the fall time he would rake up huge piles of leaves with his strong arms, grunting while he worked, and when he was done he would let me jump in them. When I was done playing around in the leaves, he would rake them up again. Then he would let me jump in them all over again.
>
> He used to babysit me while my mom went to school and when she would come out to pick me up, I would always run away and hide because I wanted to stay with my grampy. My mom would say, "If you don't come right now I'm going to leave you."
>
> And I would say, "Fine."
>
> She would come and get me and make me go home anyway. My grandpa was really important to me and I wish he was still around so I could spend more time with him. He always said I was the smartest kid he knew. He might be right. But the little time I did spend with him makes me realize that he is my most appreciated hero.

I remember reading those lines in the final draft and smiling to myself. Channing was there, on the page, speaking to me. It was content as well as the nurturing environment that helped put Channing's voice into the writing. Peer and teacher edits had eliminated major errors. Woven throughout Channing's story was an honest presence. My experience with Channing echoed Lane's (1993) observation that "voice seems to develop out of practice and having something to say" (p. 160). When students are allowed to choose topics that reflect a personal interest in their subject, they write expressively, and often with voice.

The Multigenre Research Paper Assignment

The multigenre research papers my eighth-grade students write (inspired by Tom Romano, 1995, 2000) are good examples of how voice can assert itself into the writing when students are allowed choice of topic and genre. This is especially true if students are given the responsibility for what they will learn and how they will present what they have learned.

For example, while reading Mildred D. Taylor's *Roll of Thunder, Hear My Cry* (1991) in English class, my eighth-grade students study the Civil War in their history classes. This gives the history teacher and me the perfect opportunity for a collaborative project. We spend several days in the library as the students pour over periodicals, histories, and related Web sites. Upon completion of their research, students choose three genres through which to present their information.

As they study the Civil War and read *Roll of Thunder, Hear My Cry*, they are struck by the social injustices inherent in society. Students question the devastation of the war, the cruelty of slavery, and the treatment of minorities. By the time they are ready to write the final drafts of their multigenre research paper, they have developed a passion for the topic—and their voices sing out clearly through their writing. Following is an excerpt of a poem written by Jessica that demonstrates how powerful genre and topic are to the development of voice:

Those Brave Souls: A Tribute to the Brave Men at Gettysburg

> Those men,
>
> They were so brave,
>
> They did not fear,
>
> Their death to come.
>
> We wish we could be
>
> As courageous as they,
>
> Then we would be able
>
> To face our fears.

Because I receive many multigenre research papers with poems, essays, and stories with voices equally strong as Jessica's, I find myself nodding in agreement with Barry Lane (1993), who tells his students that there are thousands of ways to write an interesting research paper and only one way to write a boring one (p. 160). It was only after Jessica was allowed to choose her own topic and genre that she was able to write passionately about an event that touched her heart. If students are excited about what they are researching, it shows in their writing. If they have the choice of genre in which to write, their curiosity and voice come through.

A Read and Retell Assignment

Another tactic for helping students to find their voices is "read and retell," a reading-as-a-model-for-writing strategy developed by Hazel Brown and Brian Cambourne (1987). Read and retell is a collaborative activity that demands intense listening and evaluation of a writer's use of voice and meaning. This strategy can be used to meet a variety of objectives, but I use it here to help students see how it is possible to model their own writing voice after that of a published author.

An example of one read and retell lesson is based on a selection from *Hatchet*, Gary Paulsen's award-winning novel (1987). Paulsen's use of grinding details, haunting images, vivid description, and long, complex sentences springboard a discussion of several stylistic devices that effective writers use to develop voice in their writing. We begin by looking at the title of the selection, "The Terrible Crash," to help us predict what will be in the selection. Working in groups of four or five, students predict in writing what they think the story might be about based only on the title. I tell them not to worry about correctness or neatness at this point. Next the students share their predictions with their peers. There is some discussion about each one, how some are similar and some are quite different. Finally, we read the following selection together:

> Then a wild crashing sound, ripping of metal, and the plane rolled to the right and blew through the trees, out over the water and down, down to slam into the lake, skip once on water as hard as concrete, water that tore the windshield out and shattered the side windows, water that drove him back into the seat. Somebody was screaming, screaming as the plane drove into the water. Someone screamed tight animal screams of fear and pain and he did not know that it was his sound, which he roared against the water that took him and the plane still deeper, down in the water. He saw nothing but sensed blue, cold blue-green, and raked at the seatbelt catch, tore his nails loose on one hand. He ripped at it until it released and somehow—the water trying to kill him, to end him—somehow he pulled himself out of the shattered front window and clawed up into the blue, felt something hold him back, felt his windbreaker tear free and he was free. (1987, p. 29)

We then compare our predictions with the actual text to see how closely their predictions matched. Next, the students read the story several times silently to themselves, making sure they understand it well. Finally, I ask them to pretend that they must write the story for someone who has not read it, to retell as much as they can without referring back to the text. There is no pressure to get it exactly right; they are simply trying to help the person hear the story so that they might enjoy it, too. They may express the meaning in their own words. Again, as they share their retellings with a partner, we spend time discussing the ways

Paulsen creates the unmistakably strong voice in his writing. His choice of words and phrases conveys the terror Brian experiences during the crash. The students can hear Brian's voice, laced with tension and panic, in the long, breathless sentences.

Trying to emulate this award-winning author's use of anticipation, friction, and voice in their own story is a task worthy of the effort. In this way the students will not just be borrowing an author's voice, but internalizing a strategy that will help them to write more effectively. Proof that this strategy actually works is shown below in an excerpt from David's story. He had been reading Terry Brooks's *Sword of Shannara* (2000) series during our fiction-writing unit:

> In weeks past CothRock had been proven as the greatest warrior in the land, with his shining blade, "Whisperer of Good," an enchanted blade which no other weapon in the land could equal. This weapon would release an odor that only its wielder could smell. That would warn him of the danger. CothRock had a son, Tallamon, who had the potential to become an even greater warrior. King Leoric immediately saw those qualities in Tallamon and sent CothRock on a mission that would lead him through the Gates of Palinor, the Orc Headquarters, and the dreaded Black Forest.

Several of David's words and phrases are unmistakably the result of his fascination and admiration for Brooks's writing style—for example, "no other weapon in the land could equal" and "on a mission that would lead . . . and the dreaded Black Forest." David is able to capture the same quality of fantasy and mysticism found in Brooks's fantasy genre. David's read and retell has helped him to practice the voice of a renowned fantasy writer.

What I Think of This Class Right Now: An Audience-Voice Awareness Activity

In the following letter-writing activity, students become aware of how audience shapes their writing voice. The students pair and write a note to their partner on the topic "What I think of this class right now." I assure them that the partner is the only person who will ever see the note. When the students have finished writing, they exchange notes with their partner. The students then write again on the same topic. This time I am the audience. I collect the "teacher papers" and read anonymous samples aloud to encourage a discussion of how the intended audience affects their writing.

Our discussion reveals that the notes are written in informal language, are concerned with ideas, and are less concerned with form, mechanical correctness, or neatness. For example, one student may write to another, "This class rocks! I love the way she is always telling personal stuff."

The "teacher paper," on the other hand, is written to please the teacher, uses more formal language directed to the teacher-audience, and places more emphasis on form, mechanical correctness, and neatness. For example, the same piece rewritten for the teacher looks like this: "There are several things I really like about English class. First, I love how you relate personal experiences to us."

When students compare the piece they wrote for their partner to the piece they wrote for the teacher, they are able to draw several important conclusions about voice. Voice depends on word choice and an awareness of the intended audience. Writers who use voice effectively know their audience and write with that audience in mind (Brandvik, 1990). By examining their choice of words and phrases in each letter, the students analyze how they create voice in their writing. We can hear them on the page. When they write more freely and unencumbered, as in the letter to the friend, a very distinct voice comes through. It is important that students understand that formal writing, such as the letter to me, also contains voice. Beginning writers, however, will recognize the voice used in the friend's letter as the one that really identifies them: "Yeah, that's me; that's what I really sound like."

Taking the letter writing–voice activity a step further, the students select an idea from a list of story ideas they keep in their writing folders and write a short narrative using their familiar voice, the one they used in the note to their friend. Once again, before the students begin to write, they tell their partner the story they have chosen. In this activity their designated audience is a good friend who is not concerned with correctness. Their goal is to write the story so the reader can experience it firsthand. Brad demonstrates by his choice of words an awareness of audience:

> I sat down to watch TV, and just then the phone rang. I jumped from my seat, tore through the house, hurdled my little brother, and then grabbed the telephone. My mom had picked up the other phone. Eavesdropping, I heard Earl Harris, who lives two or three miles up the road, say he had some ornery steers in his corral. I love a challenge. My brother, sister, aunt, grandma, and I jumped into our '78 Ford pickup (tight squeeze), and headed off up the road.

The phrases "hurdled my little brother," "ornery steers," and "tight squeeze" are evidence that Brad is comfortable with his audience. His style is familiar and friendly. He has succeeded in creating voice in this short piece of writing.

Brad's experiences echo those of Nanci Griffith, the popular folksinger, who maintains, "Your own voice is the best voice to carry you through life." I believe that as teachers we need to foster this expression of self so the students will have a voice to carry them through life, and especially through the various types of writing they are asked to do for assessment as well as for the personal writing they do. Barry Lane (1993) points out, "Finding a voice is a slow process that begins with teaching students to value their own experiences and perceptions and to write them down. Students with the strongest voices often have kept journals for years" (p. 159).

Nature Observation and Poetry Assignment

As an example of applying Lane's advice, I turn to a nature observation and poetry unit I do collaboratively with the seventh-grade science teacher. This unit is a way to help students develop their own voice by taking passages from their science notebooks directly into a piece of writing. The science teacher assigns the students 8 hours of nature observation in different environments and at different times of the day. Students record this information in their observation journals.

During this unit I rely heavily on published poets—Mary Oliver (1992, 1994), Gary Snyder (1992), William Stafford (Stafford & Bly, 1994) and many others—who have themselves kept journals and demonstrate a wide variety of voices. We are able to look at their notebook entries and see how they were able to turn those entries into poems and how their voices change between genres. As we look at professional writers' journals and poems, students are able to see the connection between the voice in the journal and that in the poem. The inspiration for this activity came from reading Vera John-Steiner's *Notebooks of the Mind* (1985). When John-Steiner interviewed various creative people, she found that "diverse records exist of the beginnings of new work in the writer's life" in their journals and diaries (p. 127).

I share with my students an example from poet Mary Oliver's journal (1994) that resulted in her poem "Some Questions You Might Ask." In her journal she has recorded such phrases as "a brown moth with battered and fragile wings" and "there is evidence here that a large bear has been gathering leaves" (p. 65). John-Steiner (1985) contends that remembering such carefully observed details gives a starting point for weaving together resonant language with their poetic themes (p.127). How the poets' purpose and word choice affect their voice is what I want the students to recognize as they transfer their journal thoughts to their poetry. We discuss the presence of the poets' voices in their entries, their almost casual talking voices. I challenge students to carry that voice through the words of their own poems. Following is Mary Beth's journal entry:

> This reminded me of the book we read in class about the girl who wanted to hear rocks breathe and sand laugh. The old Indian man told her she had to be patient and listen for a long long time. I just wasn't patient enough. I watched that old beaver and he didn't even know I was there. His dark brown fur just sort of appeared out of the water. He was being sneaky—he didn't know I was watching.

Here is the poem she wrote as a result:

Still Waters

Breathing cool, crisp air,

I sit waiting,

Lulled by the rushing water from the stream.

A small ripple appears on the surface,

Staying there shortly,

Replaced by a larger one.

Regarding me,

Keen-eyed from the water's surface,

Tiny droplets glisten on the mahogany fur.

I fail the inspection.

Tail slapping,

The beaver disappears into the depths.

The water is still,

An echo and a memory remain.

In the transition from journal entry to poem, Mary Beth's voice changes somewhat, becoming more formal. She expressed a desire to "sound like a real poet." Using words from her own journal, as Oliver did, Mary Beth is able to turn her science observation journal's notes into poetic phrases that require a more formal voice—at least in Mary Beth's eyes.

Good News and Bad News

As you can see from the above activities and examples, my students and I have discovered ways to understand and develop voice. However, I wish I could say that using and adapting the strategies we found improved their performance on our state's eighth-grade direct writing assessment. It has not. My students, quite frankly, often lack the maturity as writers to take a specific prompt on a single day and then write an essay that uses "a strong, effective, vibrant, and consistent voice." I've had to face the fact that our state's eighth-grade direct writing assessment actually negates students' voices with its rules, regulations, and test-taking genre. During the test students are not allowed any of the following:

- To write on topics of their choice
- To take ownership of their writing
- To talk about their writing before and during the writing process
- To have the time they need to formulate their ideas and practice their writing
- To choose the form
- To choose the audience
- To "try it out" on their peers and the teacher in a risk-free environment

Nevertheless, I've learned to live with the test because even though my students' scores on our state's writing assessment have not improved, they have become more comfortable with their writing. The risk-free environment we create is a success. My room is often abuzz with readers and writers sharing, editing, revising, and reflecting. Because of these outcomes, I can accept the fact that many of my students cannot yet transfer their successes as classroom writers to the writing assessment. I believe that it is more important for my eighth graders' writing to come alive than it is for them to be able to define and apply voice to their writing for assessment. I also feel more comfortable and better equipped to talk to each of my students about their writing, their voice, and how to find it.

There is a Buddhist saying, "Before enlightenment, chopping wood, pumping water. After enlightenment, chopping wood, pumping water." It is only through continual modeling and constant writing practice that students will gain the maturity and ability to write with a recognizable voice. Unfortunately, it will be long after they have left my care.

References

Albers, R. (1998, March). *The pedagogy of voice: Putting theory into practice in a story workshop composition class.* Paper presented at the Conference on College Composition and Communication, St. Louis, MO.

Bogel, F. V., & Gottschalk, K. K. (1994). *Teaching prose: A guide for writing instructors.* New York: Norton.

Bowden, D. (1996). Stolen voices: Plagiarism and authentic voice. *Composition studies/freshman English news, 1–2,* 9–10.

Brandvik, M. L. (1990). *Writing process activities kit.* New York: Center for Applied Research in Education.

Brooks, T. (2000). *Sword of Shannara.* New York: Putnam.

Brown, H., & Cambourne, B. (1987). *Read and retell.* Portsmouth, NH: Heinemann.

Burke, C., & Tinsley, M. B. (1993). *The creative process.* New York: St. Martin's Press.

Elbow, P. (1981). *Writing with power: Techniques for mastering the writing process.* New York: Oxford University Press.

Elbow, P. (1995, March). *Voice as lightning rod for dangerous thinking.* Paper presented at the Conference on College Composition and Communication, Washington, DC.

Graves, D. H. (1994). A fresh look at writing. Portsmouth, NH: Heinemann.

Hashimoto, I. (1987). Voice as juice: Some reservations about evangelic composition. *College Composition and Communication, 38* (1), 70–80.

Hickey, D. (1993). *Developing a written voice.* Mountain View, CA: Mayfield.

John-Steiner, V. (1985). *Notebooks of the mind.* New York: Harper & Row.

Lane, B. (1993). *After the end.* Portsmouth, NH: Heinemann.

Murray, D. M. (1990, March). *All writing is autobiography.* Paper presented at the Conference on College Composition and Communication, Chicago.

Murray, D. M. (1996). *Crafting a life in essay, story, poem.* Portsmouth, NH: Boynton/Cook–Heinemann.

Oliver, M. (1992). *New and selected poems.* Boston: Beacon Press.

Oliver, M. (1994). *A poetry handbook.* San Diego: Harcourt Brace.

Paulsen, G. (1987). *Hatchet.* New York: Penguin.

Purves, A. C. (1994). *Encyclopedia of English studies and language arts.* New York: Scholastic Leadership Policy Research/National Council of Teachers of English.

Romano, T. (1995). *Writing with passion.* Portsmouth, NH: Heinemann.

Romano, T. (2000). *Blending genre, altering style: Writing multigenre papers.* Portsmouth, NH: Heinemann.

Routman, R. (1996). *Literacy at the crossroads.* Portsmouth, NH: Heinemann.

Smith, F. (1990). *To think.* New York: Teachers College Press.

Snyder, G. (1992). *No nature.* New York: Pantheon.

Stafford, W., & Bly, R. (Eds.). (1994). *The darkness around us: The selected poems of William Stafford.* New York: Perennial Publications.

State of IdahoDepartment of Education. (1995). *Performance summary: Guidance/assessment and evaluation.* Boise, ID: Author.

Taylor, M. (1976). *Roll of thunder, hear my cry.* New York: Dial.

Turbill, J., Butler, A., Cambourne, B., & Langton, G. (1991a). *Theory into practice.* New York: Wayne Finger Lakes Board of Cooperative Educational Services.

Turbill, J., Butler, A., Cambourne, B., & Langton, G. (1991b). *Theory of others.* New York: Wayne Finger Lakes Board of Cooperative Educational Services.

10

"All Such Beautiful Sweet Things": An Expanded Definition of Literacy in the Poetry Writing Classroom

Scott Minar

I have a friend who tells an interesting story about something that happened in a creative writing classroom in the 1970s. Anyone who has taught poetry writing at the high school or university level will recognize some of the forces at work here. His story goes like this.

There was a creative writing professor at a large state university in the Midwest. He was African American, a Vietnam War veteran, and had been raised in tough urban neighborhoods. Not unexpectedly, there were considerable differences between his life experiences and those of his suburban or small-town students. As this teacher tried to explain the aesthetics that had become for him a lifeline of expression, a crucial part of his existence, a way to explain (and therefore live with) an entire array of injustices that he knew about personally, he encountered significant frustration. His students just didn't get it: They were mostly from suburbs, or small towns, and they certainly had never been to war. The bitter truths that he felt the need to transcend or express through his art, and the views of other writers he respected, were as far removed from these young people as a polar bear is from the equator. One day, out of frustration and because he had failed to move them through other means, he walked into a small seminar room on the second floor of a beautiful ivy-covered building and lay a snub-nosed .38-caliber revolver on the table in front of those same students. The gun was loaded. Now he had their attention. He said to the terrified class, "Do you understand *this?* This is what the world is like for some people. This is how some of us are forced to live. Are you afraid? Good, now you understand." His story ends there abruptly with his immediate removal from the classroom. Subsequently, he was of course detenured, and eight months later he was removed from teaching. It is a sad but important narrative in many ways.

Personal Definitions of Literacy

What's intriguing about all of this, it seems to me, is that the character in this story, the teacher I've described, has a very specific sense of what it means to be "literate," and his definition of literacy is not concerned with poetry alone. We can assume that his concept of literacy is tied to his perception of his own culture—the culture with which he grew to be familiar—and to his subsequent sense of his own cultural identity. Like everyone else's cultural identity, his is quite strong and plays a central role in his life: It tends to dominate his perceptions. That identity and those perceptions draw his aesthetic principles along a certain line, one that mirrors his experiences. He likes what he thinks is important; he is drawn to language that seems real to him and that makes the words and ideas beautiful and truthful. In the end, his aesthetic principles themselves are probably driven by his definition of literacy. How can his students not "get it" after all? Can't they simply look around and see how things are? Having done that, won't they see the beauty and truth of shouting all that darkness out there into a poem or two? This teacher's sense of literacy is entrenched in his cultural viewpoint, however, and the more polite utterances of his students probably strike him as boring at the least or loathsome at worst. Literacy, however, is a thing that must be taught, and this partly explains the desperation in what ended up being his final strategy in that classroom. Perhaps one lesson here is that where these three meet—aesthetics, literacy, and culture—there is significant opportunity for misunderstanding and a considerable challenge for teachers at any level. There is almost certainly, however, an equally strong and important opportunity to promote understanding and to learn something from one another.

The Idea of Aesthetics

As both a teacher and a poet, I find the idea of aesthetics a fascinating focal point here. In considering the subject, inevitable questions arise: How much of our aesthetic viewpoint is culturally or subculturally based, even in a postmodern age? How does this affect the way we teach the art of poetry, particularly the aesthetic side? What can we do to bridge the apparent gaps we're likely to find in answering these questions?

First, how culturally based are our aesthetics, even those of teachers and educated people? Consider my own experience with Gwendolyn Brooks's "We Real Cool" (1999). This is a powerful poem, in dialect, that I would have assumed I appreciated as well as anyone: I, too, was raised in the city. My parents were poor. The streets I grew up on were tough. So I should "get this." Recently, after hearing Michael Harper's reading (Moyers, 1995) of this poem (and subsequently discovering an exhibit at The Women's Hall of Fame in Seneca Falls, New York, where Brooks's voice can be heard reading it), I felt as if I were listening to something new and very different from the verse I thought I knew. For one thing, as much as I appreciated this poem, I didn't hear the "living" voice behind it: the dramatic, rhythmic representation of the people to whom the poem refers and for whom it was written (the pool players at the Golden Shovel). Brooks's rendition emphasizes the *w* in *we* in a jazzy version of the ³/₄ time rhythm in which the poem is composed.

We Real Cool

<blockquote>
The pool players.
Seven at the golden shovel.
</blockquote>

We real cool. We
Left school. We

Lurk late. We
Strike straight. We

Sing sin. We
Thin gin. We

Jazz June. We
Die soon.   (p. 73)

Brooks and Harper take the last sentence, "We / die soon," as a decrescendo, a descending sound quality that emphasizes the end of the poem in a very dramatic way. The effect, then, is to establish a jazz rhythm and end it abruptly in a decrescendo. In hindsight, the "music" in this poem seems essential to a full appreciation of it.

Understanding the Differences

One way to understand the difference between my earlier and later readings of the poem may be to consider this: Take a favorite song and change the melody while leaving the words as is. When we do that, it's not the same song at all. Perhaps the point here is that Brooks's cultural viewpoint and experience, in addition to her authorship, allow her to hear voices that those lacking that experience do not hear. The people she refers to, that she gives voice to, are real for her. I literally have to know a little bit more about Brooks's world, to be more intimate with it, in order to gain a clearer vision of the poem she created. Here's the important part: In doing so, I put a voice and perhaps even "flesh" on the characters the poem represents. This makes my sympathy for their lives, the pathos the poem wants us to feel, more intimate and, I would argue, perhaps more accurate. My own culturally based aesthetics—in the form of my ability to read or hear poetry—may thus have limited my response and my understanding of the poem itself.

I am not suggesting that one can't appreciate the poem before hearing Harper's or Brooks's reading of it, but it is true that one won't know it as well. Poetry is an oral art form, but in the absence of an authorial reading we are left on our own. This example suggests something of the need for multiple literacies in a creative writing classroom. To the extent that any literary aesthetic is limited or defined by our enculturation, it is incumbent upon us to learn all that we can about cultures, people, and voices that produce or inhabit poetry and apply what we learn to our appreciation and understanding of poems in general. Otherwise, we serve neither art nor our students' education very well.

How Aesthetics Affect Teaching

How does our culturally defined aesthetics affect our teaching of creative writing? My example sheds some light here as well. Those of us who teach creative writing are usually trained in one school of poetics or another; sometimes, if we're lucky, we come to know several schools as part of that training. This probably influences what we like in a significant way. It's no secret that teachers are often acculturated to defend particular "turfs" with zeal, and aesthetic turf tends to be very well guarded. So, if we're not careful, literacy itself may become a "blinder," of sorts. We teach what we think will make our students literate in poetry, but without a multicultural viewpoint (i.e., multiple literacies), we won't be sharing the whole picture with them. In this sense, we may be cheating them of both literary culture and inheritance. I suspect that many of us in the creative arts, like our colleagues on the scholarly side, may need a little push toward multiculturalism, and I know that this is a delicate issue, particularly with regard to the idea of academic freedom. Nevertheless, we teachers also have to deal with the very real notion that thought itself is not stagnant. This is an undervalued yet critical point. To be a responsible educator requires an awareness of the progression of humanity's thinking, generally speaking, and our methods should reflect that progression in some way. Thus, questions of academic freedom must always be weighed alongside academic responsibility and the need for education to find its best form.

The case of rap music provides a good example here. Academic literati have typically been slow to accept what popular culture might define as "good" or "essential." In the past, I have tried to steer students away from writing poems in the rap form, but is this the right thing to do? At what point do I become the orthodoxy that holds a good, albeit unorthodox, artist back? More important, rather than writing in rap form or not writing in it, are there other options? Is a blending of forms possible? These are good questions, perhaps even essential ones for teachers to ask. Here are some of the complexities involved in this particular example as I see them.

Certainly, all rap is not the same, so sweeping judgments of it tend to be unfair and biased. The place of rap—at least some of it—in our society can pose problems for people who are familiar only with its aggressive forms. On the one hand, if the complaint is that some rap is sexist or advocates violent aggression, then the complaint may seem justified. However, what happens when we consider what drives rap's popularity and proliferation? Everyone knows that rap is very "real" and energetic. Thus young people who naturally love to rebel admire it for these qualities, whereas others far removed from the forces that generate rap music might view it as obnoxious, obscene, or offensive. I am not trying to oversimplify here. It is a sign of the complexity of rap that both admiration and condemnation of it may be validated according to the broader evidence. Like all music, rap encompasses a wide range of approaches. Opinion is therefore based on *which* rap one has actually heard. Wisdom suggests, then, that rap should not be ignored or discarded out of hand by educators or anyone else. If we hope to be wise, then the poetry of the street deserves at least our attention and the reservation of judgment until we can understand it fully.

Some implications for teachers of creative writing clearly apply here. To put it in personal terms, if I can see a poem I've known for years in a new light through more immediate exposure to the culture that produced it, what might we learn about street poetry or rap by seeing these through the eyes of those who produce and revere them? No matter what the answer, there are compelling reasons at the least to ask these questions along with others like them. The worst thing we can do, it seems to me, is hide behind an uninformed notion of a monolithic "literacy," as if it actually represents some absolute artistic truth.

Bridging the Literacy Gaps

Finally, what can we do to bridge "literacy gaps" that occur in classrooms like the one I mentioned at the beginning of this chapter? How can we serve literacy *and* our students best? As I have implied, we should probably start with ourselves, with an inventory and investigation of our own aesthetics and their origins, with how much they reflect our worldview and enculturation. The more that we, as teachers, understand about the origins and relevance of literacy and the communicative arts, the more we have to pass on to our students. We also increase the number of options we have for generating exercises that will encourage greater understanding across cultural or subcultural boundaries, wherever we find them. The end result of this search will not be a mere acceptance of other aesthetic points of view; in fact, this may not be part of the result at all. Some of us may never like rap poetry; likewise, Carolyn Forché or Denise Levertov may never be massively popular in the Bronx, East St. Louis, or South Los Angeles. It may, however, very well be possible for us to understand one another's aesthetics and the various literacies they generate or represent better than we do now. Any argument for further understanding, no matter what one does with it, is inherently good and valuable.

Techniques

Here are some techniques we might use to accomplish these goals. Reading and listening help, certainly—the more, and the broader the representation, the better. Talking to people about what they admire in certain styles of poetry is also a good thing. One of the more effective methods might be to introduce unfamiliar styles of writing to students. A good example of this may be found in Sandra McPherson's "Bad Mother Blues" (1993):

>When you were arrested child
>and I had to take your pocket-knife
>When you were booked
>and I had to confiscate your pocket-knife
>It had blood on it
>from where you tried to take your life
>
>It was the night before Thanksgiving
>all the family coming over
>The night before Thanksgiving
>all the family coming over
>We had to hide your porno magazine
>and put your handcuffs under cover
>
>Each naked man looked at you, said
>"Baby, who do you think you are?"
>Each man looked straight down on you
>like a waiting astronomer's star
>Solely, disgustedly
>each wagged his luster
>
>I've decided to throw horror down the well
>and wish on it
>Decided I'll throw horror down the well
>and wish on it
>And up from the water will shine
>my sweet girl in her baby bonnet
>
>A thief will blind you with his flashlight
>but a daughter be your bouquet
>A thief will blind you with his flashlight
>but a daughter be your bouquet
>When the thief's your daughter
>you turn your eyes the other way

> I'm going into the sunflower field
> where all of them are facing me
> I'm going into the sunflower field
> so all of them are facing me
> Going to go behind the sunflowers
> feel all the sun that I can't see. (p. 49)

This poem's example could easily be turned into a creative writing exercise: McPherson takes the traditional form of the blues lyric and turns it into a complex and moving contemporary poem. McPherson "borrows" the structure of African-American blues artists, and the marriage of her writing style with the blues form is both wildly successful and an example of the artist reaching outside her own aesthetic to create a sort of bridge, a meeting place where shared human concerns are highlighted.

Aside from producing a stunning poem, the result here is also an effective and wonderful blending of cultures, an intercultural "child" of sorts. The artistic merits of such cross-cultural experiments have long been acknowledged, but the educational benefits should be equally glaring. If we take our differences and create syntheses from them, how can we deny the potential benefits of that? McPherson blends contemporary poetry and blues at the point where they most frequently and naturally meet: human suffering, anxiety over our fates, concern and confusion over our own acts along with those of the people we love. We share these things no matter what our cultural contexts or origins may be. Are we truly literate, in any larger sense of the word, if we fail to understand this?

Another useful technique might be to let our students hear a variety of voices and approaches to the art of poetry. Bill Moyers has given us a great resource for this with his *Language of Life* (1995), both a video series and a book documenting a particularly diverse venue, the Dodge Poetry Festival in Waterloo, New Jersey. Consider the kinds of discussions that students and teachers can have after reading and hearing Victor Hernandez Cruz's "Problems With Hurricanes" (1995). In Moyers's video, Cruz reads this poem with an intentionally strong accent, highlighting the sound of English from a native Spanish speaker's voice:

> A campesino looked at the air
> And told me:
>
> With hurricanes it's not the wind
> or the noise or the water.
> I'll tell you, he said:
> it's the mangoes, avocados
> Green plantains and bananas
> flying into town like projectiles.

How would your family
feel if they had to tell
the generations that you
got killed by a flying
Banana.

Death by drowning has honor
If the wind picked you up
and slammed you
Against a mountain boulder
This would not carry shame
But
to suffer a mango smashing
your skull
or a plantain hitting your
Temple at 70 miles per hour
is the ultimate disgrace.

The campesino takes off his hat—
As a sign of respect
towards the fury of the wind
And says:
Don't worry about the noise
Don't worry about the water
Don't worry about the wind—

If you are going out
beware of mangoes
And all such beautiful
sweet things.   (p.148)

Students should be asked to re-create this poem as it might be written to apply to their hometowns and particular environments. "Problems With Brush Fires or Mud Slides" for Californians, ". . . With Floods" for anyone along the Mississippi River basin, ". . . With Blizzards" for upstate New Yorkers, ". . . With Empty Factories" if students are from Youngstown, Ohio, or Detroit, Michigan, or Allentown, Pennsylvania. (See Appendix 10-A for some examples.). As students manifest and experience each other's worlds through such exercises, their own perspectives are expanded and redefined. They and we have a chance at understanding the immediacy of each other's lives a little better.

Reflection

In the end, one helpful principle applies to whatever techniques we may use: Offer opportunities to our students that extend beyond their own individual definitions of poetry, their own individual literacy. We should also foster this practice in ourselves. One of the ways students succeed is by becoming more in tune with the connections between themselves and others. Citizenship, in all of its higher, communal aspirations, is a less complex matter than we might imagine. It begins by making meaningful connections between one person and another and nurturing these. An expanded definition of what it means to be literate can help create such connections in a student's consciousness and mind, and that's exactly where we want to be in a constructive way. Moving toward these general goals, a class might spend a day at a downtown bus station reading rap poetry and generating responses by writing some of its own. The next week that same class might spend an afternoon in the grass reading a field guide and writing nature poetry. Students should do both if the opportunities can be generated. The implementation of these principles may not always be easy; in fact, expanding one's aesthetics and therefore one's catalogue of literacies requires a great deal of work. The real question, however, is "What is the cost of not doing so?" The divisions that already plague our country will remain exactly as they are, in all likelihood, or grow more severe because we will have done too little to bridge them.

We teachers, like many but certainly not all of the artists I know, seem to accomplish most when we stretch ourselves a little, when we keep our own minds open and take risks, as much of a pain in the neck as that can sometimes be. The same may be said of our students, of course. Where we take them when we are modeling artistic work is an important place and affects them more than many of us know. Unlike the teacher I mention at the beginning of this chapter, we will not bring a gun into the classroom, but the lesson that his weapon brought, albeit wrongly delivered, is worth translating. The world is filled with "beautiful, sweet things." We should help our students to learn to pick a rich and varied bouquet.

In order to give the students feedback on their work, I developed a rubric (see Appendix 10-B) and grading criteria (see Appendix 10-C).

Teaching is a difficult task and a worthy one. As my students and I struggle with contemporary poetry together, it's interesting to observe how glad we are to do it. Poetry and poetry writing seem to touch a need in human beings for some intimacy or freedom of expression that we don't find in other parts of our lives, generally speaking. One of the most attractive things about poetry may be that it is by definition both private and communal, both intimate and a way of sharing intimacy in a social framework. That is part of its gift and its responsibility. As poetry writing and the teaching of it promote understanding, explore art's possibilities, and make or keep learning a vital feature of our lives, they are essential educational tools, part of the humanity of teachers and students alike. Expanding our definition of literacy in the poetry writing classroom, then, builds bridges that can carry us forward.

Appendix 10-A. Student Examples of the "Problems With..." Exercise

(These poems are modeled on Victor Hernandez Cruz's "Problems With Hurricanes.")

Problems With Baskets

An unemployed weaver once said:

The trouble with weaving baskets
Is the monotony, withered dexterity, and carpal tunnel syndrome

How do you tell your family
Your pay was reduced
Due to a cramp received during a snowflake basket creation.

Easy money—
Education not needed
Talk about putting all your eggs in one basket

Corporate spending, declining economy
Easy money—hard to get

What do I have?
Skills limited, old hands

The weaver looks down at the want ad and mutters
Damn them, damn me.

—Mary Gibson, 2002

Problems With Rocks

A farmer looked at the field
And told me:

With rocks it's not the wind
Or the pollen or the seed.
I'll tell you, he said:

It's the multiplication, overabundance
Gray ones and large ones
Slinking in overnight.

How would your family
Feel if they had to tell
The generations that you
Got killed in shale
Reproducing

Death by combine has honor
If the tractor impaled you
And crushed you
Against a silo
This would not carry shame
But
To suffer a rock attacking
Your skull

Or a boulder bruising your ego
You swear
That field was clear
Something you cannot explain
Where do they come from?
How do they manage?

—Janice Wallenberg, 2002

Appendix 10-B. Poetry Writing Rubric

For years in my composition courses, I have been using what we in English call *rubrics*—handouts for guided self-evaluation of student work, plus a section for specific responses from the instructor regarding individual aspects of that work. The materials I use now are adapted from those distributed by the composition program at Bowling Green State University in Ohio. Students receive copies at the beginning of the course. The rubrics are handed in along with writing assignments.

When using the rubric, poetry-writing students seem a bit clearer regarding course expectations, and they have more details and insight regarding poetic techniques and practices. Student response to the rubric has been almost unanimously positive and enthusiastic.

Student's Name: _____ **Poem Title:** _____

Questionnaire: (To be completed by the student and presented to the instructor on the day of the workshop; use other side of page if needed.)

1. How much time did you spend writing this poem?
   _____

2. How many drafts of this poem have been written?
   _____

3. Were there any particular difficulties you encountered in writing this?
   _____
   _____

4. What questions do you have that remain for this draft (likes, dislikes)?
   _____
   _____

5. What is your strategy or hope for this poem?
   _____
   _____

Checklist: (To be completed by instructor: 1 equals "not effective"; 2 equals "adequate"; 3 equals "better than adequate"; 4 equals "good"; 5 equals "excellent"; "NA" stands for not applicable)

Originality of language and imagery   Evaluation:_____
Instructor's Response:
_____
_____
_____

Ability to evoke emotion or stimulate thought   Evaluation:_____
Instructor's Response:
_____
_____
_____

Sophistication of language or concept   Evaluation: _____
Instructor's Response:
_____
_____
_____

Manipulation of line and stanza breaks, form   Evaluation: _____
Instructor's Response:
_____
_____
_____

Awareness of sound or tone   Evaluation: _____
Instructor's Response:

_____

_____

Effectiveness of narrative   Evaluation: _____
Instructor's Response:

_____

_____

Appendix 10-C. Grading Criteria for Poetry

Grading criteria are also given to students at the beginning of the course and can be referred to at any time. These criteria provide general indicators used in assessing the range of a poem's grade. The student's grade is based on an assessment of the poem's or portfolio's individual features. Because students often find it intimidating, I sometimes revise the order of the criteria on the page so as to present the C grade first, followed by the B, the A, and finally the D or F. Presenting the A criteria—certainly the most challenging—in the third slot may make the information easier for students to encounter for the first time. I make certain to explain that these criteria attempt to describe the range of a grade according to certain features, and that because grading itself is very complex, only an assessment of their works' individual characteristics will produce the grade they eventually earn.

An A poem demonstrates a superior sense of the art of poetry. It is thoroughly original in its use of language, images, and statements, but it may also employ conventional language or imagery in a way that makes these original through context. It evokes powerful emotion and is sophisticated in its ideational concept. Manipulation of line breaks, stanza breaks, and other features regarding form demonstrates a high degree of selectivity and strongly enhances both the language and the content of the poem. Moreover, craft is clearly demonstrated through a superior awareness of poetic techniques— such as personification, transference, irony, double entendre, assonance, and alliteration—and/or significant contributions to poetic movements or philosophies, such as the deep image school, surrealism, and nature writing. Grade A poetry surprises and delights the reader and often includes phrases that make people want to respond with "I always thought that but could never have said it so well." All features of both content and style combine to form a unified whole that is greater than the sum of its parts.

A B poem demonstrates a sense of the art of poetry. It is far more than competent and is largely original in its use of language, images, and statements. It evokes emotion and is relatively sophisticated in its ideational concept. Manipulation of line breaks, stanza breaks, and other features regarding form demonstrates selectivity and enhances both the language and the content of the poem.

Moreover, craft is demonstrated through an awareness of poetic techniques—such as personification, transference, irony, double entendre, assonance, and alliteration and/or sound contributions to poetic movements or philosophies, such as the deep image school, surrealism, and nature writing. Grade B poetry is a pleasure for a reader to encounter and often includes memorable and interesting phrases. Most features of content and style combine to form a unified whole, leaving the reader with a sense of unity and strong purpose in the work itself.

A C poem demonstrates an adequate sense of the art of poetry. It is competent and its use of language and imagery is fairly interesting, although the poem may lack a sense of unity, some images or statements may be less than effective, and it may contain an occasional cliché. It possesses emotion and an ideational concept, although these may not be as sophisticated as those of the A or B poem. Line breaks, stanza breaks, and other features regarding form have been considered. Grade C poetry is generally competent, though not as engaging as poems at the A and B levels.

A D or F poem contains serious flaws in language, craft and construction, possesses a number of clichés either in phrasing or approach, lacks competent imagery and an ideational base commensurate with high-school-level work, and is generally in need of revision and refinement.

References

Brooks, G. (1999). *Selected poems.* New York: Harper Collins.

Cruz, V. H. (1995). Problems with hurricanes. In B. Moyers & J. Haba (Eds.). *The Language of Life.* New York: Doubleday.

McPherson, S. (1993). *The god of indeterminacy.* Chicago: University of Illinois Press.

Moyer, B. (1995). *The language of life* [Video series]. New York: Public Broadcasting System.

11

Stokely Was Right: Writing August Wilson Into the High School Curriculum

Patricia M. Gantt

"Those who can name are the masters."
—Stokely Carmichael

A few semesters ago Kristen, one of the best-read students in my Multicultural American Literature course, raised her hand and spoke out vehemently. "This class makes me so angry," she said. "Almost everyone whose work we study is a complete stranger to me. I graduated from what is supposed to be a fabulous high school, took the toughest courses it had to offer, and I never even *heard* of August Wilson!" Glancing about, I saw the majority of students nodding their heads in assent. Others spoke up, too: "We read almost no contemporary writers." "My survey on American literature ended with John Steinbeck." "The only modern writers we read much were poets."

This was a class of future English teachers who all realized that we were in the middle of what Nancie Atwell (1987) calls a "teachable moment," so we took the next few minutes to conduct an informal survey of titles and authors read, just to see which ones they had studied to some degree in high school. At the end of the day, it seemed that those English education students, who will shape so much of what gets read in the next generation, could profess only limited familiarity with works other than those by William Shakespeare, Charles Dickens, Emily Dickinson, Robert Frost, Edgar Allan Poe, and Ernest Hemingway. Still, we agreed that we should not trust our recollections implicitly, knowing that memory can definitely be faulty. We acknowledged, too, that even the most assiduous students might forget even those readings studied in depth, regardless of the skill with which they are taught.

I teach in the English Department of a state university whose teacher preparation program has just been ranked 15 in the nation. There, besides general literary surveys and specific topics courses on themes, writers, or genre, American literature and pedagogy are blended in three courses required for future secondary school English teachers. These courses—Young Adult Literature, Multicultural American Literature, and Teaching Literature—are intended to give our students a depth of perspective and practical teaching strategies that their survey courses are not meant to offer. Yet Kristen's comment that day suggested an important project that my students were soon participating in with full enthusiasm. Taking August Wilson as our touchstone, we decided to conduct an inquiry into where his work is taught in high school, which courses most frequently study it, and what we can do to make reading his plays a given for secondary school students. Doing so, we thought, would enable us to find ways of including a host of gifted writers disregarded in a traditional high school canon.

Introducing Writers Into the Curriculum

This chapter is a bit of a departure from others in this anthology. To begin with, it offers suggestions about how to work a contemporary writer of merit into a high school curriculum, including both philosophical issues and practical ones. In addition, it is not my creation only. Rather, it is a combination of the research and creativity of several people who were or are preparing to be English teachers. Looking at the best practices of a wide range of teachers, we developed a number of teaching ideas that can be implemented immediately, either for use with Wilson's drama or translated into approaches for teaching other literary works. My students and I collated these ideas when they were on the threshold of their teaching careers; in fact, several of them are now working in classrooms of their own. The solidity and usefulness of their lesson ideas is to me a gratifying indicator of the capabilities of new teachers across the country, as well as a reminder of the numerous literary recoveries we *all* need to undertake.

We had considerable resources to bring to bear in this project. Although none of my students was at the time involved in student teaching, all had substantial familiarity with teaching. For some, my class was the last they would take before actual student teaching began. Many of them were doing what we call a practicum. This preview of their professional experience puts future educators into classrooms as teaching assistants, and sometime team teachers, for an extended period while they fulfill a requirement of contact hours. Others had frequent access to teachers in schools they had graduated from or ones where their parents taught, and could interview them. Still others were taking an education course that in part trained them to evaluate textbooks and Web sites. All were willing to do Internet research. We decided to focus on August Wilson's *Fences* and *The Piano Lesson* as the two plays that high school students could most identify with. Here is what we found.

Overview of Research Findings

August Wilson's plays are taught most frequently in three areas of the country: the East Coast, Chicago, and the West Coast, especially California. Even there, we discovered, they are mainly part of a curriculum in drama or of specialized courses in African-American literature; they are less frequently part of the surveys of American literature that most high school students take during their junior year. That fact alone cuts the majority of high school students off from a formal study of Wilson's writing. The one course that *is* highly likely to read and analyze his drama is Advanced Placement Literature (AP Lit). Partial credit for AP Lit students' familiarity with Wilson's plays can be attributed to his having been included on previous AP Lit examinations, a move guaranteed to increase readership in related high school classes. A number of my students were pleasantly surprised to discover the cultural work done in AP Lit—a course that, rather than being the elitist one they had perceived it to be, has probably done more to expand the high school curriculum than any other single offering. (Nevertheless, it remains true that much of the canon-busting that AP Lit examinations encourage rests in the hands of an individual teacher. I have observed a so-called AP Lit class in which the most "contemporary" work studied was *Gulliver's Travels!*)

Solutions to Particular Issues

My students informally interviewed teachers to ask them whether they taught Wilson's plays, which ones they taught, and if they did not teach them, why not. Several teachers interviewed admitted that they did not teach Wilson for six key reasons, each of which produced a firm response from my prospective teachers.

1. *Teachers are not familiar with Wilson's plays.* Many who have taught for more than a few years may not have studied the works themselves, despite the prominence of his drama for two decades and the fact that he is one of only seven American playwrights to have won multiple Pulitzer prizes. My students enthusiastically suggested *Fences* and *The Piano Lesson* to these teachers and mentioned such resources as the interviews with Wilson shown recently during prime time on the *McNeill-Lehrer Report* (April 6, 2001) and *60 Minutes* (Janurary 27, 2002). They also recommended the Hallmark presentation (1995) of *The Piano Lesson*, featuring an excellent cast headed up by Alfre Woodard and Charles Dutton and released on video in January 1999. Its 104-minute run time is very well suited to a three-day showing in a typical secondary school class period of 55 minutes. Presented with a day of introduction, 35-minute segments for three days (with discussion and/or writing each time), and a day of concluding discussion, Wilson's play could be introduced to high school students in only 1 week. The cost of the video, $14.98 for a new copy and $6.49 for a used one, is not prohibitive at all, even in these days of severe budgetary cutbacks.

2. *Teachers do not have enough texts.* Here we had a little more difficulty, but some sleuthing solved this problem. Investigating the common publishers of high school literary texts, such as Scott, Foresman and McDougal Littell (and even one publisher who claimed to be "your complete guide to American literature"), we were able to locate few anthologies that include Wilson's plays. More typical dramatic selections are Arthur Miller's *The Crucible* and Lorraine Hansberry's *A Raisin in the Sun*. Textbooks that do include Wilson usually contain *Fences*.

"All right, then," my students said. "How much do texts cost from Amazon, Barnes & Noble, Borders, or other places like them?" We found that new copies are roughly $8.80 each, with used ones only $3.99. The cost adds up to $264 plus shipping for a standard class of 30, a considerable sum in a tight budget. "How can librarians help to provide texts?" my students wanted to know. They were told that most secondary school libraries are allowed to purchase no more than five copies of a single title. Students then suggested that half the class read *The Piano Lesson* and the other half *Fences*. Teachers could get their librarians to purchase five copies of each play and the department could buy used ones for the 10 remaining students in each group. This scheme reduces departmental cost to $79.80. If teachers in two nearby schools would work together on such a plan, each school could, by trading, have a full set of each play. Such professional networking can definitely create opportunities for student learning.

3. *Teachers do not feel confident about their own critical backgrounds for teaching Wilson's plays*. We found a tremendous variety of critical material available to teachers, including the groundbreaking work done by Sandra Shannon (1996) and Marilyn Elkins (2000), as well as important criticism by Alan Nadel (1994). Shannon's annotated bibliography, a product of her ongoing relationship with the dramatist, is a particularly rich resource. Wilson himself has been most generous about giving interviews, and several are readily available in print and Web sources. A general Internet search revealed 595,278 sites for Wilson material. Even if one third of those should be duplicates, that still leaves close to 400,000 resources. I dare say that is more than most of us refer to when preparing to teach an author's work! Two of the most helpful sites are one maintained by Mark William Rocha at Humboldt University (www.humboldt.edu/~ah/wilson/index.html) and the K–12 learning connection for the Kennedy Center's Performing Arts Series (www.3rdwaveweb.com/pwtv/theater/wilsoncurric.html). Both of these have direct classroom applications.

4. *Teachers protested that their students were mostly Latino or "white middle-class Americans," and did not "need" to read work by African Americans like August Wilson*. This reply was the one that made our blood pressures rise the most. I hope I do not have to tell this reading audience how false an argument this excuse is. Admittedly, it is axiomatic that reading the work of authors whose cultural identity reflects one's own is essential. Yet my students quickly got into a hot discussion over this specific teacher response: "Are we supposed to deny our students all authors whose gender, ethnicity, or class they do not share?" they argued in class. "Is it not just possible that those writers are the very ones whose work our students *need* to read with the most urgency?" Rather than leaping upon their soapboxes with heartfelt zeal, however, these teachers-in-the-making decided to come up with strategies for studying Wilson, connecting his work with other writing their students would be likely to read. They based their approach in part on Joan E. Kaywell's (1993) notable strategies for young adult literature, a procedure she champions for pairing traditional and modern texts as a means toward a more inclusive curriculum. Several of their teaching ideas are in the appendixes of this essay.

5. Teachers said they had decided not to teach Wilson just to avoid any possible "controversy." They feared that they might stir up racial conflict by teaching his plays. Some even self-censored *A Raisin in the Sun*, despite its brilliance and long-esteemed standing in the American canon. Others, when required by their departments, administration, or state curricular standards to teach a work that can in some way be construed as "multicultural," sidestepped Wilson's verbal intensity to choose what was perceived to be the "safer ground" of, for example, Chaim Potok's *The Chosen*. My students found these arguments and actions the saddest, the most nebulous, and therefore the most difficult to counter. The problem of conservatism by self-censorship is one that has repeatedly been addressed by the National Council of Teachers of English, the International Reading Association, and other leading organizations in the profession. It goes to the root of an individual teacher's stand in the classroom. In the end, it is difficult to induce teachers to extend their personal canons unless student and peer pressure or the sheer dynamism of individual writing pushes them to do so. Wilson's drama clearly provides the dynamism; my students have vowed to provide the quiet pressure on their future colleagues. They are confident that when they teach Wilson's work, the playwright himself will win their students, as he has won them. From that small fire, knowledge will spread.

6. Finally, some teachers acknowledged that while they are personally passionate about Wilson's plays, they end up not teaching them because they have no approaches or activities for his work. They may have three filing cabinets full of materials on, for instance, John Steinbeck's *The Red Pony* but have no lesson plans for teaching *The Piano Lesson*. For many of them, professional development opportunities that might allow them to team up with fellow teachers to create new teacher resources did not exist. Before we take the high moral ground with our high school colleagues, however, let's consider what secondary teachers are up against across the nation: Many of them teach 180 students or more in a single day, working from 7:30 a.m. to 4:00 p.m., 5 days a week, for a salary of not more than $25,000 a year. In addition, they put out the school newspaper, coach the soccer team, sponsor the prom, serve on countless committees, and grade, grade, grade! How many of us in the field of secondary teacher preparation might lose the courage of our convictions against such odds? How many of us once taught high school but left?

My students decided to remedy the problem of few or no lesson plans by creating several, to have for their own use in days to come and to share with present classmates and future colleagues. Appendix 11-A gives you our suggestions about how to work a new author (in this case, August Wilson) and his or her writing (in this case, plays) into an existing curriculum. Appendix 11-B provides a selection of specific activities that teachers can use in teaching *Fences* and/or *The Piano Lesson*.

What We Learned

Doing this research and following it up by creating practical activities for student learning proved a valuable experience for all of us. Quite a few commented, "Until we did this project, I had no idea how writers are chosen for inclusion in a curriculum." Others realized for the first time how important an individual teacher is in determining "what gets taught." A young man remarked that he had been unaware of how much control an individual teacher can exert in selecting literature and writers for instruction. One young woman said, "The realities of pinched school budgets came home to me for the first time. I thought teachers just ordered whatever they liked." Others had been under the impression that some amorphous "they" handed everything necessary for teaching a curriculum over to incoming teachers! Students also discussed the critical need for inservice development activities to nurture continuing professional growth, including those that teachers themselves would plan, rather than ones planned for them.

I believe, then, that this mode of professional inquiry has been immensely productive in giving students realistic insights. An additional outcome is that it opened prospective teachers' eyes to the importance of the cultural power an individual classroom teacher wields on a daily basis—more than an anthology, a publisher, a principal, a curriculum director, or even state and national standards.

In reviewing our project and sharing it with you, I am led full circle to the title of this chapter—"Stokely Was Right: Writing August Wilson Into the High School Curriculum." The particular insight of Stokely Carmichael that inspired my students and me to design the teaching approaches we are sharing is "Those who can name are the masters" (Ture, 1992). We cannot forget that teachers *are* the masters in the classroom. Whether we are preparing tomorrow's high school English instructors or offering surveys in American literature, studies of drama, or courses in 20-century literature and thought, we must be mindful of our political and cultural power. Our syllabi do not simply define what *we* will teach; the texts we require often become central to our students' curricula when they have classrooms of their own. Our selections and omissions become, for our high school students, a de facto canon of what has literary merit.

As teachers, we know that the most political document our students read is the one we create and revise every time we teach: the syllabus. Although curricular frameworks may bind us to a certain extent, for each new group of students who come to us, we have the power to determine what gets taught. Our syllabi, our everyday teaching activities, and our classroom enthusiasm tell our students which writers are important, which ones are the best, which ones should have their work implanted into our national consciousness. As we ensure August Wilson's necessary presence in the high school canon, we use our considerable power as teachers for acts of naming. Stokely was right: The responsibility for the cultural work of naming is ours.

Appendix 11-A. Teaching August Wilson's Drama in the Secondary Classroom (Thematic Approaches)

Themes and Controlling Ideas

1. In a recent interview with Wilson, Gwen Ifil (2001) comments on his reputation as "the American Shakespeare." Make a comparative study between the two playwrights, perhaps using *Fences* with *King Lear* (parent-child issues) or *The Piano Lesson* with *Macbeth* (use of the supernatural).
2. Discuss Wilson's use of the vernacular in his plays. With *The Piano Lesson*, Wilson's 1930s play, examine vernacular speech in the interviews conducted during that decade by the Federal Writers' Project, available on the Web from the Library of Congress (www.loc.gov).
3. In a unit on dreams, read *A Raisin in the Sun* (Lorraine Hansberry), *The Great Gatsby* (F. Scott Fitzgerald), *How the Garcia Girls Lost Their Accents* (Julia Alvarez), and *The Piano Lesson* (August Wilson).
4. Investigate the topic of finding a woman's voice in Wilson's The Piano Lesson, Zora Neale Hurston's *Their Eyes Were Watching God*, Amy Tan's *The Bonesetter's Daughter*, Michael Dorris's *A Yellow Raft in Blue Water*, and Lucille Clifton's poetry.
5. Explore Wilson's work in the context of cycle plays—the Greeks, for example.
6. In a unit on the things we carry with us, read Julia Alvarez's *How the Garcia Girls Lost Their Accents*, Wilson's *The Piano Lesson*, Amy Tan's *The Bonesetter's Daughter*, Helena Maria Viramontes's *Under the Feet of Jesus*, and Chang-rae Lee's *Native Speaker*.
7. Read *The Piano Lesson* and John Steinbeck's *The Grapes of Wrath* for their views of the Depression Era in America.
8. Read Hansberry's *A Raisin in the Sun*, Tennessee Williams' *The Glass Menagerie*, and Wilson's *The Piano Lesson* as plays where absent characters play pivotal roles (the absent and the present).
9. Examine the roles of children in drama and fiction. Read *Fences* and two or three other works such as Miller's *The Crucible* or Helena Maria Viramontes's *Under the Feet of Jesus*. *A Raisin in the Sun* would also work beautifully.

Appendix 11-B. Teaching August Wilson's Drama in the Secondary Classroom (Activities)

Specific Activities for Students and/or Groups of Teachers

1. After they have read one of Wilson's plays, have students write a brief (approximately 150-word) review and post it on one of the national bookstore

Web sites (Amazon or Barnes & Noble) or publish it in the school newspaper.

2. For teachers: As a reading group, study and discuss one or more of Wilson's plays. Investigate whether your school district will allow inservice credit for creating teaching materials for distribution throughout your school system.

3. Watch for the appearance of a Wilson play in your area. Set up the viewing of the live drama the day students are to go. Offer extra credit for going and participating in the follow-up activities you will do the day after they see the play. For those who cannot go, (a) get video copies of other plays and check them out to students or (b) arrange for a video showing in your room or auditorium after school.

4. In a unit focusing on the works of Rita Dove, Robert Frost, and Julia Alvarez, read just the introductory remarks and stage directions to *Fences*. Discuss them for their poetic qualities, realizing that Wilson was a poet before he turned to writing drama.

5. In your daily work, interweave Wilson's voice—in sentences on vocabulary, in suggested paper topics, and elsewhere.

6. Examine a series of Wilson's interviews, looking at him as an author who is also a literary critic, in the manner of Paula Gunn Allen and Toni Morrison. Several interviews with each of these are available on the Web. How does their critical commentary shape their work, and how does their work inform their critical views?

7. Create a class Web site that students can add to throughout the year, with links to information on each author. As they study each writer, signal "new" information on the home page.

8. As an introduction to *The Piano Lesson*, ask students to bring an object to school that is significant to them (or a photo of it or a digital picture captured on file, if the object is too precious or too bulky to carry to school). Have them write about the object, why they treasure it, and what it means to them or their families. Share in small groups or classwide. Introduce the piano as a symbol in Wilson's play and ask students to be alert to what it means to various characters.

9. Before you begin your study of the play, have interested students act out, audiotape, or read selected scenes from *Fences* as readers' theater. Tape the scenes for class use, allowing student voices to take center stage, rather than those of professional actors or unknowns.

References

Atwell, N. (1987). *In the middle.* Portsmouth, NH: Heinemann.

Elkins, M. (2000). *August Wilson: A casebook.* New York: Garland. (Original work published in 1994).

Ifil, G. (Anchor). (2001, April 6). "August Wilson." New York: PBS.

Kaywell, J. E. (Ed.). (1993). *Adolescent literature as a complement to the classics.* Norwood, MA: Christopher-Gordon.

Nadel, A. (Ed.). (1994). *May all your fences have gates: Essays on the drama of August Wilson.* Iowa City, IA: University of Iowa Press.

Shannon, S. (1996). *The dramatic vision of August Wilson.* Washington, D.C.: Howard University Press.

Ture, K. (Carmichael, S.), & Hamilton, C. V. (1992). *Black power: The politics of liberation.* New York: Vintage. (Original work published in 1967).

Wilson, A. (1986). *Fences.* New York: Penguin Books.

Wilson, A. (1990). *The piano lesson.* New York: Penguin Books.

12

Graduation Time for the Literary Analysis Paper

Danette DiMarco

In an essay published in *Change*, Barr and Tagg (1995) highlight a critical move that has been taking place in teaching and learning in the last decade. According to them, this shift from seeing instruction as an end to a means brings with it the possibilities of hope and fear, excitement and confusion. Our common goal as instructors of any discipline is student success in learning and life. Yet as instructors faced with a historical moment that brings an important paradigm change, we may look inward and honestly admit to ourselves that "none of us has yet put all the elements of the Learning Paradigm together in a conscious, integrated whole" (p. 14). As educators, it is, however, our duty to "shear the wool" and help our students to see what it means to "grow new coats." Take the following as an example.

Have you heard your students voicing responses similar to these: "I just don't understand what the author is trying to tell me" or "What good will writing a paper on Shakespeare's sonnets do to help me to be successful in my future career"? If so, what has been your response? Have you tried to explain to those voicing such complaints how the *process* of honing interpretation and argument skills will ultimately cultivate a better person or citizen, one who is able to draw deeper insights and far-reaching connections? Although this sounds like a fruitful answer, admittedly the one I have given before, I would now like to challenge it. I would like to suggest that we begin growing a more effective response—what we might call our "new wool." What if our old responses are not the most successful way to make our point about the value of reading, discussing, and writing about literature? It may be time that those of us teaching such courses relinquish our grieving for "the way it used to be." Nevertheless, this does not mean that we should admit defeat. Instead, we should challenge ourselves to create new ways of integrating important facets characteristic of a traditional liberal arts education with evolving ideas about a "real-world" education called for by a rising generation of future college graduates.

A Real-World Assignment

In this essay I would like to offer a real-world assignment that is learning- rather than teaching-focused and that has been successful numerous times in my own classroom. This assignment seeks to revitalize the most common of assignments, the literary analysis paper. The assignment demands that students do the following:

- Situate themselves within a "real-world" scenario where they might reach Bloom's (1984) highest levels of cognitive thinking: application, synthesis, and evaluation
- Present to a real audience their completed document for the course, which will be cast in memo proposal format, the genre of in-house business communication
- Match visually appropriate graphics or drawings to their verbal (i.e., written) documents, enabling them to use technology in productive and practical ways whenever possible.

With the above objectives outlined for them, students can be transported to a place that does not seem so much like a literary wonderland far beyond their daily experience. Many literary artists, after all, write to shed light on human conditions. Having their works written about in a more "real" manner, rather than simply within the confines of the ivory tower, might make those same works seem far more accessible and able to contribute to a common goal, the cultivation of a better individual within a more intelligent community.

Facilitating the Case (Materials and Methods)

The Assignment

On or during the first week of class, students receive instructions for a final, out-of-class writing examination. Providing them with the question early in the semester allots them enough time to begin contemplating what class material seems appropriate for the project. They are to supplement their own opinions with notes from class discussions and lectures. The case under discussion here is one that students might see in an introduction to literature course, a general one that the curriculum designed not simply to introduce students to a wide variety of authors but to teach students about the multiple ways that readers approach and interpret texts. Students not only reflect throughout the semester in writing and oral discussion about what they read, they are also expected to learn how to distinguish between the interpretive modes that they apply: reader response, historical, and psychological. The completion of the following assignment is a culminating moment for students, a forum for showing how they make connections, synthesize ideas, and understand audience. To ensure a more polished final product, we take some class time to share drafts through peer review processes. The assignment—which my students and I refer to as a *case*, to use the language of problem solving—is an invitation, as follows:

An Invitation for You

[School X]

invites you to

Spring Graduation

May 2002

Come celebrate with this year's graduating seniors

and salute our theme

"Life Can Be Like Literature:

Reading Our Past, Our Present, and Our Future."

Instructions to students accompany the invitation. They assume the following premises and complete the instructions as given.

Instructions

Numerous graduates, their families and friends, and other prestigious guests will be attending. Among those taking part will be a select group of literary figures. Because of your expertise in interpreting literature, you have been selected as the student representative who will sit on this year's graduation planning committee. Your job is twofold:

- To select a graduation keynote speaker, writing a rationale for your choice, which will be presented to the rest of your committee
- To design a seating chart and written rationale for the celebration reception dinner that will follow the formal graduation ceremony.

Please see the back of your invitation for more specific details.

List of literary figures who will be attending: [Insert authors studied here.]

Draft of proposal due for in-class peer response on_____.

Final R.S.V.P. (i.e., your final proposal is due to the committee) by the last day of class.

Further Directions

Please present your suggestions to the graduation planning committee in memo proposal format, making sure that you have done the following:

- Stated your top choice for a keynote speaker (selected from the list of literary figures on the front on the invitation)
- Provided textual evidence for why this figure "fits" with the graduation theme effectively. This means that you must use hard evidence like direct quotes and paraphrases (in your own words) from the chosen speaker's text(s) that we have read in class. After quoting the writer's work, make sure to analyze or interpret meaning for the planning committee. Without this close textual analysis or interpretation, you will be unable to convince the committee that the writer has something interesting and worthwhile to offer the graduates
- Included a visual seating chart for the celebration reception dinner to follow graduation and a written rationale for why you have placed people at par-

ticular tables with particular individuals. Remember to include a seat for yourself (since you are helping to plan this important event) and to explain why you wish to sit there. The committee expects that you will design a general seating chart for your top 10 picks (including the keynote speaker and you). In your written rationale, however, make sure to speak "deeply" about three of the guests' and their literary works, besides the keynote's, which you have already discussed.

The "Key" to Convincing the Committee

As I have suggested above, do not speak generally about the literary works by the keynote and three other writers. Rather, be specific. Analyze works by looking at them closely. You are free not only to apply what you have learned from classroom discussions but to include additional insights. Make sure to use parenthetical documentation within your proposal. On a separate sheet of paper at the end of the proposal, include Works Cited documentation in MLA style.

A Note on Memo Proposal Format

Those of you who use Microsoft Word will find templates for memos ready for your use within the software. Simply go to File, New Memos, and make a selection from one of the templates. Then all you need to do is fill in the blanks and type. Using this style of memo proposal gives the document a professional flair, which you will want to do since you are submitting this to a university-wide planning committee.

A Note on Seating Chart Format

Many of you will opt to design a seating chart on your computer. If you do, feel free to choose appropriate graphics and clip art that represent an individual author's texts from our class readings. Those of you without access to a computer can choose to complete the seating chart work by hand, making sure that it is neat and readable.

Student Assignments Prior to Class Meetings

1. Read through the case (see above assignment).
2. Read through each assigned text (story, poem, drama), making notes to yourself as necessary about how it corresponds to the graduation theme.
3. Rank each text from 1 to 5, with 1 being your top choice, and list your reasons for your rankings. Remember to include the strengths and weaknesses of each text in regard to the graduation theme.
4. Compose a memo to the graduation committee and be prepared to share your findings orally with your small group and the collective class on "memo review day."

Note: This review procedure will take place approximately every 2 weeks. You will be ranking only the collection of texts studied over that time period. At the end of the semester, there will be an overall review of the "top" candidates who are selected from these 2-week meetings. Also, these response memos should be written to your group members. Only your final memo for the class will be written to the schoolwide planning committee.

Questions to Facilitate Case Discussion

Introduction (for the Individual Student)
1. What is the task before the graduation planning committee?
2. Who is the audience of graduation and what will be their expectations regarding a keynote talk?
3. What challenges do the graduation planning committee have? Remember to consider diversity issues.
4. What are your suggestions for the graduation planning committee? What topics do you suggest that they look for when selecting the keynote speaker?

Small-Group Challenge (for Groups in Class)
1. Decide on a strategy for choosing the best candidate.
2. Share your memo report with group members and then collectively rate the candidates.
3. Who is your top candidate? Give two or three reasons or justifications for your choice. (Give at least one justification for why each of the others was given a particular ranking.)
4. What most motivated your group to make this decision?
5. How did your group arrive at a consensus?

Pitfalls to Avoid During Class Discussion
Should a class unanimously vote for one text (and thus one author) from a particular unit, the instructor might elicit from students what the particular qualities of the piece were that led them to such a decision. This discussion is dependent upon the qualities of the other pieces of literature and thus reengages them in the talk. Some of the groups may wish to recast their votes after this discussion.

Analysis of Key Subjects (Discussion of Data)

Samples From Final Student Papers (Keynote Speaker Selection)

After the initial shock of a scenario-based assignment, students will more often than not begin to explore the possibilities of it with open and creative minds. Questions that quickly arise include but are not limited to the following:

- What authors do I choose or leave out?
- What are my reasons behind such choices?

- What diction and tone will I use to persuade my audience, the graduation planning committee?
- How will I design my seating chart to capture my audience's attention?
- Will I be able to employ technology in a productive way?

Below are some samples from student writing that re-create students' responses to the final assignment.

After discussing the many possible interpretive strategies that could be used to study Shirley Jackson's "The Lottery"—including reader response and historical criticism in which specifics of the Cold War were interwoven with Jackson's main theme of fear and change—one student, Tate, decided upon Jackson as the keynote speaker, drawing parallels from Friedrich Nietzsche to convince her audience of the author's intuitiveness. She attempts to convince the planning committee of her choice by tying in her understanding of Jackson's work with the committee's graduation theme. Tate writes the following:

> As the student representative for this year's graduation planning committee, I would like to recommend Shirley Jackson as the December graduation keynote speaker. After thoughtful consideration of all the candidates on the list, I believe that Jackson would make the best speaker on this year's theme, "Life Is Like Literature: Reading Our Past, Our Present, and Our Future." [Close textual analysis omitted here] . . . . The lottery may be symbolic of any of a number of social ills that mankind blindly performs every day. As I was contemplating her work I could not help but recall the German philosopher, Nietzsche [who] said that the masses, or "the herd or crowd," as he called it, conform to tradition . . . . "[The] crowd hides our true individual identities and weakens our sense of responsibility. A crowd does not have hands." This means that no individual person can be to blame. Together they act as one. But one person would be able to break this crowd. Had one person spoken up and refused to partake in the ritual of the lottery, he would be true to himself and could have ended the negative tradition. Only the crowd as a whole is able to stone Tessie to death. In "The Lottery," Jackson emphasizes the fact that "Life Is Like Literature." Her theme of breaking away from the crowd is a recurring [one] . . . Much we do is done merely out of tradition or because it is what the majority does . . . Jackson will be able to present her ideas, and the graduates will leave feeling inspired to be individuals, to break away from the crowd.

Another student, Dominick, also capitalizes on the graduation theme. By focusing on "The Unknown Citizen," a poem written by his pick for keynote speaker, W. H. Auden, Dominick claims like Tate that a "herd" mentality will not make a better world. Dominick emphasizes how Auden's poem invites the reader to reflect upon revolution and innovation, aspects important to graduating seniors. He writes the following:

It is my recommendation that Mr. W. H. Auden be selected as the keynote speaker for the upcoming Winter Graduation Ceremony in December 2000. Mr. Auden will make an excellent representative for this year's theme, "Life Is Like Literature," because for him, life is literature. [Close textual analysis omitted.] Auden is trying to tell us that life is made up of vital experiences, and if one does not really experience life then one cannot truly live. I believe that our graduates can benefit universally by internalizing this lesson. Life is all about the experiences that we have . . . Our graduates are the future leaders of this world, and as leaders they must not be afraid to break the mold and explore new, unorthodox ideas. Nonconformity is the mother of invention, revolution, evolution, and inspiration. I can think of no better advice to equip our graduates with than this invaluable lesson.

Samples From Student Papers (Verbal Explanations for the Seating Chart)

After taking part in an introductory literature class that focused specifically on gender, Andrea determined that she would sit between the Chicana writer Sandra Cisneros and the Mexican author Laura Esquivel. While she is, in this particular discussion, providing reasons for designing her seating chart, her explanation alludes to her graduation theme, "The Gender Lesson." (The theme title is inspired by Toni Cade Bambara's short story "The Lesson"). Andrea examines the gendered aspects of the text as follows:

I seated myself between Sandra Cisneros and Laura Esquivel because they are two of my favorite guests. [Cisneros's] short story "Eyes of Zapata" is a reflective, historically fictional account of life in Mexico [told by] the wife of Emilio Zapata, the leader of the revolution. The speaker, Ines, talks of a strong, controlling man as though he were a child. When he is with her, she controls how the reader sees him. Cisneros's perspectives of gender beautifully rise to the surface of this story with phrases like "You don't know your own heart, men. Even when you are speaking with it in your hand." She says the women of her family "love as strong as we hate . . . We never forget a wrong. We know how to love and we know how to hate." These women are thought to be witches by the community: Ines's mother is even killed by the men of the village, tricked by a lover. Cisneros brings to light the weaknesses of powerful men and the powers of humble women. Spun into a short, poemlike account of adventure, family, and love, it captures the heart and imagination of the reader and enchants him or her with dreamlike images to illustrate that love is stronger than anything else in the world.

Samples From Student Papers (The Seating Chart)

Finally, three student-designed seating charts are attached.

Figure 12-1: Seating Chart Sample A

* – John Cheever  * –	* – Milcha Sanchez-Scott  * –
* – Charlotte Perkins Gilman  * –	* – John Updike  * –

While Figures 12-1 and 12-3 were technologically enhanced, Figure 12-2 was mostly completed the "old-fashioned" way, glued and handwritten. As a side note, instructors enabling students to use more advanced technology to serve justice to the final project might opt to do so. I received one chart that applied new media technologies taught by professors in the Art Department, a digitally inscribed, three-dimensional cyber rendering of what the banquet hall would look like. The student, Man, created the clip so that the viewer could navigate the hall with a mouse, to see what the tables looked like, where particular guests would sit, and even where the keynote speaker would stand. Regardless of how students aesthetically enhance their written projects, however, the point is to have them recognize how the visual should balance and supplement the verbal, not overrule it.

Figure 12-2. Seating Chart Sample B

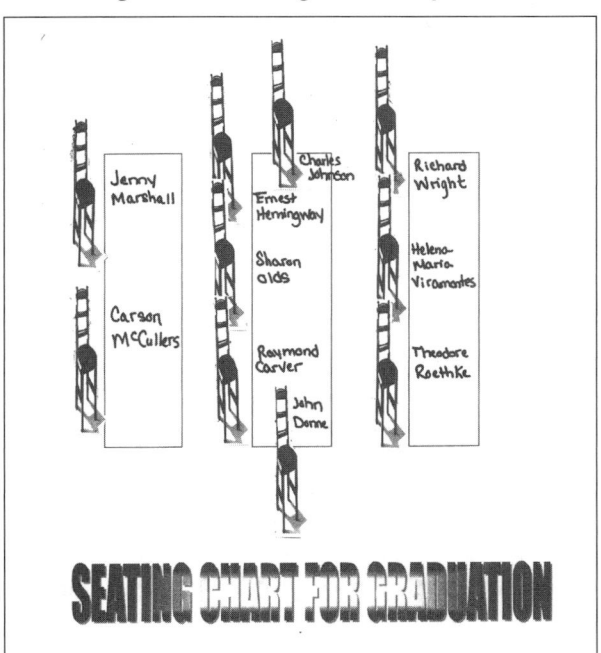

Figure 12-3: Seating Chart Sample C

Analysis of Key Subjects (Reflections on Data)

Even though students are constantly reviewing materials throughout the term—a must because of the final examination expectations—they still have difficulty with note taking and recognizing the value of traditional lecture alongside information derived from group discussions. Instructors utilizing a problem-based approach need to devise ways to encourage students to develop a vision of transactional pedagogy balanced with a transmittal style.

Although students might more readily be able to pick their top candidates, even providing strong reasons for why they do so, they are not used to thinking of argument as a "conversation," to use Deborah Tannen's (1986) idea. Instructors must devise ways of getting students to see the importance of other voices in their own arguments, including the writers of the texts they are studying.

Student Response

As I am now teaching in a university, I asked my introduction to literature students (a class of 44 consisting mostly of sophomores, first- and second-semester students, and one high school student who was enrolled in two college classes) if they thought our memo proposal approach would work in a high school classroom. Not far removed from their own high school experiences, they are some of the best resources for testing pedagogical effectiveness. The response was overwhelmingly in favor of adapting how we handled the assignment to fit that particular audience. One student believed that teachers and students could make the assignment even more real in high school by not only having the class choose a keynote speaker for graduation but by having students focus on a favorite theme presented in their authors' writings. Then this theme might be able to be linked to the actual high school graduation.

For example, a student who was excited about the possibilities of this idea for a high school class noted how many writers focus on the complexities of life. Others agreed and stated that a theme such as "Life Is Like Art" could easily be used in graduation planning: Graduating seniors could write essays, make banners, take photographs, or paint to present their interpretations of life through art. These could be shared during a pre-or post-graduation gathering or celebration. Another student wrote a message that he handed to me on his way out of class: "The memo reports are a good way to tie different ideas together and draw some conclusions from the whole." Similarly, another student wrote about how he believed it was important to find ways that high school students could "organize things into groups so the material is not horribly overwhelming," and thought that the memo proposals could help students in this capacity. Personally, I believe that those teaching middle or high school students might use the seating chart assignment alone to assist students in learning to draw relations between texts and their messages. Helping students to make this important connection early can show them how strong critical thinking skills depend on making connections between seemingly disparate things.

Generally, students respond very well to this problem-based assignment. Although it may have been useful to include written assessments of the project, gleaned from student evaluations of the overall course, it seems more fitting to use the everyday, informal language of one particular student whom I overheard in the hall. After a peer review session that focused on drafts for the final presentation of this assignment, this particular student was speaking to another in the course. His comments support the validity of the graduation banquet project. Completely unaware that I overheard his remarks, he said to his friend: "This was the most fun I have ever had working on a 'paper' in my life." Fun or not—and it is nice for students to actually think that the work they are doing is fun as well as instructive—revising the traditional literary analysis paper to serve a wider variety of today's non–English majors seems to be a good idea. This approach bears particular dividends because it engages students in active learning and problem solving and assists in rejuvenating their interest in reading. It seems, too, to deepen each participating student's overall understanding of why it is important to cultivate the enriched livelihood a liberal education brings. For my students and me, this project has continued to be a success.

Note

My special thanks to the students who gave written permission for their work to be used in this chapter: Tate Berner, Dominick Anselmo, Adnan Mahmood, Seden Kulga, Andrea Sack, Jenny Marshall, and Matt Main.

References

Barr, I., & Tagg, E. (1995). From teaching to learning. *Change*, November/December.

Bloom, B. S. (1984). *Taxonomy of educational objectives handbook. Vol. I: Cognitive domain*. Boston: Addison-Wesley.

Tannen, D. (1986). *That's not what I meant: How conversational style makes or breaks your relations with others*. New York: William Morrow.

Part III

Projects and Pedagogy

13

Gatsby Galas and Elizabethan Extravaganzas: Cultivating Higher Order Learning and the Personal Intelligences

Kimberly R. Myers

What better way to engage 11th graders in the romance of F. Scott Fitzgerald's *The Great Gatsby* than to invite them into the romance of the Jazz Age itself—to enable them to experience something of the zeitgeist that sustained Fitzgerald as he wrote the novel? This was the rhetorical question that dominated my professional musings as I entered the spring semester of my first year as a high school English teacher. I had taught the novel in a traditional way as a student teacher, discussing passages and themes, images, and characters with the class as a whole. At 16—especially when idealism is fundamental though sometimes couched in apparent cynicism—students read the story with abandon, eager to see whether Jay finally wins Daisy's love. In turn, the compelling love story is an entrée into various critical interpretations of the novel, and I dutifully marshaled my sponsoring teacher's students through complex considerations worthy of New Critical, Marxist, feminist, psychoanalytic, and reader response critics.

Having my own students, however, I sought a way to bring all these critical stances together in a holistic framework. For me, New Historicism has always been an eminently sane critical approach because it provides the context for a work and sets it in a cultural frame. I believed that if I could guide my students to an understanding of the Roaring Twenties, then the novel would take on a whole new dimension for them. How could I encourage a broad awareness of the 1920s, and what point in their reading of *Gatsby* would be the appropriate time?

I was fortunate to work with the teacher who has been my greatest inspiration since the time I was a student in her 10th-grade Honors English class, Ann Simpson. She seemed to me then (as she did when I was her student teacher, later during our 6 years as colleagues, and even now) to possess a kind of magic that enables students to "live" what they are doing in class. Now that I was Ann's colleague, I was eager to complement her creativity with my own.

Because both of us taught several sections of 11th-grade college-preparatory English, we began co-designing unit projects that centered around a particular writing activity or novel, or around several pieces of literature with a common theme. As such, the focus was tight and easily manageable, and each of us implemented the unit in our respective classes. I wondered what would happen if Ann and I could team-teach and allow our students to forge work groups of their own choosing across classes. Surely this would create an esprit de corps not unlike that which exists among teammates of a given sport—a bond that can unite an entire school in task and temperament. I proposed to Ann that in order to immerse our students in the ethos of the 1920s, we require them to "re-create" the period so that they would understand the era and Fitzgerald's novel more fully. We agreed to the challenge, and I turned to the task of writing a project that would allow students intellectual and creative freedom while also requiring them to demonstrate the academic validity of their group's chosen focus.

Bloom and Gardner: A Pedagogical Rationale for the Gatsby Gala

The work of two educational theorists, Benjamin Bloom (1956) and Howard Gardner (1993, 1999), was the driving force behind the project. Acknowledging the wisdom in Bloom's famous taxonomy, I determined that the Gatsby Gala would focus almost exclusively on the complex mental processes of analysis, synthesis, and evaluation. In addition to analyzing various facets of the novel, students would also have to break down the historical period into its component parts: discover why prohibition was the law; learn the political, economic, and social factors contributing to the pervasive carpe diem mentality; and explore the roots of jazz music. In short, students were required to dissect the period to discover what precisely made it what it was.

We consulted the research librarians and asked them to conduct an informational workshop for our students, pointing out seminal materials and offering strategies for more specialized research. Students then had 2 days for research in the library when librarians and teachers could offer individualized help. After that, research groups were on their own, working independently outside class, while in class we discussed *The Great Gatsby* and went about the business of vocabulary development and composition. Coordinating their personal schedules for the 3-4 weeks required for the project would be each group's initial (and ultimately most daunting) challenge.

Analysis should lead naturally to synthesis, and brainstorming to publication: This was the function of the Gala proper. Weeks of outside research and planning would culminate in an evening when all 11th-grade college-prep students would gather and share their understanding of the 1920s in a creative presentation, demonstration, or display. In combining their newly acquired knowledge, students would view the 1920s differently, better understanding relationships previously not evident but inherent to Fitzgerald's novel. The Gatsby

Gala was also the perfect opportunity to foster what Howard Gardner calls multiple intelligences. The first eight of them are linguistic, logical/mathematical, musical, spatial, bodily/kinesthetic, naturalist, interpersonal, and intrapersonal. In *Frames of Mind: The Theory of Multiple Intelligences* (1993a), Gardner graphically reveals how the Western educational system (perhaps especially that in America) privileges the linguistic and logical/mathematical intelligences while consigning the other forms of intelligence to the status of mere talent. Defining intelligence as the ability to solve problems or make things that are valuable in at least one culture or community, Gardner reminds us how critical it is to help our students cultivate their nonlinguistic, nonmathematical intelligences as well. To do so results in more well-rounded individuals and a richer culture.

Demonstrating the Intelligences

This project encourages students to demonstrate various intelligences as worthy complements to linguistic and literary analysis. Students gifted in music can compose a new work and perform it, and they can compile a soundtrack to use as background music for the evening's festivities. Demonstrating spatial intelligence, artists can sculpt Gatsby's main characters in clay, draw floor plans for the various mansions, build a model of Jay's automobile, reproduce the interior of a speakeasy, or design and build a stage for a group that performs an original skit or dramatizes a scene. Because the 1920s spawned so many distinctive rhythms, students with a high degree of kinesthetic intelligence can choreograph a dance performance as a prelude to teaching the audience the basics of the Charleston and the Jitterbug. Although the literary 1920s is decidedly urban, naturalists can provide a replica of cultivated gardens maintained by the wealthy or decorate outdoor spaces for the Gala. Moreover, all students dress in period costume in order to transform themselves and the surroundings into a vision of the 1920s. (See Appendix 13-A for the Gatsby Gala assignment.)

Emphasizing the Personal Intelligences

Even among those who share Gardner's advocacy of musical, spatial, and kinesthetic intelligences, the personal intelligences often get short shrift. Gardner succinctly explains that interpersonal intelligence "look[s] outward, toward the behavior, feelings, and motivations of others," intrapersonal intelligence is "involved chiefly in an individual's examination and knowledge of his own feelings," and "under normal circumstances, neither form of intelligence can develop without the other" (1983, pp. 240–241). Gardner argues that although our current educational structure slights the personal intelligences, they are in reality the "highest," most important of all forms of human intelligence. He writes as follows:

> It is appropriate to question whether personal intelligences—knowledge of self and others—should be conceived of as being at the same level of specificity (and generality) as the other intelligences.... Perhaps it makes

more sense to think of knowledge of self and others as being a higher level, a more integrated form of intelligence, one more at the behest of the culture and of historical factors, one more truly emergent, one that ultimately comes to control and to regulate more 'primary orders' of intelligence.... A developed sense of self often appears as the highest achievement of human beings, a crowning capacity which supersedes and presides over other more mundane and partial forms of intelligence. (pp. 274, 242–243)

One reason for viewing the personal intelligences as superior to all others is that although a person is not regularly called upon to employ some intelligences (Gardner mentions the musical and spatial intelligences as examples),

the premium for acting upon one's particular personal intelligence is far greater.... [I]t is the unusual individual who does not try to deploy his understanding of the personal realm in order to improve his own well-being or his relationship to the community. (p. 241)

To be sure, cultivating and demonstrating sophisticated interpersonal and intrapersonal intelligences is vital to any successful life. As Gardner says:

The less a person understands his own feelings, the more he will fall prey to them. The less a person understands the feelings, the responses, and the behavior of others, the more likely he will interact inappropriately with them and therefore fail to secure his proper place within the larger community. (p. 254)

How the Gatsby Gala Honors All Intelligences

By its very nature, the Gatsby Gala fosters various intelligences, as students must learn not only how to locate, gather, and process historical and cultural data but also how to navigate the sometimes delicate dynamics of a group endeavor. In turn, this knowledge gives students insight into themselves: the values they hold and the ways in which they compromise preferences to accommodate the needs of others and maintain group harmony. Evaluation is already operating as students utilize the personal intelligences, and a pivotal requirement of the project is that students assess the degree of success of their final product as well as the process that engendered it. Students write narrative evaluations of the strengths and weaknesses of their formal contributions to the Gala and consider what they would do differently the next time. Then they must provide a written evaluation of all members of the group, including themselves. To ensure candor, each group member's evaluation is strictly confidential. Nevertheless, students often find this part of the project the most troublesome. Even more difficult than making distinctions about the quality of other group members' contributions to the project is a student's self-evaluation—usually not because he or she cannot acknowledge shortcomings, but because discussing one's own strengths seems to many students inappropriately immodest. Nevertheless, requiring such metacognition and self-reflection ensures that the students operate in the cognitive domain most highly supported by Bloom and Gardner.

Students Laud the Gatsby Gala

In their evaluations of the project, students consistently asserted in strong terms how valuable the experience had been for them. They talked at length about how much they had learned about the historical context of the novel and how such knowledge enhanced their study of the text. In-class discussions had confirmed their assessment, as even the more reserved students eagerly shared information garnered outside class. Because everyone was involved in such intense research, the sense of competition that sometimes mars class dynamics didn't exist. Instead, students saw themselves as vital members of a collective enterprise where shared knowledge benefited everyone concerned. Figure 13-1 shows a student picture.

Figure 13.1: The Gatsby Gala

Students also expressed delight at being able to incorporate into their academic lives their talents that had traditionally been relegated to extracurricular activities. Being recognized as gifted visual artists or performers seemed especially important to those students who weren't usually singled out for superlative performance in English or math. Several students said that this was the first time since they were young children that school, social, and family life had been so fully integrated. Working in teams, they met both during and after school hours, taking their questions and ideas with them. In dance class, for instance, they asked the instructor to help them count out the steps of a dance they planned to teach the audience-participants at the Gala. In their homes, they consulted their parents on how best to construct a working fountain for the replica of the Gatsby mansion they were making. In these ways, students understood how such integrative learning is vital to their intellectual and social development.

Because enthusiasm, experimentation, and risk are key factors in student learning at the secondary level, this project rewards process as much as product and therefore provides students with ample opportunity to enhance their grade. Aside from major grades students receive on their proposal, presentation or production, and evaluation, they can do additional work for extra credit: design a formal printed invitation for the evening's events, propose a name for the Gala space, dress in period costume, host a fashion show, or prepare food from authentic recipes of the 1920s.

Extending the Project to Other Grades and Eras

The Gatsby Gala was the success that Ann Simpson, our students, and I had hoped it would be, and consequently it became a staple of the junior curriculum, eventually expanding to include seniors. Indeed, junior and senior college-prep students began asking from the first day of school when it would occur. Having heard stories from their college-prep friends, students in the honors program petitioned for the same kind of holistic project, and during the second year they too began the extravaganzas. Honors extravaganzas were easier in some ways. Because Ann taught 9th- and 11th-grade honors English, and I taught 10th-grade honors and advanced placement for 12th-grade, we shared between us all the students involved, which enabled us to coordinate all facets of the project more completely.

With their advanced academic ability, voracious curiosity, and desire to live up to their own reputation for superlative work, our honors students were typically even more self-directed than the college-prep students. Initially honors students participated in several different groups, so that exhibits and live demonstrations requiring a seated audience multiplied exponentially. This addition significantly lengthened the evening and presented a formidable challenge to teachers trying to evaluate each student's contributions. After the third year, we had to stipulate that students could be part of only one group.

An additional challenge with the honors students was working across all grade levels, from freshmen to seniors. To require such independent, self-reflective work of freshmen might have been too ambitious except for the fact that they were shepherded by their older, more experienced peers who had gone through the process in previous years.

After the first year, the Gatsby Gala was redundant. Unlike college-prep students who experienced the Gala only during their junior year, sophomore, junior, and senior honors students would already have studied *The Great Gatsby* and researched the 1920s and would therefore not repeat this particular project. This promised a new challenge for them, and they began proposing a cross-grade area of study and work(s) of literature each year. Advocates campaigned for their choices, and the debate was extremely vigorous. Once the vote was so close that honors students chose the topic for the following year as well. Among the most successful areas of study were Chaucer's *Canterbury Tales* and the Middle English period, Shakespeare and Early Modern England, and the Beat Movement of the 1950s. Appendix 13-B describes the Elizabethan assignment.

Year by year, the scope and sophistication of the extravaganzas grew so much that we allowed an entire evening for the event. Students began setting up at 3 p.m. and finished cleaning up by 11:30 p.m. The space required for the event also grew. What was initially localized in a suite of two classrooms burgeoned to encompass the English wing and ultimately the entire top floor of the building and an adjoining mini-auditorium. Fortunately, our administration and our colleagues were fully supportive and allowed students to transform their classrooms, often in radical ways.

Benefits to School and Community

The spirit of this event spread throughout the school, and its popularity rivaled the junior-senior prom. At first we considered it a measure of the project's success that students from other grades and ability levels came to witness the events. Parents came, too. Even though ours was primarily a working-class neighborhood, parents supported their children by donating time to help them set up (and in some cases actually constructed sets, scaffolding, and the like) and also to watch the range of activities. Many stated that their children had not participated in such a creative research project since elementary school.

Eventually the local television station came to shoot footage for a special feature on our English program. Clearly, our students' intelligence and creativity had resulted in excellent public relations for the entire school. More important, the quality of their work had been lauded by peers, faculty, family, and community. Students consequently took themselves and their schoolwork seriously in a whole new way—and they had fun.

At first glance it might seem that such extravaganzas could occur only in communities with lavish resources, but quite the opposite is true. Even schools with modest library holdings, for example, can provide students with myriad research materials through the Internet. Furthermore, rewarding creativity encourages students to use items they already have at home instead of purchasing something new. Converting an old dress into a flapper costume by sewing on fringe, or building a model of the Globe Theatre from scrap wood from the family's farm or workshop, is far more impressive than buying new things that require less creativity in design and construction. These were the kinds of "real-life" resources on which our students could draw.

Our school is a somewhat unusual blend of professional and working-class families, and the extravaganzas were perhaps the most equalizing academic activity students experienced. One student, with the help of his father who is a construction worker, built an impressive façade for our speakeasy. This was a unique contribution to the Gala, a valuable complement to the opulent heirloom crystal and china from the 1920s, for example, that a local politician's niece brought to decorate a banquet table. One of the strongest appeals of such holistic projects is that they work so well with students of various levels of ability. With certain modifications, these projects could also provide all students of literature with a meaningful and rewarding challenge.

The cost of the project in actual funding was minimal, as the major expenditures were our students' time, creativity, involvement, and ability to work as a team. The gains for our program and our school were extensive. First, student learning increased exponentially, as it always does when students are challenged to stretch themselves to contribute to a hands-on learning experience. Besides that, the entire school and community gained a sense of pride in the arts and in our students' accomplishments that has endured across the years.

The following appendices represent a version of the Gatsby Gala for juniors and a version of the Elizabethan Extravaganza for honors students in grades 9–12. So that teachers may use each assignment in its entirety, without cross-referencing, I have included all the material that we gave our students. There will necessarily be some repetition between assignments, particularly in student responsibilities for the evening of the event itself.

Appendix 13-A. The Gatsby Gala Assignment

The Gatsby Gala:
The Ultimate Junior Experience

Engagements

Dates for each aspect of the project are given, from the date assigned, April 27, to the post-Gala review, May 22. Included in assigned dates are the following: date given, discussion of project requirements and pictures, library research done as a class, due date for the plan, proposals & agenda posted, name-that-speakeasy contest entries, design-the-invitation contest entries, written test, the Gala premiere, and the critics' rave review.

Hoopla

1. Read a minimum of 100 pages related to the Roaring Twenties.
2. Write a detailed step-by-step plan of what you intend to do.
3. Organize and practice your performance.
4. Implement your plan.
5. Write an objective analysis of how well you did what you said you would.

Rah Rah

1. Read as much as possible to determine the "feel" of the era.
2. Individually or in groups of no more than four, select one (or a combination of several) of the following categories to research in minute detail. Your groups may be made up of people from any Myers or Simpson college-prep English class.
   - *Music*: What was the music of the 1920s? Perform or bring examples.

- *Dance*: What were different dances of the period? Choreograph a performance.
- *Art*: What was happening? Who was doing what? Prepare a discussion of several important pieces of art or create something in similar style.
- *Décor*: What were typical furnishings and furniture? Decorate our Gala space accordingly.
- *Architecture*: Who was creating important buildings; What and how? Make a model.
- *Culinary Delights*: What did they eat at their hotsy-totsy parties, at home, at ballgames? Use actual recipes.
- *Entertainment*: What was going on in radio, theatre, movies, vaudeville? Who were the famous actors, actresses, dancers? Offer us a sampling of burlesque or slapstick, prepare displays, or share excerpts or clips.
- *Literature*: Who were the most important writers of the period? Prepare displays.
- *Newspapers*: What were the most important news items? Make a replica.
- *Comics*: What was considered funny or worth satirizing? Draw your own.
- *Magazines*: What appeared in features, advertisements? Design your own magazine.

3. Everything must be authentic and documented.
4. You may participate in only one group.
5. Your performance will not exceed 5 minutes.

The Plan

This is a proposal that states what you will be contributing to the Gala.
1. You will type one proposal per group, using the attached form. Complete each section. Leave nothing blank.
2. On Friday, May 12, we will post the order of performance. This will be followed exactly.
3. We will also post on the bulletin board across from Ms. Myers' classroom all proposals for your perusal. Ensure that your presentation does not infringe on that of any other group. There should be absolutely no repetition.

Remember: 1920s art, literature, theatre, food, clothing, architecture, food, magazines, dance, politics, television, famous people, fads, food, cultural trends, economics, style, food, food, food.

Note: Turn in only one proposal per group, even if you are working with someone in another class. The instructors will jointly evaluate these proposals. All group members will receive exactly the same grade. This will count as a major test grade.

The Premiere

Do it!
1. You may begin setting up immediately after school on Thursday, May 18.
2. Block off your area and arrange your stage.
3. Be prepared for any and all disasters. (If Jordan has the starring role and Jordan is sick or otherwise encumbered, you will perform without Jordan. Be prepared to cope.)
4. Bring with you everything that you might even remotely require. We will provide nothing except our supportive selves. (Our record players and tape decks are rejects from pre–World War II days; bring your own.) Remember how much better electrical equipment works when it is plugged into some sort of socket. Bring extension cords.
5. Be organized. When it's your turn you will perform, ready or not.
6. Carry out your proposed plan. This will be presented in Speakeasy [which you will name], a.k.a. classroom suite C-320 and C-321, on the evening of May 18 from 6–8 p.m.
7. Your presentation will not exceed 5 minutes. This applies to everyone. Your time begins when your group's name is called, and you will sit down when time is up. If you do not finish, you will be penalized.
8. If your presentation includes something edible or potable, you must place a sheet under your table to catch spills.
9. Bring garbage bags to take away everything that you bring. Clean up after yourselves and take your garbage bags home with you. It is imperative that we leave nothing for the mice.
10. Bring cleaning materials to tidy the area prior to your departure. No one leaves until we have a white-glove examination.

The Critics' Rave Review

The review is an evaluation of your performance.
1. You will turn in one evaluation per group.
2. You will type your evaluation using the attached form.

Historical Significance

This is your chance to earn many extra credit points. If you are willing to work, you will be amply rewarded for fine participation in this gala event. You should take advantage of each and every extra credit opportunity given to you, especially those of you who might be on the verge of enjoying this project again next year. You win only if you choose to play.

You will receive separate and distinct major test grades for (a) the plan, (b) the premiere, (c) the critics' rave review, and (d) sartorial enrichment (see below).

Each group member will receive exactly the same grade on everything except sartorial enrichment, which is graded on an individual basis.

Other Stuff and All That Jazz

Name-That-Speakeasy Contest: Entries should reflect your originality, creativity, knowledge, love of life, fun and games, and appreciation of your fellow classmates. Remember who and where you are, as well as the era that you are studying. These entries may be submitted individually or as a group. The winning entry will be selected by a totally unbiased, distinguished panel of judges, and the winning entry will earn an extra 100 major test grade to those responsible for its creation. The entry should be designed as a marquee with the name emblazoned on it to welcome the guests to our speakeasy. All entries will receive a daily grade of 100; the winners will receive an additional 100 major test grade for actually making the marquee. (Winner's total: three 100s!)

Design-the-Invitation Contest: Guests of our speakeasy need to be formally and cordially invited to partake of our gracious hospitality, preferably in a style that would have pleased Jay Gatsby himself if he were inviting Daisy Fay. Thus, submit entries (either individually or as a group) that reflect your artistic, creative, (see list above) abilities. Include all pertinent information. Make the invitation a masterpiece that can easily be reproduced on a Canon copier. The winning entry will earn its creator a 100 major test grade. Every serious entry will receive a 100 daily grade. (Winner's total: two 100s!) Note: Submit separate entries for each contest on white, unlined paper, using the most appropriate aesthetic device, with a cover sheet.

Sartorial Enrichment: On the night of the Gala, if you are dressed from head to toe in an authentic, documented costume, you will receive an extra 100 major test grade!

The Judith Challenge (named for the student who issued the challenge to her fellow students)**:** Plan and execute a show of the fashions of the 1920s.

Culinary Delight Dare: You receive extra credit for preparing some tasty 1920s morsels for us to munch! You should prepare enough to feed about 25 people.

Please remember the following:
- Plan to be here by 5:30 p.m. to set up your table and ensure the most choice location.
- Decorate your table in a manner that is commensurate with the plushness of the period (e.g. silver, tablecloths, china.)
- Include a minimum of one candle.
- Bring everything that you will need to serve your food. Nothing will be provided.
- Bring a drop cloth (an old sheet will do) to place under your table to catch spills.
- Bring many garbage bags to clean up your leftover delights.
- Clean up everything and take your garbage bags, filled and tied, home with you.

Note: Every student will be required to stay until the very last inch of the

Gala space is clean and ready for students at 8 a.m. the next day. Ms. Myers and Ms. Simpson do not plan to attend the Gala in janitorial attire. If you leave before the space is entirely clean and straight, understand that your grade will reflect our disapproval. This is *your* project. We designed it especially for you so that you could show off your best talents. We sincerely hope that you enjoy yourselves and that you *jazz*!

Appendix 13-B. The Elizabethan Extravaganza Assignment

Elizabethan Extravaganza:
All the World's a Stage (and You're on It!)

Date Given	Thursday, January 3	
Due Dates	Research or Book:	Monday, January 28
	Proposals:	Monday, February 4
	Acceptance or Rejection:	Wednesday, February 6
	Auditions:	Thursday, February 14
	The Production:	Thursday, February 21
	Critique:	Monday, March 2
The Entertainment	**9th Grade**	**10th Grade**
	Romeo and Juliet	*Romeo and Juliet*
	Julius Caesar	*Julius Caesar*
	Macbeth	*Macbeth*
	A Midsummer Night's Dream	*The Taming of the Shrew*
	11th Grade	**12th Grade**
	Hamlet	*Othello*
	Henry IV, Part I	*King Lear*
	Macbeth	*Macbeth*
	As You Like It	*The Tempest*
After-School	*Romeo and Juliet*	Tuesday, January 15
Film Festival	*Hamlet*	Wednesday, January 16
	Othello	Thursday, January 17
	Julius Caesar	Wednesday, January 23
	King Lear	Thursday, January 24
	Macbeth	Thursday, January 31
	In local theaters: Mel Gibson as Hamlet!	January 18–February 15

The Pageantry
1. Read and savor four different Shakespearean plays.
2. Research William Shakespeare and Elizabethan England.
3. Demonstrate your expertise by publishing a book.
4. Work with a group to plan a visual representation of your knowledge.
5. Participate in an Elizabethan presentation.
6. Write an evaluation of your group's performance.

Historical Background
1. Become experts on William Shakespeare and the Elizabethan Age.
2. Each group member is responsible for reading 100 pages related to the period (thus five members read 500 pages).
3. Each group member must read an overview of the period.
4. Research the art, literature, theatre, food, clothing, architecture, publications, dances, politics, famous people, important events, fads, cultural trends, economics, style of the period. In other words, everything.
5. Do not rely on your own slim knowledge of this period. Study. Delve. Discover. Verify. Explore. Document.
6. Demonstrate your group's expertise by publishing a book about this period. Your book will include: (a) an original cover, (b) an original title, (c) a table of contents, (d) articles, (e) art work, (f) summaries, (g) anything else that will enable you to flaunt your knowledge, (h) bibliography that lists every source used by every member of your group (MLA style), and includes page numbers read for each source. (Remember: Each group member is responsible for reading 100 pages), and (i) an addenda (who read what and who did what toward the publication of the book).

Note: The research should prepare you to plan your project. The book should demonstrate what you have learned about Elizabethan England and William Shakespeare.

The Proposal
1. Turn in one typed proposal per group.
2. Use the attached form.
3. Your performance will not exceed 8 minutes.

The Groups
1. Compose your group of no more than five people.
2. You may work individually, but why? Part of the fun is group anxiety!
3. You may participate in only one group.

4. Your group members may cross grade levels. Be adventurous! Choose exciting, interesting members.
5. Choose dependable, congenial, creative, compatible people.
6. Understand that every member of the group will receive exactly the same grade. Do you remember how angry and frustrated you became last year when you did all the work and they received the same grade? Your best friend might not be the person with whom you would like to work. Avoid such problems. Be selective.
7. Choose a chairperson who will coordinate the group's activities. That exalted person will receive an extra 100 daily grade for his or her efforts.

The Audition
1. Groups who plan projects that require stage time (i.e., performances in front of a seated audience) must audition.
2. The audition will take place in the class to which the majority of performers belong.
3. The group will receive its performance grade for that in-class performance.
4. Groups that are selected to perform on the night of the eloquence will receive an additional 100 major test grade.
5. If your group is not chosen to perform, you may still earn extra credit by preparing food for the night's feast.
6. Come properly attired for additional credit.

The Performance
1. You may begin setting up immediately after school on Thursday, February 21.
2. Block off your area and arrange your space. Ms. Myers' and Ms. Simpson's rooms will be used primarily as stage area. Only four groups will set up in that space. The hallways around the English Department will make excellent backgrounds for your displays, simulations, re-creations of actual places, or whatever your brilliant minds can conceive. Limit yourselves to the top floor of the school and the minitorium.
3. If you plan to use another teacher's space, then you are responsible for asking permission of that teacher. You are further responsible for replacing that teacher's classroom to its original splendor exactly as it was before. Take a before photo to compare to the after, if necessary. That's how serious we are.
4. Be prepared for any and all disasters. (If Ophelia is scheduled to star and Ophelia actually drowns prior to the performance, you will continue without Ophelia. Be prepared to cope.)
5. Bring with you everything that you might even remotely require. We will provide nothing except our supportive selves and our undying admiration.

Our audiovisual equipment is laughable; you would not even want to use it. Bring your own. Remember: Electrical equipment works far more efficiently when plugged in. Bring extension cords.

6. If your presentation includes food or drink you must place a sheet under your food table to catch any spills.
7. Bring garbage bags to take away everything that you bring. Janitorial Science 101 is not part of our educational backgrounds. You bring it; you take it home.
8. Bring cleaning materials to purge the area prior to your departure. No one leaves until we have a white-glove inspection.

Costumes

1. To receive a major test grade of 100, come to the eloquence dressed head-to toe in a costume that is an accurate reflection of the Elizabethan Age or appropriate for one of Shakespeare's characters.
2. Do not spend tons of money; be creative; use your imagination.

Critique

You will evaluate your completed project and your group members (including yourself) on the form provided.

Evaluation

You will receive major test grades for the (a) book, (b) proposal, (c) presentation, (d) costume, and (e) critique. You will receive additional grades for various events to be announced, including attending an after-school film festival.

Quotation Board

On the bulletin board outside the Myers-Simpson complex, place your favorite Shakespearean quotation, graffiti, or parodies. What fun! Let's bring more erudition to the English wing! On the night of the performance, the only people who are to be here are members of Honors I, II, III, and AP and the parents of these students. For management reasons, this event is not open to the general population.

Proposal

1. List all group members. Beside each name, identify that person's teacher.
2. Provide a title that describes the nature of your project.
3. Itemize every single step of your project. If it includes dialogue, print a detailed outline of what you will say.
4. Does your project require stage time before a seated audience? If so, how much time?
5. How much space do you require and where you would like it to be? (No

guarantees, but preferences will be noted.)
6. List audiovisual equipment and other supplies that you need (and will provide for yourselves).
7. Mention anything else that we need to know or anticipate.

Evaluation
1. Your name
2. Names of other group members
3. List dates, times and places of meetings. Be specific. How long did you meet each time? Which members were present at each meeting?
4. Write a paragraph evaluating each member's contribution to the overall project—his preparation beforehand, her participation during the actual presentation in class. Give specific details. After the written evaluation, rate each group member on a 1–5 scale (5 is highest) in terms of overall contribution.
5. Be sure to include yourself in number 4.
6. Assign yourselves an overall group grade (scale of 1–5, 5 is highest) . How well did you do what you planned to do? How much did the class learn and enjoy? What would you do differently if you had the opportunity to do this project again?

References

Anderson, L. W., & Sosniak, L. A. (Eds.). (1994). *Bloom's taxonomy: A forty-year retrospective*. Chicago: University of Chicago Press.

Bloom, B. (Ed.). (1956). *Taxonomy of educational objectives. The classification of educational goals*. New York: McKay.

Gardner, H. (1983). *Frames of mind: The theory of multiple intelligences*. New York: Basic Books.

Gardner, H. (1993). *Multiple intelligences: The theory in practice*. New York: Basic Books.

Gardner, H. (1999). *The disciplined mind*. New York: Simon & Schuster.

Hunter, M. (1982). *Mastery teaching: Increasing instructional effectiveness in elementary, secondary schools, colleges and universities*. Thousand Oaks, CA: Corwin Press.

Hunter, M. (1994). *Enhancing teaching*. New York: Macmillan.

Kaplan, L. D. (1994). Teaching as applied philosophy. *Teaching Philosophy* 17 (1), 5–17.

Lazear, D. G. (1992). *Teaching for multiple intelligences*. Bloomington, IN: Phi Delta Kappa.

McKeachie, W. J. (1963). Research on teaching at the college and university level. In N. L. Gage (Ed.), *Handbook of research on teaching*. Chicago: Rand McNally.

Palmer, P. J. (1983). *To know as we are known: A spirituality of education.* San Francisco: Harper & Row.

Palmer, P. J. (1998). *The courage to teach: Exploring the inner landscape of a teacher's life.* San Francisco: Jossey-Bass.

14

The American Museum Project

Jeff House

In the 1960s, we were fond of saying that if you give a man a fish, you feed him for a day, but if you teach him how to fish, you feed him for a lifetime. So it is with teaching. When we give our students information, we "feed" them for the unit test. When we teach them how to apply that information, we prepare them for life outside the classroom.

In the summer of 1997, at the urging and nagging of five juniors, I took a vanload of students on a tour of New England. Amid the shared and disheveled hotel rooms, Dunkin' Donuts breakfasts, and backroads we stumbled on because my navigator couldn't read maps well, the kids fell in love with the museums. Of course, we have museums in California, but nothing like the interactive Plimoth Plantation ("The Dutch midwife was the coolest," pronounced Missy), the history-drenched Lower East Side Museum of New York City ("The best part was the clothing orders scrawled in pencil in the door jambs," noted Talia), or the dark-as-a-dungeon coal mines of Scranton ("Mr. House was too chicken to go down with us," correctly observed Tim). This, of course, got me thinking about how to transfer that interest to the classroom.

After my first year teaching an American literature course that combined literature, history, and the humanities, I wanted to develop a long-term project that would force students to link the various units so that they would arrive at a focal idea about America. As we covered nearly 4 centuries of literature and history, I wanted students to focus on a concept so that tracking its development would provide a connecting idea between the nation's past and present. They would establish a focal point as the course started, tracing that focus throughout the year and, in charting its evolution, see a way to sew up the disparate parts of the course into a kind of quilt. Like most good ideas, the answer arrived unexpectedly.

Coming Up With a New Teaching Plan

On a visit to Philadelphia, I dropped by the Philadelphia Museum of Art. The museum's objective—detailing the evolution of American painting over the last 2 centuries—was met in its layout, a series of rooms divided into historical periods in American art. Each room contained representative paintings with annotations. That, as it happens, is a metaphorical representation of a typical writing assignment: The museum's goal acts like a thesis, each room operates as a developing point for that goal or thesis, and the paintings become examples of the points for each room.

This structured approach to a museum's learning experience is often detailed in its brochures, from simple flyers to more elaborate booklets. Here was the model for my yearlong project: the production of a brochure for a student-created museum, the brochure's layout, focal point, and annotated exhibits would enable students to transform research into an imaginative creation.

Several years later, the museum project is still one of the more exciting methods I have employed. Students remark on its high level of work but often say it is the most rewarding experience they have had in high school. "The museum project was exciting for me," noted junior Vicki Chan. "I learned more about American literature and history doing that than anything else."

Background for Student Work

As part of the project, students must visit and become familiar with museums themselves, so my first presentation concerns the innate structure of a museum's setup. Traveling in recent years throughout New England, the South and the West, I have noticed different museum structures, from traditional "viewing" types to living museums (Plimoth Plantation in Massachusetts), interactive museums (The Museum of Intolerance in Los Angeles), and geographically based museums (Gettysburg, or the Lowell Mills in Lowell, Massachusetts). I explain these differing museum types to the students, emphasizing their structure:

- *A Focal Point*: Museums are rarely haphazard layouts of material. They marshal exhibits and garner items that work to produce a single idea or impression. The Barbie Museum in Palo Alto, California, argues for the relevance of Barbie as a postmodern and feminist icon; the Gene Autry Museum in Los Angeles critiques the mythologies of the West; Old Sturbridge Village in Massachusetts documents life in a New England village in the 1830s. Sometimes implied, often directly stated, a museum's thesis is conveyed in its structure.

- *Supporting Ideas*: A museum's layout is the means by which it presents the sub-ideas that support the focal idea. Its collection of rooms or particular areas works to produce this single impression. Even a living museum like Plimoth Plantation is divided into different sites and areas, and the village itself is further divided into the individual houses and working areas of its

inhabitants. Visiting all of these areas, the tourist inductively begins to understand the pilgrims' way of life.
- *Exhibit Items*: The specific items within each viewing area are the concrete examples of that area's theme. In Cooperstown, New York, the Farmer's Village—a re-creation of an early 19th century village—features a series of buildings, each containing artifacts germane to that building's history. The printing shop contains a hand press and printed materials; the country store sells handmade items and home products that both decorate the shop and detail the habits of country living; the schoolroom houses desks, writing materials, and instructional aids that convey the atmosphere of a one-room schoolhouse. In this way, the selected items clarify the specific way each building was used and operated.

Again, what each museum replicates is a traditional research project: a focal point (thesis), supporting thematic areas (points), and concrete items (examples).

Project Structure: Our Six Stages of Learning

A yearlong project requires two things to make it work. First, it must be monitored and produced in stages, so that students don't attempt to produce a 9-month-long monster in one weekend. Second, it should be composed of various sections so that students do not become bored repeating the same task. Therefore, the first task is to structure dates and assignments, informing students in advance of your expectations.

Stage 1

In the first week I pass out a packet consisting of the following:
- A sheet detailing the project's purpose, assignments, and due dates (Appendix 14-A)
- The grading sheet to be used at the project's completion (Appendix 14-B)
- A suggested list of local museums and historical sites (Appendix 14-C)
- A sample write-up of a visit to a local museum with recommendations on what to look for (Appendix 14-D)

I also make overheads of both professional and student-produced brochures to illustrate the range of approaches and topics. The brochure should minimally contain the following: an opening statement wherein the museum's purpose is explained and detailed; an annotated layout; annotations for each area or room in the museum, including a partial listing of items to be found in each area and their relevance to that area. I encourage students to explore their interests, noting that past students have produced museum brochures on the Harlem Renaissance, cartoons in American history, the 1950s (and other decades), notions of the frontier, the women's movement, Native American culture, the history of fast foods, utopian experiments, ecological movements, immigrant experiences (including specific groups), MTV and the 1980s, dance (from classical to folk forms), radio, and sports. In short, students should feel encouraged not only to explore areas of interest but, in doing so, to ultimately see how that interest is related to larger aspects of American literature and culture. This was a selling point for the project. "I loved the museum project," wrote Erica Ruggiero. "I was already studying a part of American culture that I was interested in, and the project allowed me to pursue it in more depth." I tell students, "Pretend you're bringing a Martian to your museum. What experience would you create for it so that, at its conclusion, it would come away with a representative sense of American culture?" This is a key idea. It is not enough simply to document rock 'n 'roll; one must also clarify how rock 'n 'roll is emblematic of American culture.

In this way, students explore ideas related to class readings. Holden Caulfield's experiences can lead to an exploration of alienation in the 1950s and Beat culture; Edna Pontellier's frustrations both reflect and contrast with the fight of the suffragists in the Progressive Era; John Steinbeck's Joads critique the economic policies of the 1930s; Huck Finn's plight details the tension between urban development and western expansion; Hester Prynne's punishment comments on the values and lifestyle of Puritan New England; James Fenimore Cooper's English, French, and Native Americans symbolize the cultural conflicts of the frontier; *Sister Carrie* dramatizes the cultural value shifts of a newly urbanized America; Toni Morrison's *Beloved* epitomizes William Faulkner's notion that the past never dies. All these works, and many others, are wonderful starting points for further cultural explorations that both expand the discussion and reflect back on the texts themselves.

Stage 2

In the first semester, I require students to visit at least one local museum. It is wise to clarify what constitutes a legitimate experience. For instance, the Barbie Museum is small enough that I insist it be one of two museums that a student visits; by contrast, the three-story, three-section Oakland Museum of California would qualify as the only visit that a student has to make in a semester. Students must follow the directions on the sheet contained in their packets that explain what to look for. This visit is then written up in a format similar to the example provided in the packet. It asks them for their impressions of the museum, an explanation of its focus, how that focus is achieved, and an evaluation of the success of that focus. It's a good idea to require proof of attendance (such as a dated ticket stub) attached to the paper. If you're not located near a metropolitan center or a region that has museums that will work for your project, many museums now offer Web sites that can act as a supplement to student research. Plimoth Plantation, for example, has an on-line site that also features a virtual tour (http://www.plimoth.org/), as do such museums as Colonial Williamsburg (http://www.history.org/), The Holocaust Museum (http://www.ushmm.org/), Chaco Canyon in New Mexico (http://www.ghcc.msfc.masa.gov/archeology), The Gene Autry Museum (http://www.autry-museum.org/), and the Birmingham Civil Rights Institute (http://bcri.bham.al.us/).

Stage 3

By the end of the semester, students should begin developing some idea of what they want to create. I assure them that this is an ongoing project, and any decisions they make at this stage are not written in stone. I require a one-page write-up describing their museum's focus, general layout, and possible items, including their relation to class readings. This enables me to determine early on if a student needs help.

Stage 4

As the second semester starts, students should begin their research. What kind of research you desire is subjective. Intending to make my students media literate, I insist they supplement printed materials with CD-ROMs, on-line sites, and cultural items that can range from photographs to music to ads to music sheets. In this I am asking them to act like historians, gathering a wealth of various items from which they will induce a proposition that becomes their focal point. By the end of the third quarter, they must submit an annotated bibliography of their sources. This MLA-formatted sheet must be accompanied by a short paragraph for each source that both summarizes its content and explains its relevance to the project. Again, turned in at this early date, the bibliography can tip me off to potential problems.

Stage 5

By the end of the third quarter, students should begin to visualize their museum's layout. I often review layouts presented at the beginning of the year, encouraging students to design a museum that is both creative and practical. Within a month, students should turn in a detailed, annotated layout. It is also helpful to review with them the different approaches to a museum's layout and construction. (It is also helpful if students have recently seen a range of museum types.) Their museum might be organized like a traditional setup, as with the Smithsonian, wherein objects are on display for viewing. Living museums, like those at Plimoth Plantation and Williamsburg, enable visitors to experience and "step into" another world. Still other museums (like the Museum of Intolerance in Los Angeles or the U.S. Holocaust Museum in Washington, DC) provide a number of interactive experiences that require emotional, not passive, participation. Finally, museums like San Francisco's Alcatraz Island and Hawaii's Pearl Harbor are true historical sites that allow direct interaction with places that stand out in our nation's memory. The layout that students hand in will become part of their brochure.

Stage 6

In the fourth quarter students work on their brochures. It is helpful to point out basic elements of presentation, so that typefaces, arrangement of visuals and text, colors, and the structure of the brochure itself will complement each other.

Providing class time enables students to see how peers are exploring their visual presentations. This is also a good time to allow students to share what their museums look like and what they are discovering. This tends to be the most harried and compelling part of the year.

Advantages of Project Learning: Student-Teacher Reflection

The are several advantages of the museum project. First, students are required to explore texts to see them as emblems of a particular time, region, and culture. Second, the myriad writing experiences allow students to transform research into a variety of formats and tones. Third, the notion of research is expanded, suggesting that other forms of media, as well as visitation and interview, can supplement printed materials. Fourth, students are required to represent research in sophisticated ways and inductively arrive at ideas garnered from research and observation. Finally, as junior Jackie Martin noted, the project is fun: "The project forced me to rethink the way I gather information and process it. It was a lot of work, but it's the thing I most remember from high school."

Assessment is about determining a student's comprehension of the material, but it is also about communicating our level of expectation. Asking a student to repeat definitions, dates, names, or facts requires thinking skills on the level of memorization and identification only. By contrast, asking students to manipulate information requires higher order thinking skills. Projects that pose a question or problem force students to arrange information in a manner that will achieve a solution, to apply their knowledge. The more open-ended such work is (in contrast to objective testing that insists on a single answer), the more students are forced to abandon formulas and arrive at original approaches. With this project I hope students both remember what they learned and how they learned it. If they do, then I've taught them how to learn for a lifetime.

Appendix 14-A. Project Purpose, Assignment, and Due Dates

Purpose

This project is intended to help you focus on what you will be learning, and will have learned, about American culture this year. In providing a detailed description of a museum intended to convey American culture, you will need to detail two ideas: first, what is the most important aspect about America and its history; second, what historical events, documents, or people best convey that aspect.

Overview

This final project will be a brochure that consists of the following:
- A schematic overview of a museum you have designed
- Accompanying descriptions and background that explain the workings of your museum

This project will be developed throughout the year; a number of smaller assignments (including one or two museum visits of your own) will prepare you for the final project due in the fourth quarter. Your map or schematic drawing must look professional. I recommend PageMaker for this, although you can use freehand art if the design is effective. The brochure should be typed. However you prepare this, both the brochure and the map must be incorporated into one document.

Procedure

Pretend you have visitors from another country who know little or nothing about America. You are going to take them through a museum that will convey the most important point about this country. Your visitors will see a variety of items that all work together to reinforce this one impression. The first thing you must do is to decide on the one idea you want your visitors to have about this country after they finish touring your museum.

Make a list of the items to be found in your museum. If there is a particular impression you wish to convey, what items will produce that impression? This list could include any kind of object or media; use your imagination.

Design your museum. In doing this, consider what design would best convey your idea. Remember that museums can be designed any number of ways. Some are simply visually oriented, so that the viewer wanders from object to object. Others are interactive so that viewers can play with media or computer programs or engage in activities that re-create particular episodes. Still other presentations are known as "living museums," communities that re-create particular places and are filled with actors and sights that make the tourist feel transported to another era. You might use any one of these, any combination of these, or anything else that will make an effective impression.

Prepare your map or schematic drawing. This should be an aerial view of your museum, indicating where sights are located and how the movement of tourists goes. You must decide how you want to convey your information. For instance, you might want to present information chronologically or thematically, or you might want to present it as a series of encounters with groups or communities. As you lay out your museum, consider if you want to direct your tourists in a particular way or allow them to follow their own paths.

- Prepare a brochure that your visitors will receive at the opening of the museum. This should give them a specific idea of what they are about to encounter and should include the following:
- An opening statement that indicates the purpose of your museum and what you wish them to think about as they tour. Be specific here, as this is where

you make clear the impression you want to convey.
- A listing of each area in the museum that visitors will encounter. Specify the main purpose of each area, indicating both the impression that the area should convey and how it reinforces your museum's overall impression.
- For each area, identify and explain at least three or four things the visitor will encounter. Again, be specific here, stating what these objects symbolize and how they help to create the overall impression.
- State what visitors may purchase in your museum store as they leave. Again, be specific about the contents, indicating the importance of what you offer.

Dates

Your museum visit(s) will be due _____ and _____.

By _____ you should have found your basic research sources and turn in an annotated bibliography of these sources. These must include four Internet sites (one CD-ROM may be substituted for one site); two periodicals, newspaper accounts, or books; two literary sources; at least two visual items that are nonprint (ads, cartoons, film clips, photos); any other sources.

On _____ you will turn in a two-page write-up of your projected topic, indicating what attracted you to this area of study and how you will cover it in your brochure.

An initial annotated design of your museum will be due _____. Though not a finished layout design, it should show the design or structure of your museum and include explanations for all your sites and what will be included in each area.

Your brochure is due _____.

Appendix 14-B. Grading Sheet

Problem areas are checked below.

Written Content (60 points):
An overview that includes the following:
___ Purpose of your museum
___ Statement of how the museum is to be used or explored
Smaller areas (rooms, locations) that meet the following requirements:
___ Make clear their relation to the overall purpose of the museum
___ Makes a clear statement about their central idea
___ Include at least three items that effectively illustrate this idea
___ Explain how these items represent the theme of this specific area

___ Are relevant to the room in which they are contained
___ Include a museum shop containing items that underscore your main idea
___ Include museum essentials: hours and days; fees; location of bathrooms, phones, info center, coat room
___ Make evident your research

Brochure (50 points):
___ Contains an annotated layout
___ Evidences an integrated design (font, structure, layout) and reflects the museum's theme
___ Shows imagination and creativity
___ Is plausible
___ Makes your museum look fun and interesting to see
___ Is well prepared and interesting to look at

Style (20 points):
___ Writing is clear and makes sense
___ Sentences are varied, not simplistic and repetitive
___ Word choice is effective, not mundane
___ Writing stays focused, doesn't ramble
___ Writing is lively and interesting
___ Writing isn't sketchy; it explains your ideas fully

Usage and Mechanics (20 points):
___ Correct spelling
___ No run-ons, comma splices or fragments
___ No tense shifts
___ No pronoun reference problems
Correct use of the following:
___ Commas
___ Capitalization
___ Apostrophes
___ Colons
___ Semicolons
___ Titles
Total: ___/150

Appendix 14-C. List of Museums and Historical Sites

(Note: These museums are in areas adjacent to my high school, so teachers should take them only as suggestions of the wide range of facilities their students might explore closer to their homes—or on-line.)

American Museum of Quilts and Textiles
Location: 766 South 2nd Street, San Jose, CA
Phone: (408) 971-0323
Web site: http://www.sjquiltmuseum.org/
Project Weight: B

Quilts are displayed here as art forms, social commentary, and historical documentation. Works from the area and around the world are featured.

Barbie Doll Hall of Fame
Location: 433 Waverley Street, Palo Alto, CA
Phone: (415) 326-5841
Project Weight: B

More than 16,000 items of Barbiana fill this small house dedicated to the most successful doll in toy history.

California Antique Aircraft Museum
Location: 12777 Murphy, San Martin, CA
Phone: (408) 683-2290
Project Weight: A

Twenty aircraft from World War I through the 1950s are on display here, as well as instruments, replicas, and models.

Campbell Historic Museum (The Ainsley House)
Location: 300 Grant Street, Campbell, CA
Phone: (408) 866-2119
Project Weight: B

A perfectly preserved 1920s mansion owned by the Ainsleys, a Campbell pioneer family, whose fortune was made in fruit orchards and canning. All original furniture and family artifacts.

Hearst Castle
Location: Highway 1, San Simeon, CA
Phone: (800) 444-4445
Web site: http://www.hearstcastle.org/
Project Weight: A

The famed mansion of newspaper magnate William Randolph Hearst is so big that not even four tours can cover its extensive grounds. This is where the Hollywood crowd once came for weekend parties.

Lighthouse Surfing Museum
Location: West Cliff Drive, Santa Cruz, CA
Phone: (408) 429-3760
Web site: http://www.cruzio.com/~scva/surf.html
Project Weight: B

More than 100 years of surfing history are featured in this lighthouse, including videos, photographs and surfboards.

Los Altos History House Museum
Location: 51 South San Antonio Road, Los Altos, CA
Phone: (415) 948-9427
Web site: http://www.losaltoshistory.org/
Project Weight: B

What was life like in Santa Clara Valley during the Great Depression? You can see it preserved in the Gilbert Smith farm and orchard house.

Monterey State Historic Park
Location: Visitor Center, Custom House Plaza, Old Monterey, CA
Phone: (408) 649-7118
Web site: http://www.mbay.net/~mshp/
Project Weight: A

This restoration of Old Monterey allows you to walk through and past more than a dozen buildings, including homes, businesses, and political centers. Monterey in the days of its Mexican heritage is the focus.

Appendix 14-D. Sample Write-Up of Museum Visits

Purpose

This assignment is intended to acquaint you with local history and assist you in designing your museum. By noting how history and culture are presented, you should become better acquainted with techniques of presentation you can incorporate into your own project.

Preparation

As you look over the list of museums and historical sites, keep in mind three things:
1. You should pick a museum that will help you in creating your own American museum. This doesn't necessarily mean that you can't pick a museum of immediate interest to you, just one that might also be of help.
2. When you visit, you need to be observant. This will require you to bring a notepad and jot down observations as you move along.
3. Your write-up should be more than a dry recitation of facts. Be creative.

Include yourself and your responses. You should also do the following before you make your visit:
- Call the museum in advance to confirm times and cost.
- Ask what is available for viewing and leave yourself enough time to see everything.
- Take advantage of what is there to be seen. Some museums offer introductory films, which can be valuable. Some offer lectures or tours. Others have special exhibits. All of these will help you gain a fuller understanding of the museum.

The Work

Although you do not have to choose a place from the recommended list, you must clear any visit not on the list in advance with me; please note that any museum you visit must have an American angle (the Rosicrucian Museum doesn't count). Failure to do so will likely result in no credit for your work. In addition, your paper must have an attached admission ticket or reasonable proof of your attendance (date of visit), or credit will not be given. You may make the visit alone, with friends, or with family; the only expectation is that your write-up follow these rules:
- Contain descriptions of the physical setting and layout.
- Contain behavioral descriptions of other people.
- Narrate specific events or actions occurring at the museum.
- Follow an appropriate rhetorical strategy for organization.
- Open with an interesting and effective intro.
- Reflect on the museum's purpose and effect on you.

Also note that each museum carries a specific project weight, A or B. To fulfill the requirement of this assignment, you either visit one A museum or two B museums. All museum A and first museum B visits are due _____. Second museum B visits are due _____.

Ellis Island Museum Visit

by Jeff House
American Literature
Date of visit: July 9, 2002

Because I do not believe we were meant to fly or sail across the water, I nervously walked up the plank of the ferry that would shortly embark for Ellis Island. Moments before I had walked through The Castle, a small, stone fortress at The Battery—Manhattan's southern tip—to purchase my ticket and then moved into the line that hugged the steel rail along the wharf. Manhattan skyscrapers behind me, I leaned against the rail to gaze across New York Harbor, past the copper green Statue of Liberty, to a series of Victorian buildings that seemed to float on the water.

This was my first impression of Ellis Island, deliberately set apart from the mainland, as if to first screen the immigrants, protecting Americans from undesirables. In fact, it was only "lower-class foreigners"—those who could afford to travel only in steerage—who passed through Ellis Island; immigrants with more money were immediately let off at Manhattan.

Under the raised, guiding arm of the Statue of Liberty, we chug to the island without incident and made our way to the main building. Built in 1892, this three-story brick structure echoed the Victorian wedding of form and function, its steel-rimmed windows and white brick corners contributing to its demeanor of sobriety and beauty. Decades ago, immigrants disembarked where we were, some seeing the glory of the building, others remembering the state authorities they'd left behind, wondering if they'd be deemed unacceptable and forced to sail another 2 months back across the Atlantic. The huge entrance hall stretches to a series of doors to the left—beyond which accepted immigrants once purchased ferry and rail tickets—and to the right, where a theater, cafeteria, and gift shop are located. In the middle of the hall is an exhibit of baggage: Gladstone bags, traveling trunks, B-4 bags, duffel bags, small armoires, cardboard boxes, fruit boxes, leather suitcases, cane straw contraptions, rounded barrels, purses, pockets, billfolds, paper bags, envelopes, cases for glasses and hats; baggage that carried clothing, photographs, heirlooms, furniture; baggage that reflected the wealth of the rich and the forced improvisation of the poor.

The hall is relatively silent. For all the people who mingle here at the visitor's center, the information desk, the exhibits, the tour booking site; for all of these and for the echo created by the vast, tiled room, there is little noise. People often speak in whispers, and parents do not let their children run. Couples will bend their heads together, one pointing at a television screen where an immigrant tells her story, the other nodding in understanding. By consensus, by space, perhaps by ghosts, the hall is made sacred. Structurally, the second floor is an echo of the first, but here the rooms on both wings bookend the Great Hall, and from the third floor balcony that rings the room, I gaze down and remember the pictures I have seen of this room: how, arranged in benches and railings, immigrants waited in lines to be inspected, to be questioned, to be inventoried, to be entered onto the rolls of America. By this point, some had already begun to fear they would not be admitted when doctors, stationed atop the stairs at the second floor landing, had placed chalk marks on their backs to indicate a problem. Perhaps this one evidenced trachoma (discovered by a medical examiner's using a shoe button hook to lift the eyelid); this one seemed mentally slow; this one appeared tubercular; this one was blind, the next one deaf; this one just suspicious. Such a one might be taken to the island's hospital to be quarantined and detained until a final diagnosis could be made, while his family waited in quiet terror through each day, hoping they would not have to decide whether to enter Manhattan without their loved one or return home with him.

There were more tests to pass. The immigrants had to answer questions demonstrating mental competence, financial solvency, and proof of a sponsor. Some spoke English; many did not and required an interpreter. Some took comfort from the officials who guided them through the lines; some saw the uniforms and remembered state police who had brutalized, pillaged, or murdered family members. Perhaps this hall was as sacredly silent then as now.

The exhibits on the second and third floors detail the immigrant experience: booking steerage on a transatlantic journey that induced nausea, illness, and occasionally death; leaving behind the clothing and furniture of the Old World to acquire the new; finding employment and housing in urban tenements, country houses, midwestern farms; creating communities around religion, theater, food, philosophy, and work. Glass booths contain personal belongings, song sheets, newspapers, pipe collections, religious works. On the walls hang signs advertising jobs, music titles, theater shows, and invitations to find land and homes out West. Hanging from the ceilings, quotes on plexiglass fill in the human detail. "They told me the streets of America were paved with gold," one reads. "But when I got here, I found out three things: first, the streets weren't paved with gold; second, the streets weren't paved at all; third, they expected me to pave them."

Italian opera wafts through one room, Slovak folk music from another, an Irish jig from another. Flags in more colors and combinations than I can imagine hang suspended. Mannequins in period dress and international styles are woven throughout the exhibits, standing like sentinels or with ease or with apprehension. I am most touched by the stories. Millions of immigrants passed through Ellis Island, and most of their voices were lost; so it is the placards of anecdotes that stop us all, people staring reverently at the words before slowly moving on. One is the story of a young English girl, who describes the day she left her mother and friends at the Liverpool dock. The tradition at this leavetaking was for family members, those leaving and those staying, to carry a ball of yarn to the pier. There one member would hold the yarn at one end of the ball, and the departing member would take the yarn from the other end, walking up the plank and unfurling the string, still holding the other end as she leaned over the boat's side. The many people doing this created a silent symphony of color from shore to ship. Then the boat would pull away, and each string, alone or in tangles of twos and threes, would float to the ocean, a rainbow of colors, as lovers, friends, and family waved to those they would never see again.

After 5 hours, I embark on the ferry back to Manhattan, and this time the journey doesn't seem so unnerving. I have been in the company of courageous ghosts who risked and endured so much for the possibility of greater happiness. Surely I can cross a mile of water.

15

Survivor, the Literary Edition: A Suggestion for Concluding a Literature Class

Elizabeth Teare

I have always found the last day of class even more intimidating than the first. On the first day, neither my students nor I really expect more than the usual opening business: confusion about who's on my roll sheet, an introduction to the syllabus, a sketch of my expectations, and two or three jokes. The last day of class demands more of us all. The end of a course needs closure, a look back that puts all our daily work into a long perspective that clearly shows what it all means. Many of my favorite teachers gave brilliant closing lectures, but after spending the term trying to play down my authority and to play up my students', I'm not comfortable concluding with a lecture. The problem is exacerbated in my survey courses, which, like most surveys I've attended or observed, get about two thirds of the way through the anthology or, as a historian friend once put it, "barely through Watergate." How, I asked, could I help my students see the big picture for themselves on the last day of class?

Survivor: The Literary Edition

The solution I've developed is an activity called "Survivor: The Literary Edition." This title capitalizes on my students' obsession with the CBS television program *Survivor*. I use the show's vocabulary of *tribes* and *challenges* as shorthand to explain the lesson, but it will work under another name when its television precursor has faded from memory. Other "reality" programs, like Fox's *American Idol*, offer other possible models. (I have also simply framed the exercise by asking students to help me choose the readings for next year's class.) Under any name, the lesson solves the problems of time and student participation that we face as the term winds down, and it even turns the large chunk of the anthology that we haven't covered into an advantage. By choosing an unfamiliar author who intrigues them and by placing that author in the literary tradition we've explored, students come up with their own summaries and interpretations of that tradition. In effect, each of them writes his or her own concluding lecture.

Initially I developed the Survivor lesson plan in its current form for postsecondary students, but it works equally well in secondary and middle schools. In fact, versions of the Survivor lesson work even better in secondary-level surveys, where the more frequent class meetings allow more time for the teacher to unfold the lesson and more opportunities for students to respond to each other's work. In high school, where surveys are more likely to last a year than a semester, it is important to help students cast their minds back to works they read in September as 8 months may have obscured thematic and symbolic connections. Having students choose their own conclusions to the course gives the survey something of the feel of an elective rather than of an inevitable requirement. It may even—especially if the teacher or school can offer some reward—encourage students to read more of their chosen authors over the summer.

The Game Begins

The Literary Survivor game begins on or about the next-to-last day of class, although students don't know it. I spend the last 15 minutes of that class piloting students through the final pages of the table of contents of the anthology. Having begun with William Blake, Mary Robinson, and other writers of the French revolutionary period, we have read together up through W. H. Auden, Dylan Thomas, and World War II. I refer to the post–World War II writers we did not study as "postcolonial." These writers offer different perspectives from those we have been studying at the end of the imperial period. I give the most intriguing sketches I can of the writers remaining in the anthology, from Doris Lessing to Paul Muldoon. (A history teacher might provide students with a list of important recent political and social developments.) I send students home with this assignment:

> Pick any postcolonial writer in the anthology who looks interesting to you. Read both the introduction to that writer and his or her work. Then write a page explaining what you like (and perhaps dislike) about the writer you chose. Make sure you answer the following questions: How does your writer fit into the scheme of British literature we've been establishing? To which other authors that we've read can you compare your writer, in content and in style?

My students have written similar brief response papers throughout the term. They know that they must provide examples from the texts they discuss, that their responses can be informal but should be proofread. They also expect that I will collect responses and record them with a checkmark or, if they are exceptionally interesting, with a checkmark and a plus sign. These responses have figured prominently in students' participation grades throughout the course, so everyone knows to take them seriously.

On the last day of class, I surprise students with the game, which involves a series of three elimination rounds that leave one Literary Survivor—the writer that students decide best caps off our survey. I begin by announcing the prize: for the writer, a big cardboard check for $1 million; for the writer's successful sponsor, whatever home-baked treat he or she requests, to be shared with the class at the final exam. Announcing this prize at the beginning of the lesson has been very effective in encouraging students to participate actively in the debate series.

Literary Survivor: Round 1

For the first round, I divide students into "tribes" of three and give each tribe its "challenge." (I find that three is the ideal number for a group, giving all students time to present their arguments. Other group sizes can also work, as long as the number of students in each group is odd, to avoid time-consuming ties.) The tribe has 15 minutes to discuss and decide which of their three writers would be the best one with whom to conclude the survey. Students base their arguments on the response papers they've written. As I move from group to group listening to their discussions, I encourage students to draw connections between the writers they're sponsoring and those we've read in the past. They are quick to make these links: Ted Hughes's "Daffodils" reminds them of William Wordsworth; Alice Munro's "Walker Brothers Cowboy" recalls our discussions of girls' education in Elizabeth Barrett Browning's "Aurora Leigh." After each tribe votes, the students who have convinced their tribes that their writers are the best representatives of postcolonial British literature sponsor those writers into the next round.

Literary Survivor: Round 2

The second round works the same way. The small tribes merge into three larger ones, and students again have 15 minutes to argue and vote for the most representative writer. By this point the room is usually noisy and full of energy; students' presentations of their writers are more impassioned though less careful. Some of the same problems that we have observed on the *Survivor* program crop up as students may vote along their former tribal lines rather than really allowing themselves to be persuaded by convincing arguments, but with some encouragement each group finally manages a vote.

Literary Survivor: Round 3

Finally, in the third challenge, each of the three larger tribes selects a spokesperson to give a more formal presentation in support of its candidate for Sole Survivor. I allow each speaker 3 minutes and, after all three speeches, a minute each for rebuttal. During each speech I write on the board the themes the winning writer seems to address and the connections with other writers and works that come up in the presentation. A final vote—usually a raucous bargaining session rather than a strict parliamentary procedure—determines the winner. In the remaining half hour of our 75-minute period, we review the themes and connections on the board, adding other ideas that students think are important and relevant. (With shorter class periods or younger students, the exercise might with good effect be spread out over 2 or 3 days, with the formal presentations and final vote on the second day. This arrangement would have the advantage of allowing secondary students to prepare their speeches carefully.)

I conclude by telling students that a passage from the work of the Sole Survivor will appear as an identification option on the exam, which they know will consist of a combination of identifications and short essays drawing connections between two writers. I point out that, by thinking about themes and connections, they have not only begun to study for the exam but have also begun to shape their own canon of British literature. This reminds students that they, as much as their anthology or I, can determine a canon, which makes a strong conclusion to the survey course.

Who Survives?

Finalists in the Survivor game have included Philip Larkin, Ted Hughes, Alice Munro, and Edna O'Brien. Each semester, somewhat to my surprise, Larkin has been the Sole Survivor, with students expressing particular fondness for his poems "High Windows" and "Talking in Bed." Students who have successfully sponsored Larkin argue that a poet is the best choice to cap a course in which most of what we have read is poetry, and that Larkin is appealing because his poetry speaks clearly to modern concerns in modern language. He is particularly popular among non–English majors. "We read a lot of poetry this year that took me a long time to read because of complicated language," one student wrote, comparing Larkin to the Romantics. "Larkin uses modern-day language, including curse words, but still manages to make it beautifully descriptive. His melancholy poems actually brought a small bit of light to my day because I finally felt I could identify with what a poet was feeling." Although I might not agree with this student that Larkin is a particularly "beautifully descriptive" representative of postcolonial British poetry, I was pleased to see her enjoyment of his work.

Student Responses to Literary Survivor

Students' responses to their writers are invariably thoughtful and almost invariably well written, revealing a confidence in their own judgment of writers as part of the tradition of British literature. Following are some of the student responses I have received. The first response pays close attention both to the language of the text and to connections to writers we covered earlier in the term:

> I really enjoyed reading Doris Lessing's piece entitled "To Room Nineteen." I think that she accurately portrays how some women feel in a marriage after the children have grown and the husband is at work. Women all the time suffer what is known as a "mid-life crisis" and that is just what Susan is going through. I think Lessing fits into the scheme of literature we've been reading because she portrays how women have evolved and how marriages have changed. Lessing is known for writing about feminism and psychological effects on women, and this piece does just that. Lessing can be compared to women writers like Virginia Woolf and Mary Wollstonecraft. "To Room Nineteen" is like Woolf's *A Room of One's Own* in that both stories tell of how women need a "vacation" from their busy lives in

order to find peace of mind. Woolf suggests this be a room where women can write, and Lessing creates a hotel room in which Susan can seek refuge from her troubled life at home. And finally Lessing's character of Susan is like the image of the flower Wollstonecraft uses in *A Vindication of the Rights of Women*. Susan has been successful in raising a family, and without them constantly around for her to take care of, she began to wither and die inside.

The next student uses the assignment to remind herself of both biographical and stylistic details of 19th-century writers:

> I chose Ted Hughes as a poet to analyze because he was interesting to me since he was married to Sylvia Plath and was the poet laureate of England. Things I noticed that I liked about this writing as I was reading his poems are his use of imagery and focus on nature. His emphasis on nature made me think of the Romantic poets, and his "Daffodils" poem obviously reminded me of Wordsworth. Hughes's speaker in "Daffodils" talks of remembering picking the daffodils and asks if anyone else remembers besides him. It is similar to how Wordsworth is remembering walking alone through nature in "I wandered lonely as a cloud." Both have the obvious references to daffodils and both are remembering things. However, Hughes is wondering why no one else can remember picking the daffodils, whereas Wordsworth remembers everything but no one else can because he was alone (although really with Dorothy). I can compare Wordsworth and Hughes more in content than in actual style. Hughes's style is less romantic and more harsh, focused and compact (more like Rossetti's "The Woodspurge" in style) and descriptive in his terms.

The last excerpt comes from the response of a student who decided he would not recommend his author for a place in our survey:

> Anita Desai has a short story included in the Norton Anthology titled "Scholar and Gypsy." She has a very descriptive style of writing, and while the subject matter of her story, a married couple going separate ways, is one that has been touched upon by many other writers, the setting and characters distinguish this work of fiction. In modern short stories this sort of lavish detail can be a double-edged sword. Many of her descriptions are nice, but not all of them move the plot of the story forward. This type of critique, however, is not important to a class on British literature, but rather for a short story class. Therein lies the problem with Desai's story in this class. Aside from Joyce's "The Dead," which is a beautiful story in its own right, there are few examples of the short story genre in the Norton Anthology. This is not poor planning on the part of the publisher. The short story was born in America and Russia, not in England. As a consequence of this, poetry and essays rightfully make up the bulk of British literature texts. "Scholar and Gypsy" is similar in setting to "Shooting an Elephant," although the times are different. The theme of outside influences in India and Burma is still strong in both pieces, but Desai's story is probably best left to a class on her genre.

I file copies of these intelligent responses in case I ever do manage to teach past World War II, since the students' ideas about what to teach and why are so carefully thought out and helpful.

Variations on Survivor: The Literary Tradition

Versions of the game also work well simply to review shorter units of a course, harnessing the students' expertise in the workings of pop culture to drive their ability to argue for their opinions. For example, I have asked ninth graders who have just finished reading *The Odyssey* to cast a movie version of the story. As teams of producers, they must first decide whether they want to film a blockbuster hit or a thoughtful independent film. (They always choose the blockbuster.) Then they must bargain with the rest of the production team for the stars they think would best fill the roles, an exercise that can produce lengthy and memorable arguments about the most important character traits of Telemachus, the suitors, or Penelope. The project can end with the design and display of publicity posters for their versions of *The Odyssey: The Movie*.

In other flights of TV reality show–induced fancy, I have imagined an all-star *Fear Factor* featuring the characters of *Dracula* or *Frankenstein* or a version of *The Amazing Race* across the United States with "teams" of literary and historical characters (Huck and Jim, Lewis and Clark, Daisy and Jay, Woodward and Bernstein). It would also be possible to do a version of BBC America's popular decorating show, *Trading Places*, between the castles of *Macbeth* or the mansions of Gatsby and Daisy; a hilarious take-off on *elimiDATE* could be written using the characters of an Jane Austen novel. As long as television (especially reality television) and video games remain central to our students' lives, the possibilities are endless.

Students Write Their Own Concluding Lectures

"Survivor: The Literary Edition" has been a smash success for my survey class. Not only do students enjoy the game, they also find themselves participating in class up until the last minute of the semester, using the close-reading skills we have relentlessly practiced and basing their arguments on the textual evidence they've discovered. Students have noted in evaluations that the game does help them to prepare for their final exam by reminding them of themes and issues we've covered in the course of the semester. It leaves them, too, with some sense of authority over and ownership of the canon of works they've read. The following is typical of the evaluations I receive:

> Being able to defend why my author of choice was the "best" helped me to examine the strengths of that writer more in depth. Also, having my own ideas about the superiority of my writer reinforced by other classmates was beneficial, even though my writer did not 'survive' my group. Also in the process of the exercise, my mind was actually swayed within my own group based on the persuasive arguing tactics of other

group members. I truly did enjoy the game. It was a nice change of pace during the end of the year from other professors' lectures.

Beyond Survivor: Practical Applications

My own ambivalence about making a grand summary statement at the end of the semester is clearly echoed in such student responses. The Survivor game makes the last day of class both more memorable and more empowering for students. The game also benefits students in practical ways. The standardized literature tests—from the SAT II to the AP to the GRE—expect students to feel comfortable responding to poems and prose passages they haven't seen before. As the current instructions on the College Board (2001) Web page point out:

> The best way to prepare for the [SAT II Literature test] is through close critical reading of English and American literature from a variety of historical periods and in a variety of genres. The more skilled you become at understanding and analyzing literary texts, the better prepared you will be. There is no reading list for the Literature test. It doesn't cover specific facts or background information about particular books or writers. If you have practiced your interpretive skills thoroughly and can apply them to a number of different types of literary works, you are ready to take the test.

The key idea here, as in the Survivor game, is *application*. The game, like the tests, asks students to apply their "close critical reading" skills—on their own—to texts with which they have relatively little introduction. Even more important, the game encourages students to make *connections*. It helps them to realize that they do indeed know how to apply their skills to new texts. In addition, it may encourage them to enrich essay tests by pointing out similarities between test passages and works they have studied. In these practical as well as intangible ways, the Survivor game both educates students and enables them to believe themselves educated—a goal worth a million dollars any time.

References

Abrams, M. H., & Greenblatt, S. (Eds.). (2000). *The Norton anthology of English literature* (Vol. 2, 7th ed.). New York: Norton.

The College Board. (2001). *The College Board: SAT® II: Literature* [On-line]. Available: http://www.collegeboard.com/sat/center2/lite/lite.html.

16

Empowering Students With Portfolios

Darren Perkes

I taught eighth- and ninth-grade English and French at a middle school for one year before teaching high school Advanced Placement English and concurrent enrollment English, the dual enrollment class many students take their senior year in cooperation with a local university. That was a huge jump for me—a good jump. I was excited to tackle the challenges of AP and concurrent enrollment English because such classes had not been available to me when I was a high school student. Even though I loved English in high school, paradoxically I hated to read. Rather than read, I went to the movies, watched TV, rented videos, or played video games. The problem for me was that reading required effort; it still does.

Resistance to Reading

Like me at their age, many of my students read only those novels they are forced to read by their English teachers. Many of them admit that they have never chosen a novel on their own to read just for enjoyment. A few years ago one student asked, "What's the point? I only read so I can do the assignments for that novel. What's so great about just reading a book?" I was disappointed at this student's attitude, but not surprised because that was my attitude 14 years earlier.

The students' negative attitudes toward reading prompted me to restructure my literature classes. I used my experiences as a nonmotivated reader to construct questions to use before students begin to read. Some of those questions were the following: How do I find a book I'll enjoy? What's the point of reading? What can I do to get more out of what I read? How do books differ from each other? In an effort to help students engage deeply with these questions, I developed the Novel Portfolio Project in which students are empowered to answer the above and their own questions through assignments that help them to reflect on their reading in structured yet self-directed ways.

The Novel Portfolio Project empowers students to take responsibility for making personal connections, questioning and responding to texts, creating illustrations for comprehension, recognizing and understanding literary elements in writing, and discovering writing styles of different authors. Students also use the portfolio to develop the specific skills and strategies associated with critical reading.

A portfolio is by no means a new technique. However, the Novel Portfolio Project empowers students actually to *do something* with what they've been studying throughout the trimester. With each assignment, the students apply reading and writing skills and strategies to their study of a novel. This project also serves as a final assessment of the reading skills the students have acquired over the course of the trimester. As a participant in an Eisenhower grant funded to introduce portfolios across the disciplines, I learned that effective portfolios should meet the following five criteria: (a) teach and assess learning objectives, (b) demonstrate student voice, (c) collect student work, (d) require an organizational strategy, and (e) contain student reflection. With these criteria in mind, I set about organizing and later refining the Novel Portfolio Project.

Effective Portfolio Criterion No. 1: Teaches and Assesses Learning Objectives

Using the Novel Portfolio Project to teach and assess learning objectives is probably the most important yet difficult task to accomplish. Aligning objectives to a state's core curricular standards is often a tedious but simple task. Narrowing an activity to address only one or two points of the core curriculum specifically isn't always easy, however because so many classroom activities encompass a wide range of core standards at the same time. Nevertheless, this challenge of narrowing an activity to specific core standards gives me the opportunity to discuss our state's core curriculum with my students and to develop a very explicit overarching purpose for the project itself.

For the Novel Portfolio Project, I decided to focus on two objectives from the state curriculum: (a) demonstrate competency in reading and interpreting literary texts, and (b) demonstrate competency in writing literary texts. These are the specific critical thinking skills necessary for students to acquire. Keeping the five criteria for an effective portfolio in mind, I created the activity description shown in Table 16-1.

At the bottom of the Novel Portfolio Project description page, I include the last three lines of Robert Frost's poem "The Road Not Taken" to help students understand that the items listed on the assignment description page are only a brief description of what is possible: Remember, I tell them, what Robert Frost says about what a difference our choices make.

Table 16-1: Novel Portfolio Project Assignment Description

Name: _____ Points Earned: ___/___

You will be in literature circles of five students. Each group will work on a different novel. Although you will work on this novel as a group, each member will create his or her own portfolio, which will include all measures of analysis for that novel. Through the portfolio you will demonstrate your understanding of literature (see specifics below).

Purpose: To develop and demonstrate your abilities to read, interpret, and write literary text. To demonstrate your ability to apply the skills you have learned and present those skills in a meaningful, literary fashion.

Audience: The same audience that your book addresses (as if showing your research done on the book and then submitting your own writing sample to a professional)

List of texts from which to choose:

Things Fall Apart by Chinua Achebe

Their Eyes Were Watching God by Zora Neale Hurston

The Bean Trees by Barbara Kingsolver

Monkey Bridge by Lan Cao

The Sound and the Fury by William Faulkner

Specifics: All of the following information must be included in a "nice" folder.

(Remember that you are submitting this portfolio to a professional, so make it look as if you are sending it to a professional):

- Annotated table of contents. The "annotation" in this case is a short reflection on each portfolio item.
- Questions and responses for each chapter. I will provide sample questions as examples. Remember experience, interpretation, evaluation from when we studied short stories?
- Notes and examples of the different writing techniques and elements in your book—metaphor, plot line, characters, setting, senses, outside sources, biographical information.
- Illustrations (hand-drawn, painted, collages, computer generated), with a detailed explanation for each one that makes specific reference to the text.
- Construct a "chapter" of your own. Put to use the elements you have learned and imitate the writing style of the author you read. This will be peer revised and scored by your group members.
- One-page final reflection describing your experience of reading, interpreting, and writing literary texts.
- Other material that you think would add to your literary presentation.

Grading: You will be graded on how well you present the knowledge you should have gained while studying the elements of the novel and previous genres; see the attached grading rubric for grading details [not included in this table].

I wanted my students' portfolios to be creative, innovative, and original, and by using their own voices, their portfolios would represent their own personal learning. I gave them enough directions to get started but made sure they understood that what to include in the final portfolio was their choice.

Effective Portfolio Criterion No. 2: Demonstrates Student Voice

To encourage students to create portfolios that demonstrates their voices, I gave them an opportunity to develop their own criteria for assessment. Often students "jump through the hoops" set by teachers without understanding how they will be assessed. However, when students contribute to the assessment process, they feel included in the process and therefore are more likely to develop their personal voices, because they know that their personal voices will be honored. Table 16-2 shows a blank scoring standard that gives students the opportunity to take part in developing the assessment for the Novel Portfolio Project, which in turn allows students to demonstrate their personal voices.

Table 16-2. Blank Scoring Standard for the Novel Portfolio Project

Description	Excellent	Proficient	Good	Poor	Comments
Table of contents					
Questions					
Notes and examples					
Illustrations					
Your own chapter					
Final reflection					
Overall portfolio					

Around 7 school days into the project, once the students have begun reading their novels and have started writing drafts of pieces they hope to put in their portfolios, they work in groups to develop the grading rubric. I show them examples, and we discuss how a rubric works, but they create the categories and the descriptions of how those categories meet certain levels of achievement. Once each group has created its rubric, I put all the comments together and give it t the class a few days later for review by the class. The class discusses the rubric and adds what they think are important points for assessment. They also omit what they consider nonessential criteria. The rubric then reflects the general consensus of the class on how the Novel Portfolio Project will be assessed. I type up the final version of the rubric so that each member of the class will have it in front of him or her as a reminder of exactly how the portfolio will be assessed. Table 16-3 is an example of one of the completed categories developed by the class.

Table 16-3. Example of Scoring Standard Category Developed by Class

Description	Excellent	Proficient	Good	Poor
Table of contents and annotations	Annotations provide intellectual reflection for each piece created. Reflections explain in an intelligent and meaningful manner the process used to achieve the final products. Items are organized, clear, and well written. Minimum of one complete paragraph for each annotation.	Annotations provide intellectual reflection for each piece created. Reflections explain in a meaningful manner the process used to achieve the final products. Items are organized, clear, and well written. Minimum of one complete paragraph for each annotation.	Annotations provide reflection for each piece created. Reflections explain the process used to achieve the final products. Items are organized, clear, and well written. Minimum of one complete paragraph for each annotation.	No annotations. Just a list of items in the portfolio.

I've learned that providing clear expectations and distinct objectives encourages students to use their own voices. Because students take an active role in the development of the guidelines for the rubric, they assume ownership of the project. The project is no longer my idea, but theirs. They set the criteria for assessment; they determine the content. The more opportunities that students have to take part in decision making in the classroom, the more they buy into actually doing the assignment—and the more their products are actually meaningful to them.

The basis for the assessment of their work is clearly articulated. Therefore, they can see that the grading is not based on my personal preference or whim. Because they have created their own grading criteria, they are no longer simply doing what they think I want. Thus, through ownership their Novel Portfolio Project gives them more voice in shaping the project.

Effective Portfolio Criterion No. 3: Archives Student Work

An effective portfolio archives a student's work on a particular project. Included in the archive should be a wide range of genres that the student has developed in response to the project assignment. This archive allows students to demonstrate to a variety of stakeholders (parents, administration, other students, and community members) the students' progress in attempting to master the learning objectives. Using the portfolio as an archive encourages students to demonstrate the wide range of skills and strategies they have developed while working on their Novel Portfolio Project. To get students working on a variety of genres that will demonstrate their mastery of the learning objectives, I provide daily explanations and models for only one area of focus (annotated table of contents on Monday, questions and responses and Tuesday, notes and examples on Wednesday, etc.). I model each genre briefly because I know that they will be starting points for whatever pieces the students actually decide to create and include in their portfolios. I then give the students time to read and work together as a group. Here is an example of one type of genre, asking questions and responding to a text, that a student might choose to include in a portfolio:

> While reading a novel, successful readers unconsciously question the events taking place. Unfortunately, not all readers are born with this skill. In an effort to share questioning techniques with other group members and to gain a better understanding of the text you are reading, you will consciously verbalize and write down questions and comments that occur to you while reading. Although the process might take more time than just thinking about the questions, this process, when shared, will give each group member an opportunity to reflect on how his or her understanding of the text might differ from others in the group. This will also provide a written reference for you when reviewing chapters for further discussion or for making connections.
>
> Question categories may be divided into pages, chapters, sections, themes, characters, setting, background, or plot. You decide, or decide as a group. The purpose is to develop questions that will help you to become an active participant in your reading and therefore help you to better understand the text. Consider notes you took when studying short stories. In particular, review the discussion on "Experience, Interpretation, and Evaluation." By looking back at your notes and by reviewing Robert DiYanni's *Fiction*, you should be able to generate meaningful questions that will support and extend your understanding of the text.

This is an example of one genre archived by a student—answers to questions generated by the student and answered by the student's group for Lan Cao's *Monkey Bridge*:

>1. Why is the book entitled *Monkey Bridge*?
>
>A monkey bridge is a type of bridge used in Vietnam to cross canals. It is made of "a thin pole of bamboo no wider than a grown man's foot, roped together by vines and mangrove roots. A railing was tied to one side, so you could at least hold on to it as you made your way across like a monkey" (p. 109). We compared the monkey bridge to challenges in life. Both are difficult to cross and require patience. Mai faces the challenge of adjusting to a new society when she comes to America from Vietnam. By adapting to the new society and enrolling in college, Mai had crossed a monkey bridge in her life.
>
>2. What does the poem inside the front cover have to do with the book?
>
>We took T. S. Eliot's "The Waste Land" as our comparison to Mai and her mother. Mai looks at America as the land of opportunity. However, Mai's mother sees America as a land that considers them outsiders. Just as a shadow can be seen in two different ways depending on the time of day, Mai and her mother see America in two different ways. The shadow behind Mai is the past that she has put behind her. The shadow in front of Mai's mother is the past that she can't seem to escape.

These questions and answers are archived in each student's portfolio as a record of his or her thinking about and understanding of the text. The archived materials can later be retrieved for review and reflection as students create other parts of the portfolio. Some teachers allow archived materials to be used on exams. However, putting the notes and other artifacts of learning into a file folder does not help students with essential organizational strategies that will show their archived materials to best advantage.

Effective Portfolio Criterion No. 4: Organizational Strategy

An effective portfolio demands all sorts of organizational strategies, from the meta-organization of advantageously arranging each individual piece in the portfolio to contrast with each other to the micro-organizational strategies required by note taking while reading. Arranging parts of the portfolio in a reasonable order and developing a table of contents are self explanatory, so I would like to turn to the micro-organizational strategy of taking notes while reading.

Taking notes while reading is a difficult activity for the many of the students who are involved in the Novel Portfolio Project. However, I insist that students take an active role while reading to better understand the novel they are studying. To aid in note taking, I encourage students to purchase their own novels so they can write in the margins, but many students are apprehensive about writing in a book, and many borrow books from the library or acquaintances. To encourage students to take reading notes, I give students small Post-Its® to use while reading. Unintentionally, I created a competition with these Post-Its®. Students are excited to show their group members and me all the notes they made the night before. Each day group members are quick to see who has the most Post-Its® in their book from the previous night's reading; some even judge the quality of the book by how many Post-Its® they use while they read. Many have commented on the fact that the Post-Its® give them reference points that are easily found when needed. Some have taken the experience a step further and have developed specific categories to associate with different colors of Post-Its®. I haven't researched if the Post-Its® have lasting detrimental effects on the actual pages of the books, but the overall feedback is that the students enjoy using them, and the students are doing more with their novels *with* the Post-Its® than they did without them. Table 16-4 shows the assignment directions on taking notes and looking for examples in the text that might generate a piece for the students' portfolios.

Table 16-4. Assignment Description for Taking Notes

The notes and examples section is set aside from the questions and responses, because you will discuss more about the writing techniques being used in the text than about the content of the novel. This is the section where you will demonstrate your understanding of the techniques and skills used in novels. Use notes and ideas that you have gained over the course of this trimester to support your explanations of the elements used in your particular novel. First, consider the notes for plot and structure that we discussed in conjunction with Frank O'Connor's "Guest of a Nation." Many of the same elements that we discussed while working with short stories apply to the study of the novel:

1. Irony and symbol
2. Plot and structure
3. Characters
4. Setting
5. Themes
6. Senses
7. Point of view
8. Language and style
9. Biographical information (including a photograph of the author)
10. Critical theory approaches
11. Time lines
12. Related texts
13. Critical reviews
14. Letter or e-mail communications
15. Metaphor

Overall, you are trying to determine the writing style of the author. What

cont.

> does the author of your particular novel do with his or her writing that is different from other authors? What writing techniques characterize this author's writing? Does this author use complex sentences or simple sentences? Does this author use such techniques as metaphors or foreshadowing or use interesting details with all character descriptions? If you were to read another piece of literature, how would you be able to compare it to the work of your author?
>
> This will require some actual outside researching on your part. Just like your poet presentations, however, the outside information you find in connection with your author and his or her work will influence the quality of understanding you obtain. As you read, pay close attention to these techniques because you will be asked to imitate his or her techniques in another section of this portfolio.

Each assignment description and the discussion about it is designed to give the students a few more ideas to help them reflect on what they've been doing all trimester with an overall goal to encourage them to put those ideas into their portfolios. When I first started this project, all these assignment descriptions were only in my head. Each time I delivered the information, I changed it—I added things, forgot other things, mentioned things I had already covered in another section. By actually writing down the assignments, even just the basic descriptions, I've been able to stay more focused on what I want to accomplish. I can more easily add and subtract information as I see fit, and I avoid overlapping unnecessary details. In addition, I have ready-to-go notes for students who miss or don't take complete notes in class. These assignment descriptions usually clear up any last-minute questions and provide support for the students who work on their projects at home. No portfolio—however detailed, organized, or connected to learning objectives—is worth the time and effort to put together without asking students to reflect on it.

Effective Portfolio Criterion No. 5: Student Reflection

Asking students to reflect on the artifacts in their portfolio and how those artifacts represent their learning is a powerful way to include students in the assessment process. Students are used to self-assessment. Every time they look into a mirror, they compare themselves to the "ideal" teen body, hair, and clothes and rate themselves accordingly. Given the instructions, students can also reflect on their performance in school. I consider the final reflection *the* most important aspect of the portfolio. The reflection tells me the worth of the assignment from the student's perspective; it gives me the information I need to assess what the student learned, what helped the student learn, and how I can make the activity better for future students. Initially I asked students to create a final reflection for their portfolios without a criteria guide. I soon learned, however, that guidance—even just a few reminders—results in more significant assessments that are also interesting to read.

Having spent many years as a student myself, I know how difficult it is to finish a huge project for a class and then create a final reflection with what little energy you have left. My students commented that the agony comes from not knowing where to start, not having any more ideas about which to write. So I created a list of questions to help the students generate ideas with which to finish their projects. I value student reflection highly. It is in reflection that students recognize what they have done and what they have learned and put everything together. Because students have identified their learning strengths, they are then more apt to apply them in the future. I would argue that self-reflection is our best teacher because of its metacognitive influence on learning. Table 16-5 is the assignment description for the portfolio reflection.

Table 16-5. Final Reflection Assignment Description

Tell me about your experience working on this portfolio. I want you to write a one-page, informal reflection on your thoughts and feelings about this portfolio project. Tell me anything and everything you can that will help me, as the teacher, to understand you and how you felt about this project.

Just relax and talk to me as you would to a psychologist—no, talk to me as you would to a friend of yours. Write this as the very last assignment. Finish your portfolio and then walk away. Leave your portfolio alone for a day or so; then come back and look it over. As you review your own personal creation, jot down thoughts and feelings you have about the project as a whole. Use those thoughts and feelings to create this one-page reflection about your experience with this portfolio and with the novel itself. Do this assignment as the very last item, but do it when you are not tired. I like to read coherent comments.

Here are some questions to get your thoughts going. Remember that these questions are to generate your thoughts on the subject. They are not just a list of questions that you should answer one after the other.

- Which opportunities did you enjoy the most? Why?
- Which opportunities did you enjoy the least? Why?
- How did your group function? What did you learn from the members of your group? What caused problems in the group? What worked well in the group? What could have made the group more effective?
- What are your thoughts about the novel you read? What connections did you make with the novel? What would have helped in picking a novel? What would you have done differently in analyzing the content and the writing style used in this novel?
- What was the most interesting part of this project?
- What was most helpful in increasing your understanding of literature with this project?
- How is this project more helpful or less helpful than doing other singular assignments? Explain.

cont.

> - When faced with literature in the future, do you feel comfortable approaching it in these three different ways? Explain.
>
> *One question that you must address in your reflection:* Looking at each of the goals for this project—reading literary texts, interpreting literary texts, and writing literary texts—how well do you think you learned and experienced these different ways of approaching literature?
>
> Students are not required to answer all of these questions. The questions are designed to help students reflect on the project and address ways in which the project is meaningful to them. The questions also elicit from students a description of what they have learned. Here is one paragraph from a student's final reflection:
>
>> To say that this entire assignment was easy, fun, and I wish that I could do it again would be a falsehood. To say that I learned a lot and am grateful for the "forced opportunity" would be very true. This portfolio forced me to look deeper into my novel than I've ever looked before into a novel. . . . The portfolio is, by far, one of the biggest English assignments that I've ever had to do. It's something to be proud of. Yes, it was a lot of work. Yes, it was a couple of late nights. And, yes, I feel like my closest friend right now is the computer. But I've learned a lot. I've learned things that I wouldn't trade for a few more hours of sleep.

Outcomes

The Novel Portfolio Project exemplifies the five criteria that characterize an effective portfolio. It teaches and assesses learning objectives, demonstrates student voice, collects student work, requires an organizational strategy, and contains student reflection. In addition, it provides students with the opportunity to explore a variety of genres while honing their reading skills. The Novel Portfolio Project encourages students to answer their own questions and thus take more responsibility and ownership for what they read. One of the most meaningful comments on the Novel Portfolio Project was one I received from the parents of a nonreader. They explained that their son never read books at home unless he had to for school assignments. However, not long after having a good experience with his Novel Portfolio Project, something happened. One leisurely evening when the boy was home with nothing to do, he told his parents that he was "going to find a good book to read." The parents were shocked by this sudden change of heart, so they questioned his motive. He explained that he guessed that Mr. Perkes had turned him into some kind of geek, because now he was excited about finding a good book to read instead of doing something else.

A few students dislike the portfolio as a whole, whereas others enjoy every moment. Many in both of these groups have produced pieces that astonish me with their originality and literary merit. Not one student has walked away from this project without commenting in the final reflection how much he or she learned, whether the project as a whole was enjoyed or not. Each trimester the Novel Portfolio Project assignments are guided by what I learn from the previous students—their likes and dislikes, challenges and defeats, expectations and achievements. I work with the class to promote a level of honest and open conversation that helps both the students and me to progress in our understanding of literature and of one another. This project has revealed to me how well students are able to learn when given empowering opportunities to do so.

References

Stoddart, P., Fitzgerald, K., & Ruffus, S. (2001). *The Eisenhower portfolio project: Using portfolios to improve teaching, assessment and student writing across the curriculum* [On-line]. Available: http://www.studentportfolios.org.

Utah State Office of Education (USOE) and Utah State Office of Higher Education (USHE). (1999). *Language Arts Core Curriculum for Utah, Grades 7-11* [On-line]. Available: http://www.uen.org/core/languagearts/index.html.

17

Poetic Drama: Breathing Life Into Poems and Poets

Carol F. Bender

I am an understudy. This may sound odd coming from a teacher, because we are usually center stage, right? That's what I used to think, but after one particularly enlightening classroom experience, I began to alter my thinking. Now I find that often class runs better when I'm not a principal player or even the director. I have never aspired to be an actor, so losing that status was not difficult. In fact, it was a relief. But I must admit that I like to see things run smoothly, so giving up my director's chair has not been entirely easy.

Aware of the traditional classroom dynamic—teacher as compulsive talker, student as compelled listener—I watched the last 2 decades of the 20th century sustain a good many challenges and counterchallenges to typical classroom language structures. Avoiding the disempowerment of students at the small midwestern school where I teach has required me to be responsible in the ways I speak, to be cognizant of my tendency to dominate conversation, and to ensure that students have the resources to turn their language into learning. This awareness has led to my making students' language experiences central to the classroom and to problematizing structures that ascribe expertise exclusively to teachers. Like other teachers at the secondary and college level, I strive to make connections between students' knowledge and their language practice in the classroom. This practice works best when it is purposeful and linked to authentic desires to communicate with real audiences, for in this way learners experience the risks and benefits of language decisions.

Using Poetic Drama

One form of real language experience that works for me and my students is poetic drama, which, as James Britton (1993) reminds us in *Literature in Its Place*, has the "potential to break free from habitual thought and patterns of behavior" (p. 19) and in so doing to create in the participants a true and human connection. In England, dramatic activity features prominently in secondary schools, whereas in America the educational importance of such activity has found slightly less support. Britton speculates that in England "personally accessible forms of dramatic activity" owe to the "historical continuity from early religious drama through Shakespearean times to the present day theater" (p. 19). He maintains, however, and I concur, that high school students on both sides of the Atlantic may be especially receptive to dramatic interpretation or improvisation for its potential both to individualize and to communalize the educational experience.

In his essay "Poetic Discourse: Can You Hear What I Mean?" Britton (1993) reflects upon the ways that poetry creates "contemplative reflections upon experience" (p. 54). The reflections, though not analytic in nature, tend to be closely linked to reenactment. That is, as listeners of poetry hear imagined experiences or others' experiences, they engage in a kind of rehearsal that Britton calls "virtual reenactment" (p. 55), a spontaneous contemplation of another world and time, easily distinguishable and distinct from day-to-day experiences. According to Susanne Langer, poetry will produce no real impact unless "the very first words of the poem effect the break with the reader's actual environment" (cited in Britton, p. 55). The shift from "actual" to "virtual" environment is primarily a response to the spoken word rather than to written language. In the classroom it is possible to create such an environment through a collective dramatic enterprise that takes hold of the students and moves them out of their own skins into somebody else's. Such a process asks them to call upon knowledge newly acquired, perhaps acquired specifically for the enactment and thus having the potential to extend the range and complexity of the works explored. Combining these ideas about drama and poetry has produced for me several creative class sessions in which I moved from center stage to the role of seldomly seen understudy.

The occurrence that made me retool my course is one that most teachers—secondary or not—will understand. That it happened in a university classroom does not undercut its validity for secondary school teachers. I can say that with confidence, because I have 7 years of teaching experience in Iowa and Michigan, and I know what life is like "on the front lines." For many recent years I have taught English 130: Introduction to Poetry. Classes usually consist of an equal number of 18- to 21-year-old male and female students, ranging from those seriously interested in English to those satisfying general education requirements. Class size varies from 25–35 students, on the average. Several years ago, after reading the end-of-semester teaching evaluations, I was dismayed to see comments about how "boring" the course had been. Boring! I was hurt. For me the evaluations constituted a bad review of my performance, and not just one performance, either. These critics were assessing several "shows" a week for an entire semester. Defensively I found myself wondering how *they* would like being "on stage." This question dogged me as I began organizing materials for the following year.

Revamping the Course

After much thought, I decided to revamp the poetry course, to change it from a one-woman performance to a variety show. Although I had no idea how this strategy would work, I did know one thing: It would reduce my time on stage. So on the first day of class, I divided students into six groups and gave them the following instructions: "This semester your group will be responsible for selecting one poet for presentation to the class. Each member of the group must take part, and you will have one 50-minute class period for the performance." I admit, my directorial skills were pathetically thin, but actually I wanted students to experience the challenge of presenting poets and their works in an engaging and informative way, and I wanted them to make their own language decisions.

The first group took a traditional poet, Edgar Allan Poe, and a standard approach. On the day of their presentation they arranged six desks across the front of the room. Students then read poems and spoke briefly about one aspect of Poe's life or work. From my place in the back, I looked around to gauge the critics' response. I had to agree—pretty boring. That day I could have resumed my center-stage role with little resistance. I didn't know, however, that it would be my last opportunity for the starring role.

Creative Student Performance

Two weeks later the second group was ready for its presentation. I got to class promptly at 9:30 a.m. to find the windowless classroom totally dark. I could hear the muffled sound of bongo drums being played softly, and as my eyes became accustomed to the darkness, I could see the entire class sitting quietly on the floor in a huge circle. Where were the desks? What was happening? Dumping my books and papers into the nearest corner, I eased myself into a space between two students. No one spoke. In the middle of the circle sat five students dressed in black, some wearing beads and sandals.

As they lit several candles, suddenly a bearded young man wearing sunglasses and a bandanna stopped drumming and spoke solemnly, "I am Allen Ginsberg, and these are my friends." He proceeded to introduce Jack Kerouac, Gregory Corso, William Burroughs, and Lawrence Ferlinghetti, all writers from the Beat generation. For the next hour these five students, never once breaking character, entertained and educated us about the life and writing of each of the best-known Beat poets.

"Ginsberg" told us about his childhood, his frustrations as a young writer, and the inspiration he received from literary figures who had preceded him. He read some of his poems and explained their meaning. He invited us to join hands and chant poems with him. His friends told of their travels, protests, alternative lifestyles, and writing. The class sat cross-legged, spellbound, absorbing this unique learning experience.

The 50 minutes flew by, and when it was over I found my books and slowly filed out of the dark room with the others. They were quiet, savoring the memory, reflecting on all they had learned. I was sincerely moved by the performance and impressed at how much the students' acting and role-playing had enriched the class. Each writer had been thoroughly researched, each work carefully selected, yet the total enactment had seemed like a casual gathering, the shift from actual to virtual environment accomplished seamlessly. These six students, breathing life into the poems and the poets, took us to another place and time. Since then I have added slightly more substance to my directorial instructions and broadened the scope of the assignment to occasionally include more than one poet. This decision arose in part from the Beat performance, in which the rich context of other writers and cultural influences added significantly to our understanding of Ginsberg.

The second most memorable enactment was on the larger topic of South American poets. Students in this group transformed the classroom into a fiesta complete with refreshments, a piñata, and lively music. The guests of honor were well-known poets who had gathered to celebrate their successes and read from their works. In my role as party-goer (and understudy), I was blindfolded and asked to break the piñata, much to the delight of students who watched as I wildly jabbed the air. The mood was festive, the hour filled with poetry readings and toasts. Just as we thought the celebration was ending, we were shocked and saddened by the unexpected "assassination" of one of the poets. Because we had grown to love his socially and politically compelling poems, his sudden death provided an especially poignant reminder of the power of language and the dangers of censorship. The party, and hence the class, ended in disbelief and sadness.

Impact on the Course

I must admit that over the years not all of the dramatizations have been as elaborate or memorable, but I'd venture to say that for the students participating (and for those watching), each enactment has left more impact than any typical day-to-day discussion and/or lecture. Now when I plan my poetry course, I carefully weave in poetic drama. To help students create a "virtual" environment through a collective dramatization, I give them a handout with the following ground rules:

> Your group has selected a general topic or a particular poet for research and performance. You will have 50 minutes to present the fruits of your labors. You may dramatize in any way you choose. Try to be creative and informational. Each member of the group will participate. Please have handouts of a few poems for the entire class so that we have something to take away with us from your presentation. You may include specific authors and poems in your performance as well as general information and reviews of critics, if appropriate. The content and division of tasks is at the discretion of your group. Today be sure to exchange phone numbers and perhaps set up a meeting time to start planning. I will be happy to run off copies of any handouts if you get them to me well ahead of class time. Please have two goals in mind for your 50 minutes: (1) clear, insightful information, and (2) entertaining format. Make good use of the library for your research. Good luck!

I try to schedule the performances about 2 weeks apart, both to break up class routine and to give students time to savor and reflect upon one enactment before experiencing another.

Groups, which vary in size from four to six students depending on class size, select their poet and their presentation date at the beginning of the semester. Each group is responsible for one entire class period. If they need printed handouts or media equipment, I ask that they let me know in advance so I can help to secure appropriate materials. Generally groups leave time for class discussion and questions, but, as the two examples here indicate, sometimes performers begin and end in character. If so, we try to allot time at the beginning of the next class period for reflection. Students are expected to have thoroughly researched the poet(s) and thus are able to answer most student questions after the dramatization.

Grading Performance

Grading performance is perhaps the most difficult aspect of this assignment. As a follow-up I give a narrative evaluation, highlighting moments that worked especially well and noting any gaps or any questions I may have. I try not to take too many notes during a performance but instead listen and participate in the same way as other audience members. However, I do try to write the evaluation soon after class so that I don't forget important points, and I bring it with me to the next class. Each group member gets a copy of the narrative assessment with the group's collective grade. The audience is quick to recognize a good dramatic presentation for its creativity as well as the careful research that preceded the performance. As I suggest in the assignment handout, audiences want both entertainment and enlightenment, and a good balance of both will send them away feeling better for having experienced the performance.

My evaluation of the South American dramatization was as follows:

> What a tough act to follow! Your performance was excellent. I think you should take it on the road, to other schools in the area! It would help students to truly enjoy poetry! It was very clever to focus your presentation around the life of one writer, Lorca. It points out the effect writers have on one another and the importance of knowing how poems can be (and are) connected in many ways. The presentation, by its very nature, highlighted the way South American poetry is intertwined with conflict and oppression. You certainly chose wonderful writers—many award-winning poets. The fiesta program was excellent, chronicling the writers' important achievements and books for us. Everything went like clockwork to create one of the smoothest and best presentations I have ever had in my class! Bravo! Grade: A

Students at my small school seem to enjoy group work such as this, and generally they pull their weight, contributing fairly to a collective grade. Occasionally I do get complaints from some who believe that they have done more than their share. To address this equity problem, I ask each student to fill out an evaluation of the project at its completion (Appendix 17-A). The opportunity to reflect on their group's language decisions and participation is important not only for those who worked hard but also for those who could have done more. Such reflection fosters critical thinking about successful language communities and how they operate. Although it is too late to effect a change in grade for this assignment, the reflective writing prompts them to consider how they will participate collaboratively in the future, thus extending the learning experience beyond this particular class. Their comments also prove helpful as I tinker with the structure of the assignment for the following year.

Benefits for Students

Aside from being educational and entertaining, poetic dramatization has additional benefits for students. English education researchers say that the work of teachers is to help build a discourse community wherein students take the initiative and become responsible partners in their learning. "Students teaching students" is one way to build community. Identifying objectives, deciding on the best techniques to attain them, inventing enlightening and educational presentations, and conveying the material clearly enables students to be responsible learners. Since the Ginsberg dramatization, I have had a number of good performances. Each has been unique. They are created collaboratively with little direction from me. Yet I am always there, ready to go on stage—as an understudy, I guess you could say. So far though, they haven't needed me. Somehow, I think that's really better.

Appendix 17-A: Reflections

Collaborative Poetic Dramatization

Name _____

1. Think for a moment about your own learning in this process. What did you learn about the poets and their works and, perhaps more important, about the process of working collaboratively?
2. Did you understand the process, what was expected of you, and how to proceed with the assignment? If you could redesign this collaborative assignment (and still keep it as a collaboration), what would you do differently? Explain.
3. Assess your own ability and responsibility for group work such as this. What did you do especially well? What were your own shortcomings? If you had another project such as this for another class, what would you do differently or better?
4. Now evaluate the work of your group members. Who contributed what? Was it fair? Did everyone carry equal weight? If not, why not? How could group dynamics be improved so that a good presentation can be produced?

References

Britton, James. (1993). *Literature in its place*. London: Cassell Educational Limited.

18

Powerful Poetry: Team Teaching Across the Disciplines

Annette McGrew and Ginny Dochety

Recently, high schools across the nation have been looking closely at how they can form increasing numbers of curricular connections. They have particularly focused on how traditional curricula in the arts and sciences can collaborate with vocational subjects to respond to the technological advances in business and industry. As a result, many local school systems are implementing Vocational Integration Programs whose goal is to improve the quality of the work force while equipping a wider range of students for greater successes. In such programs, teachers of traditional academic subjects work with vocational instructors to design and teach lessons that utilize academic skills within the context of real-world activities.

As a Competency English and English I teacher, I collaborated with Ginny, a keyboarding applications teacher at West Greene High School, to create Powerful Poetry, a summative activity that requires freshmen in high school to use techniques of analyzing poetry within a research project and to create a PowerPoint presentation based on their research. Our goal was to pair students from Ginny's class, who had been instructed in the basics of PowerPoint, with students from my class, who had received instruction in techniques of analyzing poetry. Both classes worked together in the school's computer lab to complete this project. Each team was assigned a poet whose work was studied during the poetry unit. Their task was to use Internet resources to compile a brief biography of the poet and to select a poem other than the ones that were examined in class. The English student and keyboarding applications student cooperatively used techniques for analyzing poetry to explicate their chosen poem. When their research and analysis was complete, the keyboarding applications student guided the English student in the creation of a PowerPoint presentation. Finally, the English student made the presentation to his or her classmates.

Planning the Lesson

This lesson required significant planning, both individually and jointly, for successful implementation. The first step was to identify poets for whom sufficient information was available using reputable Web sites. After identifying 30 suitable poets, I (Annette) designed an assignment sheet (Appendix 18-A). I assigned students from my class to a poet, and then collaborated with Ginny to pair strong students with weaker ones and to avoid known personality conflicts. We also avoided pairing friends in order to provide the students with experience working with strangers or acquaintances, thereby simulating actual working conditions.

The actual assignment contains a description of the specific task, including time guidelines and performance objectives that students were expected to meet (Appendix 18-B). When making the assignment, I gave a copy of everything I had prepared to each student. Ginny did the same for her students (Appendix 18-C). From the beginning, each student worked with two documents: the basic guidelines for the assignment and two scoring rubrics that clarified expectations of student performance. Ginny's students did the same (Appendix 18-D). Expectations and approaches to success with the assignment were thus made clear to all students from the outset. Using the same format for assignments in both classes added to the clarity.

During my preparation, I found the Web site of the Academy of American Poets (www.poets.org) to be extremely useful. This extensive resource provides basic biographical information about numerous poets as well as the texts of selected poems for each one. My students used this Web site as a focal point for their research. (Note: Though containing neither pornographic nor scatological material, some of the poetry showcased at this site does contain adult themes. As with all other teaching materials, the site should be reviewed prior to student use.)

Teachers everywhere will find this project to be an effective use of class time because it accomplishes so much in a compressed time. It contributes to the mastery of numerous learning expectations in each of the language arts content areas: writing, reading, viewing and representing, and speaking and listening. All are easy to coordinate with state core curricula.

Learning and Adjusting

The classes spent three class periods in the computer lab. The total time was 4.5 hours, or approximately 1 week for teachers with 50-minute classes. Students worked the entire first day collecting information and selecting a poem. They spent the remaining time experimenting with the graphic capabilities of PowerPoint. While the students were in the lab, both teachers constantly monitored the students' progress and assisted them as needed.

Overall, we were impressed by the creativity of the graphic effects that our students used. All of them experimented with design templates before choosing the background for their presentation. Most students learned how to save a graphic from an Internet Web site as an image file and import that image into their presentation. Many of the students used the animation and sound options for their presentation; some enjoyed enhancing their presentations with these effects, whereas others learned that the inappropriate or excessive use of such effects can be extremely annoying. A few students created custom backgrounds for their presentations. One even imported music from a CD to use as background atmosphere throughout his presentation.

Theoretically, students from the keyboarding applications class would provide technical knowledge about creating a PowerPoint presentation, whereas the English student provided academic knowledge about poetry. However, this was not always the case. Some of the English students had a higher degree of mastery of PowerPoint than their partners from keyboarding applications. Conversely, a few of the keyboarding applications students were more proficient at poetry analysis than their English I partners and offered considerable insight into thematic meaning and symbolic interpretation. The mutual benefits of these new partnerships proved immensely gratifying to our students, as well as to both of us.

Overall, the students were so excited about access to the computer lab and the opportunity to play with the capabilities of PowerPoint that they initially deemphasized the analysis of the poetry. For this reason, our first try did not completely satisfy me (Annette) that their poetry examinations represented their best efforts. Most of their analyses focused on basic form, particularly rhyme scheme. However, a few students offered insightful thematic interpretation and accurately assessed symbolic representations. I believed that my students could be encouraged to focus more on poetic analysis if Ginny and I reorganized the assignment into two parts: first the research component and then the presentation component. Restructuring the assignment for greater expectations, we thought, would create a deeper, more satisfying engagement for our students and ourselves. When we used this assignment subsequently, we developed a template leading the students to focus in a more complex way on the various tools of poets. The results were much better when students began with a solid analysis of the poems.

Reflections on Student Learning

The first time this project was completed, the students emphasized the knowledge of PowerPoint that they had acquired. Although I had told them to use at least 35-point font, some of them used smaller fonts to get more on the screen. They expressed shock when a slide that was perfectly legible on the computer monitor was too small to read on the 36-inch-screen TV used for presentation to the class. Another revelation occurred when images that had been beautiful on the monitor in the lab were so distorted that they were illegible during the TV presentation.

After being taught how to find the rhyme scheme of the poem, one student who had previously claimed that she was not capable of writing a rhyme scheme decided that it was easy. Others stated that they did not understand poetic devices until they were asked to use their definitions to find examples of them in their poems. Several times, as students successfully identified examples of figurative language, they would exclaim, "*That's* what that is" or "I've always *wondered* what that is."

Authentic Assessment

This project provided a perfect opportunity for authentic assessment, because I could challenge my verbally gifted students without intimidating students whose aptitudes lie outside traditional academic pursuits. In fact, many of the nonverbal students were the most proficient with the technical aspects of creating the presentation *and* the most creative with the use of special effects and graphics. All students found, to their surprise, that their teammates' skills made them rethink their previous narrow parameters for "gifted" and "vocational." They realized that they could learn a great deal from one another.

The value of this assignment lies not just in what our students learned about poetry or about PowerPoint. It requires every student to work cooperatively with another person, encourages creativity and critical thought, and forces each person to summon up the poise to make a presentation to a group. Many students realized their errors in presentation style even as they were making their presentations; therefore, they also taught themselves. The effectiveness of this project would be enhanced by requiring a similar presentation about a different topic, thereby reinforcing the students' learning by allowing them to apply it to a similar situation. When I teach this lesson in the future, I plan to use it to introduce the technology involved, then develop a similar project for use with a short story unit.

The Teamwork Aspect

Ginny was excited about working on this project from the beginning. As a vocational teacher, she has often found it very difficult to break into the academic teacher's realm. She believes that school systems, however unintentionally, promote this separation with their tendency to divide students both academically and spatially. This project brought both the teachers and the students together. "It was clear from the start that the students enjoyed the process," Ginny said. "With the instructions clearly given, the students went right to work."

One additional benefit of the project came as a result of our particular setting. Our students worked in the computer lab located in the school's library. Ginny reports that the librarian, who observed the students' work habits day in and day out, was amazed at the cooperative efforts all of the students displayed. There were no discipline problems from the two-person teams during the unit. Keyboarding students quickly oriented the English students to the Internet's Web browsers. Teams then worked to obtain the required information for the poetry unit, and together each team created its PowerPoint presentation. According to our librarian, teams worked diligently and seemed to enjoy the time spent in the lab. Ginny adds, "My keyboarding students all stated that they enjoyed the interaction and looked forward to similar projects in the future." The English students and Annette agree wholeheartedly. Not only did they learn both literature and technology, they learned valuable life skills that will last them a lifetime.

Appendix 18-A. Powerful Poetry Assignment Sheet

Poet	2nd English	2nd Keyboarding	4th English	4th Keyboarding
Maya Angelou				
Philip Booth				
Gwendolyn Brooks				
Robert Burns				
Lewis Carroll				
e.e. cummings				
Emily Dickinson				
Paul Laurence Dunbar				
Robert Francis				
Robert Frost				
Nikki Giovanni				
Robert Herrick				
Langston Hughes				
Eve Merriam				
Edna St. Vincent Millay				
N. Scott Momaday				
Gordon Parks				
Sylvia Plath				
Edgar Allan Poe				
Theodore Roethke				
Carl Sandburg				
William Shakespeare				
James Still				
Ernest Lawrence Thayer				
Alice Walker				
Walt Whitman				
William Wordsworth				
Richard Wright				
Elinor Wylie				
William Butler Yeats				

Appendix 18-B. Powerful Poetry Presentation

Presentation Requirements

Time: 5–10 minutes

Content:

- Basic biographical information about the poet
- Significant events in life of poet
- Honors, awards, achievements of poet
- List of published works by poet
- One poem that has not yet been discussed in class
- Literary analysis of poem: theme, speaker, rhyme scheme, rhythm, use of figurative language, etc.

Format:

- Presenters must use Microsoft PowerPoint.
- Text should be presented using 35-point (or larger) font.
- Slides should include background and appropriate graphics in addition to speaker's notes.
- The slide(s) presenting the poem should contain an audio clip of either the poet reading the poem or music that complements the mood of the poem.
- Slide show should be creatively but tastefully animated.
- Slide show should incorporate at least one example of word art.

Appendix 18-C. Keyboarding Applications

Integrated Learning Project With English Class

Expectations of keyboarding applications students are as follows:

- Assist English student with Internet research.
- Assist English student in creating a PowerPoint presentation from research gathered.
- Demonstrate respectful behavior to partner.
- Demonstrate patience to partner while helping with searches and presentation.

Appendix 18-D. Keyboarding Applications Students' Criteria

Keyboarding Applications Students' Criteria	Level 1 Meets few criteria	Level 2 Meets some criteria	Level 3 Meets all criteria
Research poet and prepare a PowerPoint presentation with partner.			
Make an accurate and thorough presentation.			
Produce a final project.			
Work together to accomplish a well-defined goal.			
Use appropriate integrated technology.			

19

Collaborative Nonfiction Unit: *Freedom's Children* and the Civil Rights Movement

Terri Rodriguez

Segregation had legally ended more than 40 years before I moved to Georgia to teach in a public high school. However, as I lived and worked in Georgia, it was clear that, like many areas in both the North and the South, de facto segregation still existed. The laws had changed, and on the surface many improvements had been made, but the law cannot immediately change people's opinions and attitudes. Only education can do that. Because people typically fear what they do not know or understand, educating students about racial inequalities, past and present, is perhaps the best way to arm them with the knowledge to fight racial prejudice.

Freedom's Children and the Civil Rights Movement

The unit I describe in this chapter on the Civil Rights Movement originated in Georgia in celebration of Black History Month. I have found that wherever I have taught since 1995—in public or private schools, in the North or South, and regardless of the ethnicity of the students—there is a need to teach the history of the Civil Rights Movement and the history of race relations in our country. All students need to become aware of the cultural assumptions passed on to them by their parents, grandparents, and the larger culture in which they are raised. This point was further reinforced to me by one of my students, who, after being disciplined for inappropriate classroom behavior, asked, "It's because I'm Black, right?" Some might argue that she was using race as an excuse to shift the blame to me, her White teacher. Call me naive, but until that moment it had not occurred to me that behavior and discipline might be perceived as connected to race.

Even though it can be a touchy subject, racism is a topic that students want to confront; the following unit gives them ample opportunity and background readings to do just that. The basis for the unit is *Freedom's Children* by Ellen Levine

(1993). *Freedom's Children* describes the struggles to achieve racial equality experienced by people who participated in the Civil Rights Movement.

For this unit, I usually team-teach with a social studies teacher. The social studies teacher provides background information on court cases, legal issues, and the freedoms protected by the Constitution of the United States. The social studies teacher also shows documentary videos to give students a realistic picture of the Civil Rights Movement and race relations prior to it. The social studies teacher and I trade students three to four times during the unit. He or she tests my students on their factual knowledge about the Civil Rights Movement. (The grade, however, counts for my class.) Finally, the social studies class serves as an authentic audience for my classes' final projects. Although this unit on the Civil Rights Movement grew out of a requirement to teach Black history in February, this unit has evolved into a staple of my ninth-grade nonfiction unit—taught throughout the year, rather than in "ghetto" fashion that limits a focus on Black history to one month. The relevance and timeliness of this study have made it a favorite with my students. Every year, students come to me with new videos, poems, songs, and books to supplement our examination of the Civil Rights Movement.

Forced-Choice Activity

While the social studies teacher is working with my students, I work with the social studies teacher's students to develop writing skills related to nonfiction. I assign some of the same writing activities that my own students work on throughout the unit, including a newspaper editorial genre and a comparison-and-contrast essay. One successful activity to prepare students to write editorials is called "Agree/Disagree." Students are given a controversial statement like "Teachers in public schools should be allowed to post the Ten Commandments in their classrooms." (Any topic that is relevant and "hot" will work for this activity.) Students stand up and move to one side of the room if they agree with the statement, or to the other side if they disagree. They also prepare to give one reason supporting their opinion. As students share their opinions and reasons, others see that there are many different sides to an issue. We examine several examples of editorials and discuss editorial style; then each student writes an editorial essay based on issues we discussed during our study of the Civil Rights Movement.

Comparison-and-Contrast Activity

We also listen to Dr. Martin Luther King, Jr.'s "I Have a Dream" speech and to an excerpt from Chief Joseph's address, "An Indian's Views of Indian Affairs." We discuss different methods of comparing or contrasting the speeches, and the students write an essay developing their ideas. Although I comment on the essays and give the social studies teacher's class the time they need to work through the writing process, the final grade on the project counts as part of their social studies grade, just as my students' grades from the social studies class count in my class.

Using Films and Documentaries

Film can be a powerful tool in the literature classroom to entice students into understanding and relating to literature. The 1998 documentary *KKK: A Secret History*, produced by Arts & Entertainment and the History Channel, immediately engages students. Although a discussion of the Ku Klux Klan stirs up strong feelings, I believe that open dialogue and education are the keys to effecting positive change. Another movie that students enjoy is the recent film *Remember the Titans* (2001), in which a Black football coach struggles to overcome the racial prejudices of a small-town community.

My favorite way to introduce the Civil Rights Movement unit is to show the video *The Long Walk Home* (1990), starring Whoopi Goldberg and Sissy Spacek. It is a powerful film dramatizing the Montgomery bus boycott of 1955–1956, which was the key event launching the Civil Rights Movement and Martin Luther King, Jr.'s involvement with it. Because there is some violence and racist language, it is important to discuss the use of racial slurs both historically and in our own time. Students become "film critics" and write a review to share with small groups of their peers. We discuss specific questions like "What did you think motivated the main characters?" and "How did the setting contribute to the overall effect of the movie?" and "Can you equate what happened in Montgomery to anything that is happening today?" Students use details from the film to support their opinions. Later, as we read the chapter about the Montgomery bus boycott in *Freedom's Children*, students are already familiar with it. We discuss the significance of 15-year-old Claudette Colvin's contribution as one of the first Blacks to be arrested for refusing to give up her seat to a White passenger. My students relate to those interviewed in the book because they, too, often rebel and push the limits of authority. The film immerses students in the setting and the powerful emotions of the time period.

Interview: Making the Past Real

Freedom's Children can also be supplemented with pieces from the nonfiction unit "Collection 5: We Remember" (Probst & Vacca, 2003). We read selections from the following list and discuss the differences between biography and autobiography, as well as interviewing techniques:

"The Struggle to Be an All-American Girl" (memoir) by Elizabeth Wong

"Not Much of Me" (autobiography) by Abraham Lincoln

"With a Task Before Me" (speech) by Abraham Lincoln

"When I Lay My Burden Down" from *I Know Why the Caged Bird Sings* (autobiography) by Maya Angelou

"Choice: A Tribute to Dr. Martin Luther King" (speech) by Alice Walker

"The Talk" (essay) by Gary Soto

"Ballad of Birmingham" (ballad) by Dudley Randall

Next I ask students to interview friends and family members who lived through the Civil Rights Movement. When I taught in Georgia, the interviewees were often adults who as children had integrated the local schools. Whether the interviewees were directly involved in desegregation or not, my students came back to class with some interesting anecdotes. For many of my students, the interview was the first time they had ever discussed the movement or the idea of racial inequality with their parents, grandparents, aunts, uncles, or friends. In this way, Levine's (1993) book can spark an important dialogue across generations.

Choral Reading: "The Ballad of Birmingham"

Another activity I often use is to involve the entire class in a choral reading of "The Ballad of Birmingham," a poem by Dudley Randall (1985) about the 1963 bombing of the Sixteenth Street Baptist Church in Birmingham, Alabama. I divide the students into groups and ask them to present a choral reading of the poem to the class. We discuss different effects, like using several voices in repeated lines or words for emphasis, or taking advantage of the differences in male and female voices. However they choose to read the poem, I emphasize to the groups that a choral reading means that everyone participates in some way. It is up to them to decide what kind of effect they want to have on the audience, then to produce a reading that creates that effect. Even though the class hears the same poem several times (an actual benefit from the teacher's point of view), they appreciate and enjoy the different interpretations.

Reading *Freedom's Children*

The most important activity is, of course, reading *Freedom's Children*. My goal is for students to read, enjoy, and relate to this collection of essays. To this end, I use the activities suggested above throughout the reading as a way to "spice" things up. Each activity can be paired with the chapter in the book to which it relates: It may be used before, as a prereading activity; during, as formative assessment; or after, as a summative assessment and/or reinforcement. Journal writing is also an essential part of this unit. Students respond to the following prompts that ask them to relate some aspect or theme of the Civil Rights Movement unit to their own experience:

1. Describe a time when you risked something important in order to stand up for something you believe in, or describe something you believe in for which you would risk something important.
2. Recall a time when you were afraid. Describe your experience.
3. Describe a time when you felt humiliated or when someone put you down in some way.

4. Do you think prejudice would end in the world if people were color blind? Why or why not?
5. Describe your vision of a "perfect" world. How might your ideas be achieved?

To encourage active reading, I also assign study guide questions for each chapter (Appendix 19-A). We read some chapters together in class; others are assigned as homework. I often begin each class session with a quiz over the previous lesson's reading assignment. I also give a final exam that includes true-false questions from previous quizzes and study guides, as well as open response questions, which prompt students to form and support an opinion about what they have read.

Final Project: Rationale and Assessment

For the final project I give the students the following choice of activities:
1. List at least three things you learned about Martin Luther King, Jr. and the Civil Rights Movement. Why do you think Dr. King is still considered a great man today?
2. Which part of the book affected you the most? Summarize that part, then tell what you felt and why.
3. How would you have reacted if you had been alive during the Civil Rights Movement? Describe what you think your actions, thoughts, and feelings would have been.
4. Choose a current issue in which social justice is a problem. Explain what needs to be done to address the social issue. How do you think you could help the people who are the direct victims of social injustice?

Students choose from three group projects with the following instructions:

> Choose a project from the following ideas for your group to present to the class. Each group member must participate equally in the presentation. You will receive an individual as well as a group grade. Presentations should be 5–10 minutes in length. Turn in a typed copy of your lines or dialogue with one copy for each member of the group.
>
> *Talk Show:* One person will host his or her very own live talk show! You have invited guests (characters from *Freedom's Children*) to come on your show and discuss their experiences as recorded in Levine's book. Prepare questions and answers, and be prepared for questions and discussion from your audience. Use props and costumes to enhance your performance. [Sample in Appendix 19-B]
>
> *Demonstration or sit-in:* Choose an incident from the book to reenact for the class. Using the actual words of the characters in *Freedom's Children*, act out an important or vivid scene. Choose a narrator to introduce your scene and use props and costumes to enhance your performance.
>
> *Oral Report:* Each member of the group will summarize a section of the chapter that you have chosen to present to the class. Be sure to include important details like names and dates when retelling the class

about your section. Each group member should prepare a visual aid to capture the audience's attention.

The social studies class makes a wonderful audience, because they too have studied the material and are aware of the issues presented in the book. The genuine interest and applause of their peers is one of the greatest rewards for my students. Because this activity is the culminating activity for the combined English and social studies unit on the Civil Rights Movement, there is often a partylike, celebratory atmosphere. Of course, this activity is also one of the students' favorites because they get to act. The costumes, the props, and the chance to do a live talk show or reenactment sparks positive creative energy in the students. The greatest reward for me, however, is that I watch the students learn and grow as they bring a piece of literature and a period of history to life.

Assessing the final projects is relatively easy. I choose four criteria: participation, performance, costumes and props, and typed dialogue or lines. Each student receives points for each of the four categories individually, then each student receives points for the group's performance as a whole based on the same categories.

This unit has been highly successful in many different classrooms. Although I began teaching in a public school in Georgia, I carried the Civil Rights Movement unit with me to a seventh-grade classroom at a mostly white private school in Kentucky and to a ninth-grade classroom in an integrated school in rural Kentucky. My students have always shown tremendous interest in the Civil Rights Movement and the topic of racism. I think that no matter where students live in the world, they are aware of the racial and cultural inequalities that exist in human societies. In my new teaching adventure in Puerto Rico, I have also carried the Civil Rights Movement unit with me. I may expand or adjust the unit by incorporating films, songs, poems, or other pieces of literature that address specific issues of racial or cultural inequality in Puerto Rico, but I think that Dr. Martin Luther King, Jr.'s message and his appeal are universal.

The South was painfully desegregated only a generation ago. Sadly, many adults shy away from this touchy subject, but I have found that it is one that students want to discuss. What better forum for discussion than the literature and social studies classrooms? The subject of racial inequality will continue to haunt us until individual attitudes and opinions are changed. The law can't address opinions; only education can do that. However, if we don't teach young people the facts about the Civil Rights Movement and the continuing racial inequalities in our society, they are doomed to repeat the wrongs of the past. Ellen Levine's *Freedom's Children* is a timely piece of literature with the power to affect our future positively if we use it wisely.

Collaborative Nonfiction Unit

Appendix 19-A: Study Guide for Freedom's Children

Chapter 1. Experiences of Segregation
1. Briefly describe, in your own words, the experiences of each of the following people:
   A. Ben Chaney
   B. Gwendolyn Patton
   C. James Roberson
   D. Fred Shuttlesworth, Jr.
   E. Roy DeBerry
   F. Thelma Eubanks
   G. Judy Tarver
   H. Myrna Carter
   I. Pat Shuttlesworth
   J. Ricky Shuttlesworth
   K. Larry Russell
2. Name some of the different emotions experienced by these people:
3. Response Journal: Write a paragraph describing your thoughts and feelings about this chapter.

Chapter 2. The Montgomery Bus Boycott and the Beginning of the Movement
1. What was the Montgomery Bus Boycott?
2. How was the arrest of Rosa Parks related to the boycott?
3. Who was Claudette Colvin? What did she do?
4. Briefly describe the experiences of the following people:
   A. Joseph Lacey
   B. Fred Taylor
   C. Princella Howard
   D. Gwendolyn Patton
5. Response Journal: Write a paragraph describing your thoughts and feelings about this chapter.

Chapter 3. Different Classrooms: Segregation and Integration in the Schools
1. What was *Brown vs. Board of Education*?
2. What was the Southern Manifesto?
3. In what ways did segregated schools differ?
4. Briefly describe the experiences of the following people:

A. Myrna Carter
   B. Larry Russell
   C. Roy DeBerry
   D. Fred Taylor
   E. Ricky Shuttlesworth
   F. Pat Shuttlesworth
   G. Fred Shuttlesworth, Jr.
   H. James Roberson
   I. Ernest Green
   J. Arlam Carr
   K. Delores Boyd
   L. Thelma Eubanks
5. Response Journal: Write a paragraph describing your thoughts and feelings about this chapter.

Chapter 4. Sit-Ins, Freedom Rides, and Other Protests
1. What was a nickname for the city of Birmingham in 1956?
2. Who was "Bull" Connor and what did he do?
3. What is a sit-in? What is a freedom ride?
4. Briefly describe the experiences of the following people:
   A. Frances Foster
   B. James Roberson
   C. Barbara Howard
   D. Ricky Shuttlesworth
   E. Gladis Williams
   F. Joseph Lacy
   G. Gwendolyn Patton
5. Response Journal: Write a paragraph describing your thoughts and feelings about this chapter.

Chapter 5. The Children's Crusade
1. What happened in Birmingham in April and May of 1963?
2. Why were these events later called "The Children's Crusade"?
3. Briefly describe the experiences of the following people:
   A. Audrey Faye Hendricks
   B. Judy Tarver
   C. Bernita Roberson
   D. Larry Russell
   E. Mary Gadson

F. Myrna Carter
4. What was the March on Washington?
5. What was the Sunday School Bombing?
6. Response Journal: Write a paragraph describing your thoughts and feelings about this chapter.

Chapter 6. The Closed Society: Mississippi and Freedom Summer

1. What is a *closed society*?
2. Why did Mississippi stand out for its brutal enforcement of segregation? (Describe several incidents that occurred there in the 1950s.)
3. What were the four major civil rights groups? What group did they form together? (Give both the acronym and the full name—e.g., NAACP – National Association for the Advancement of Colored People.)
4. Briefly describe the experiences of the following people:
   Larry Martin
   Ben Chaney
   John Steele
   Euvester Simpson
   Roy DeBerry
5. Response Journal: Write a paragraph describing your thoughts and feelings about this chapter.

Chapter 7. Bloody Sunday and the Selma Movement

1. To where did the civil rights battleground move in 1965? Why?
2. Describe the incident known as Bloody Sunday.
3. Briefly describe the experiences of the following people:
   Sheyann Webb
   Jawana Jackson
   Towanner Hinkle
4. What happened on April 4, 1968, in Memphis?
5. How did young southern Blacks describe their feelings at the time?
6. Response Journal: Write a paragraph describing your thoughts and feelings about this chapter.

Appendix 19-B. Sample Talk Show

Announcer: From Birmingham, Alabama, this is the *Liz Watson Show*!

Liz: This is the *Liz Watson Show* and I'm your host, Liz Watson. Our topic for today is "Keeping Our Schools Segregated." [*Crowd cheers.*] Today we have a very special show for you. Our first guest came all the way from Montgomery, Alabama. He is a 17-year-old high school student at Central High School in Montgomery. Please welcome James Taylor. [*Crowd cheers.*] James, how do you feel about segregation?

James: Well, Liz, to me segregation is an uncalled for and unreasonable punishment toward Black people. I don't see why we as White people think it is necessary to discriminate against them based on their color. [*Pause after loud boos from the crowd.*]

Liz: That's a very interesting point of view. What makes you feel this way?

James: When I was growing up, the road I lived on was the dividing line between the White and Black neighborhoods. I crossed the street to play with my Black friends and my parents didn't mind. Then people at church asked about it, and I was no longer allowed to play with them. From the ages of 7–16, I was prohibited from dealing with Black people.

Liz: Are there any Black students at your school?

James: Yes.

Liz: How are they treated?

James: Generally they are treated very poorly. Everything is separated: bathrooms, water fountains, lunch lines, everything. Not to mention the harassment they face from most White people. I don't know how they deal with it.

Liz: Thank you very much, James. We are going to take a quick break and we will be right back. [*Short pause.*] Okay, we're back now and let's welcome our next guest, a 16-year-old Black student also from Central High School in Montgomery, Larry Russell. [*He comes out as if trying to hide himself from boos.*]

James: Nice to meet you, Larry. [*James reaches out to shake Larry's hand and Larry reluctantly does.*]

Larry: Nice to meet you, Mr. Taylor.

James: Don't call me mister. It's James.

Liz: How do you feel about segregated schools, Larry?

Larry: I feel that segregating school doesn't do anything but worsen the problem. Having people separated only keeps people more uneducated than the opposite race. I think that it also deprives Black students of a good education. That is why it is hard for people like me to get jobs.

Liz: I agree.

Jimmy (the stage musician): I don't.

Liz (ignoring Jimmy): What makes you feel that way?

Larry: Blacks always get the short end of the stick. We get the dirty bathrooms, the old restaurants, the old and worn clothes, and the old houses. It is not that I hate the White people but I wish that everyone was treated equally.

Liz: How are you treated?

Larry: Even though I go to school with Whites I am not treated with respect. Getting spit on, called names and harassed, and being physically beaten are part of everyday school life for me. They treat me like a dog but I don't fight back because Momma taught me better.

Liz: Okay, we'll be right back after we find our guitar player, Jimmy, who has just left the set. [*Short pause.*] Okay, we're back now and we are about to join Jimmy backstage. He doesn't know he is on camera right now. Jimmy, what's wrong?

Jimmy: I am so disappointed in myself that I have been such a hateful person. I never really knew how Black people felt whenever people like me made fun of them.

Liz: I understand how you feel. Now let's go back on stage and finish the show. [*Back on stage.*] We don't have much longer so now it's time for the final thought. Today we have learned that—

Jimmy: Wait, Liz. I think I need to say something for my family, friends, and myself. Is it okay if I do the final thought?

Liz: I guess. Go ahead.

Jimmy: Before the show today, the only thing I knew about Black people was that I didn't like them because of their skin color. There were many people that I rejected because I thought they weren't up to the level that I was. I did this not only to Black people, but also to Hispanics, Japanese, Mormons, and all sorts of other people of different races and religions. What I never realized is that all of those people feel the same things I do even if they do live differently or have different beliefs. I had gone to church and they taught me to love my neighbor as myself but I didn't really think that applied to people of other races. Larry, I'd like to apologize. Will you accept?

Larry: Yes, sir. I guess so. I wish more people would feel like you do. [*They shake hands.*]

Jimmy: Everyone, join me in singing one of my favorite songs, "Amazing Grace."

Liz (as Jimmy and the others are singing in the background): Okay, that's all for our show today. Thanks for tuning in. We'll see you again on the next *Liz Watson Show!*

References

Bruckheimer, J. (Prod.), & Yakin, B. (Dir.). (2001). *Freedom's children* [Film]. Hollywood: Disney Entertainment.

Brumm, B. (Prod. & Dir.). (1998). *KKK: A secret history* [Video]. New York: Arts & Entertainment Network & The History Channel. Available: www.store.aelv.som/html/catalog

Levine, E. (1993). *Freedom's children: Young civil rights activists tell their own stories*. New York: Putnam.

Pearce, R. G. (Dir.). (1990). *Remember the titans* [Film]. Hollywood: Artisan Entertainment.

Probst, R., & Vacca, R. (2003). Collection 5: We remember. In *Elements of literature third course*. Austin, TX: Holt, Rinehart and Winston.

Randall, D. (1985). The battle of Birmingham. In R. Dudley (Ed.), *Black poets* (p. 143). New York: Bantam.

20

Challenging "Frontal Teaching": How to De-center the Classroom

Heidi Estrem

Recently I have become more aware of the geography of classroom spaces: how desks are arranged, which desks are bigger, where the light switches and whiteboards and windows (if any) are placed. The physical space of a classroom ensures that some patterns of talk and movement are more "natural" than others; if the room is a traditional arrangement, students come in and find a small desk facing forward. They turn to face the instructor at the front who stands behind the larger desk and in front of the whiteboard. They turn to a clean page in their notebooks, scramble through their backpacks for a pen—usually blue, but sometimes pink and even purple, murmuring "hello" and "what's up" to those around them before glancing toward the front. Like a conductor of a ragged, struggling orchestra, the instructor lifts her marker—and begins.

Rethinking Classroom Space: A Reformed Conductor's View

High school and college classrooms alike can share this sense of geography. Students and teachers both know what a "normal" classroom looks like; although some high school classrooms might have colorful prints on the walls or extra windows, a common sense of what a classroom "should be" dictates where students and teachers sit, move, and work. Even within nontraditional programs, this "common sense" can prevail. I once taught in a high school class for pregnant teenagers, and except for the nursery down the hall, anyone could have instantly recognized this as a classroom. As I led writing workshops, I got used to that sense of being the "teacher," of being the one all eyes turned to when a question was asked.

Yet too many times I felt keenly the boundaries of the role that classroom spaces allowed me. I confined myself to the front of the classroom, facing out. My (mis)use of classroom space meant that the pattern of interaction in my classroom was often similar to the patterns that Cazden (1988) discusses: a teacher initiates a discussion (or an in-class work project), students ask questions back, and the teacher responds. Despite my efforts to engage students in whole-class discussion, interaction patterns in this kind of class too often resemble a fan. In the geography of a "fan" classroom, the teacher is the pivot point through which all talk is monitored. This pattern also ensures that the instructor is the monitor for all work being done in class as well. It's a problem not only of talk but of the work and interactions relegated through that talk.

As I've gained experience as a teacher, I've noticed my growing ease at the front of the classroom. Many times it's just easier to run a class that way; students enter our classrooms with years of expectations about what a "good" teacher is or does. They expect that the teacher will be at the front of the classroom, that he or she will assign work, and that they will ask questions and do the work. As I gained more teaching experience, I found myself engaging in whole-class "discussions," even when I admitted to myself that I had done most of the talking and delegating from the front of the class.

I felt my conductor role. I left far too many class sessions knowing that I had "taught"—but not nearly so certain that students had learned. My students increasingly turned to me for the answers. Their eyes rarely drifted to their classmates. Their desks even began to migrate to front-facing positions, despite my efforts to arrange them in a whole-class circle. It was as though I were using the desks that I faithfully dragged into a circle as a façade for what really went on in my class: Too often, I talked and students listened.

Teaching With My Mouth Shut

I still attempt whole-class discussions, but more rarely now. As I continue my journey as an instructor, I constantly relearn how to "teach with my mouth shut," as Donald Finkel puts it (2000, p. 8). This means becoming more conscious about the "traffic patterns"—of movement, interaction, work, and conversation—in my classroom. Instead of imagining myself to be a "good" teacher when students are quietly listening and I am talking, I try to work from the perspective that "good teaching is the creating of those circumstances that lead to significant learning in others" (p. 8). This has meant shifting a bit. Instead of worrying about my performance as a teacher, I focus first on what I want students to learn, and design my classroom from there. Although this perspective may seem fairly obvious to many thoughtful, reflective instructors, it is easy to forget in the busy cycle of teaching that our primary role is *teacher* only as far as we are helping students grow as *learners*.

I now try to use the "fan" pattern for only a few reasons: to disseminate information about upcoming deadlines and assignments, to work through whole-class minilessons, and to answer questions. Although I also use small-group work and one-on-one conferences, I have found that using stations to move students around the classroom is especially useful in decentering my classroom.

Stations Defined

Those familiar with elementary schools know that stations are areas in the classroom dedicated to helping students learn skills and strategies, to practice critical thinking, to provide additional practice, or to extend a lesson. Stations may be set up throughout the classroom, in corners, on walls, or in special seating areas. Students leave their regularly assigned seats to move to stations and complete assignments, either individually or in groups. The teacher may or may not be present at a station, depending on the purpose of the lesson and the types of stations set up in the classroom. Usually students move to a station and follow directions to complete the activity. Often students are asked to complete the activities in three of five stations, or perhaps they are expected to go to a station to complete an activity after completing their regular classroom seat work.

In these classroom setups, the students' and my movements more closely resemble the ball in a pinball machine, but in slow motion. Students are able to work on task-oriented projects (in no particular order), and I become a roving consultant and timekeeper rather than the pivot point of a fan. I travel among groups, answering questions, encouraging unfocused groups to focus or reminding students to read the directions for that station. Their *work*—as directed by the focus sheets—becomes central. An additional benefit of stations is that restless adolescents can move around the room, frequently stretching and changing venues.

This doesn't mean that I am no longer in charge of my classroom. On the contrary, stations take as much planning and preparation as other classroom activities—before the class begins. While the class is in session, though, the students do all the work and activity in the classroom. Finkel (2000) writes that "'teaching with your mouth shut' does not entail teacher passivity; it requires different *kinds* of activities from teachers" (p. 17). It also requires different kinds of activities from students. I have used stations successfully in high school, undergraduate, and graduate courses.

Stations have had two main benefits for classes, regardless of grade level. They focus students' attention on the task at each station and on working with each other to accomplish that task while it shifts my role as a teacher. In classes where students are able to work independently, I can "run" one station while the others run themselves; in this way, I become a consultant to the four or five students who visit me as a group. Furthermore, the projects described in the remainder of this chapter give students the opportunity to synthesize from multiple texts and apply the principles and generalizations needed to investigate and confront complex issues and problems—strategies valued by postsecondary schools and employees.

Using All Four Walls: Station Work Works

On a day that is appropriate for station work, I bring in posters or focus sheets that direct work for a station. Students then move through these stations, working together at some stations and perhaps individually at others. Stations take two possible formats:
- Students move in groups of four or five through four to six stations, visiting each one.
- Students work independently but visit a set number of stations during a class period (usually two or three).

I use stations for two purposes, regardless of the class (composition or literature) and level (high school, first-year writing in college, or upper-division courses):
- To generate ideas (whether for a writing task or in response to a reading)
- To move students through a series of low-risk, hands-on writing activities (whether in a new genre or as a revising strategy)

Stations for Prewriting

When writing extended essays, high school and first-year college students are challenged by having to synthesize others' ideas, analyze those ideas, and even see their own perspectives in light of others. Whether they're working on integrating ideas from texts we have read, from observations, or from interviews, entering an academic conversation in this way is daunting. Stations help students to work collaboratively, generate material that can support all of them as they write their essays, and practice mastering the common problems related to depth of understanding and voice. To help students draft an essay on how their past educational experiences have influenced them, we read Mike Rose's *Lives on the Boundary* (1990) as well as a few essays from the reader *Writing Lives* (Garnes et al., 1996). Then we spend a class day preparing to write these essays by doing prewriting activities at stations. To pool their resources and help each other generate ideas, students find the focus sheets shown in Table 20-1 at each station.

After spending about 15 minutes at each station, each group summarizes the information on the poster(s) at their last station. Then, with notebook in hand, students revisit stations and take notes that will help them as they work on their essay drafts, which are due at the next class meeting. This classroom configuration helps students to work together on specific writing strategies—gathering evidence, generating specific evidence and details, and extending their reading through juxtaposing writers' ideas alongside each other. The posters stay on the walls as reminders and resources. When the entire class reads the same article, essay, or resource, stations are a low-risk way for them to work together to find meaningful citations from a source, post them, and then go back later and take notes about what other groups have posted. The intra-class collaboration and pooling of resources works much more naturally this way—either through informal individual reports or through small-group oral reports to the class.

Table 20-1. Focus Sheets

Station 1

Drawing from the chapters we have read so far in *Lives on the Boundary*, generate a list of people who influence Mike Rose's education, what kind of influence that person is, and on what page this evidence is found. Put your responses on a poster with the following heads:

Influential Person	Kind of Influence (Effect on Rose)	Page Number

Station 2

What are the qualities of a mentor? As a group, review the qualities of a mentor you listed on the poster in Station 1. Then, on the second poster, list ideas about mentors from the essays each of you read in the "Personal Literacies" section of *Writing Lives*. Be sure to note the essay and page number from which you're drawing your ideas. As this list grows, later groups should read through the whole list and put checkmarks beside ideas that are particularly striking.

Name of Essay from *Writing Lives* and Author	Page Number of Source	Qualities of a Mentor From Selection in *Writing Lives*	Read Through All Listings. Put Checkmarks Beside Interesting Ideas.

Station 3

At this station, you will find three quotes from *Lives on the Boundary*. Choose one to work with. First, list at least three questions or ideas your group has that relate to the key quote. Then list at least three quotes or ideas from Scribner's essay "Literacy in Three Metaphors" in *Writing Lives* that are in some way connected to the first quote. If the quotes you find in "Literacy" contradict the *Lives on the Boundary* quote, give more details or an additional perspective.

Lives on the Boundary quote A	*Lives on the Boundary* quote B	*Lives on the Boundary* quote C
"Literacy" quote 1	"Literacy" quote 1	"Literacy" quote 1
"Literacy" quote 2	"Literacy" quote 2	"Literacy" quote 2
"Literacy" quote 3	"Literacy" quote 3	"Literacy" quote 3

cont.

Station 4

At this station, your group will re-create an imaginary conversation with Mike Rose. This imaginary conversation begins with a quote about education from a noted educator.

Below that, you will find a question from Mike Rose based on the chapters we've read so far. As a group, continue the conversation—and make sure that as you do so, you're creating an imaginary conversation based on direct evidence from *Lives on the Boundary*. You may also want to add others' voices to the conversation. Each group should continue the conversation from where the previous group left off.

Quote from a noted educator	Question from Mike Rose from *Lives on the Boundary*
Response from educator	Response from Mike Rose
Response from educator	Response from Mike Rose

This kind of station setup works especially well in a classroom with a limited number of computers. Students rotate into a computer station—and stay for a longer period of time—to gather evidence or participate in a synchronized on-line discussion.

Stations for Poetry

Recently I worked with a group of future teachers in a summer writing course. They were looking forward to teaching English—and, of course, terrified of it as well, just as many of their future high school students will be. A few of them admitted to liking poetry and reading it on their own, but most doubted their own abilities to interpret poetry or teach it. As we immersed ourselves in a mini-unit on poetry, I used stations to focus these students' work with poetic language and to lessen their fears about writing poetry. I asked them to imagine the class that day as a hands-on museum, filled with exhibits with which they could visit and interact.

The following prompts are not new or original ideas—they will likely sound familiar to those who teach writing and literature. The traces of influence include the work of Susan and Stephen Tchudi (1999), Bruce Ballenger (1999), Donald Finkel (2000), and Peter Elbow (1998). However, it is the geography of the classroom that is important. Students immerse themselves in the task at hand and focus on enjoying the language and words in front of them. A further advantage is that they are not looking at me to tell them what to do next. The directions at each poetry station are given in Appendix 20-A.

Revision Invitation Stations

I want to highlight one additional way in which I use stations. In writing courses I struggle to show students the value of revision. Of course, we sometimes write for audiences beyond the classroom, which inevitably helps. Nevertheless, students often come to English courses with the idea that you revise a piece only if it is "bad" and needs to be made "better"—not necessarily that a piece is in process, good at this point, and merits revision.

Elsewhere I have written about encouraging revision through making students try—actually commit to paper—alternative versions of their drafts (Tchudi, Estrem, & Hanlon, 1997). These days, however, I rarely lead whole classes through writing experiments; instead, I use stations as invitations to revision and have students choose which invitations they would like to "accept" based on the piece they are revising. To encourage students to see revision as an *invitation* to resee their ideas and revisit their subject matter, when we are nearing a portfolio deadline I rearrange a writing class into revision invitation stations. I give students most of the class time to revise—to work independently on extending their pieces for their portfolios—but will set a few rules for their work. They must visit and complete a set number of revision invitation stations before the end of class (generally, two or three). At those stations—which I talk through and explain before we get to work—students take revision invitations that focus their work in specific ways. For example, the revision invitations might include the directions shown in Table 20-2.

Table 20-2. Revision Invitation Directions

Beginnings
We've discussed the many different ways a writer has of opening his or her piece, and these options should be listed in your notebook. Choose one option and spend 10 minutes trying that option for your essay. After you've drafted it, you may decide you like it better than the one you have there now.

Endings
Look at the list of possibilities for ending an essay (from Ralph Fletcher, *What a Writer Needs.*) Take 10 minutes to sketch out at least one alternative ending to your piece. Remember: You need to trust yourself enough to try it completely. If you don't like it, you don't have to use it—but you won't know until you try.

Adding Detail
Reread what you have written, looking for areas where you've told about an experience, event, image, or emotion. Experiment with one of the following to help bring immediacy to your piece:
- Add dialogue

cont.

- Drop in a scene
- Add a scene from another person's point of view within the piece
- Look for general statements ("What a gorgeous day" or "I'd never been so happy before in my life.") that don't give the reader a vivid image. Write that general statement at the top of a new piece of paper—and work on using all five senses to describe that statement.

Replacing Verbs and Nouns

Go through your piece and underline all the verbs. Then work on each one. Is there a word that more completely expresses that action? For example, perhaps you've underlined *walked*. Did the person actually *stroll, jog, stride,* or *saunter*? What image do you want in the reader's mind? Although you won't want to change every verb, you will want to try to change some.

Then go through your piece and underline all the nouns. Complete the same process: Are there more specific words you can choose?

Title

Brainstorm a list of at least 15 titles for your piece. Have you found one you like best? Circle it and use it as your working title. You may change it later, but for now it will help you to focus your revisions.

Conversations With Others

Remember that we've been working on using essays to "converse" with others' ideas. Although your ideas are central, the ideas of others are crucial as well. Many times we can add more evidence by using other writers' ideas (with proper citations, of course). For this invitation, do the following:
1. Put a star by two to four places in your essay where you could invite the voices of others into conversation with you—in other words, places where your essay would be strengthened, would be more immediate, and would give your reader a better sense of to whose ideas you're reacting.
2. For each starred area, find direct evidence from Rose or Scribner that you think would be appropriate. Write these quotes on a separate piece of paper. Under each, react by answering the following questions: (a) What do you think of their ideas? (b) Reread your essay, and as you revise think about how you might incorporate these quotes into your essay.

In a writing course, I might open the class meeting with these revision stations and then, after 45–60 minutes (or in the following class session), I will ask students to take a "response invitation":

> After you've written and revised extensively, you'll want to get some feedback. I will find someone in the class who is also ready for feedback when you are. You may want to step into the hall and visit quietly and briefly about what you are working on in your revisions. Then, read that person's essay and revisions and write a response memo.

Although I still use small-group peer-response sessions, I have also found that less formal, one-on-one response encourages revision by giving students feedback while they are in the midst of writing. Students are much more willing to try these invitations, especially after I remind them that although they need to make a good effort at trying the invitation listed, it does not *have* to become part of their draft. However, these revisions almost always do.

"Tricking Me Into Writing": Students' Perspectives on Station Work

Students invariably list station work as some of the most productive class sessions for them. For block schedules in high school, station work can be a productive way to keep students writing intensively over longer periods of time. A 75-minute class sometimes feels long, but on station days students often comment on how fast time goes—and how much writing they get done without feeling as if they've been writing and thinking for well over an hour.

The low-risk approach of station work calms students' apprehensions when faced with unfamiliar writing tasks. On class evaluations, students remark that the time in a writing class to actually write, in a wide variety of ways, is useful; in a writing class for future teachers, a majority of students mentioned the positive impact of the poetry station work, especially after the literary criticism focus of many of their English courses.

Revision, too, becomes a less daunting task when it is approached as an "invitation"—a strategy that emphasizes the rhetorical choices a writer has, rather than fixing "mistakes" a writer has made. One student wrote, "Revision is not something I have enjoyed [in the past]. During this class, probably the best 'light bulb moment' was being introduced to the idea of global revision." Revision becomes an exploration of possibilities instead of an admonition to find and correct mistakes.

What struck me most as I read over this recent set of classroom evaluations is that many students had valued their work with peers. In answering the question "What class work or projects were most useful to you and why?" nearly all mentioned some aspect of collaborative group work. One student listed the following: "the group responses [because] they helped me to get peers' feedback, and the revision stations because they helped me recast some of my work to make it better or different." Others listed "working together with my classmates" and "being able to talk and work with my peers." This surprised me, frankly, since I have had uneven results with small-group work in the past. However, many mentioned the "variety of ways we worked together" in the class. We didn't always meet in the same small groups; instead, students worked in response groups, participated in a book club with an on-line component, and worked in randomly assigned groups on station work. My conversations with students suggest that it was the variety of small-group work we did—including stations—that led them to see their peers as invaluable resources. Station work provides another configuration for this to happen as they work together in class.

Traveling Within the Classroom: Geography and Location Revisited

As I have worked on this chapter over the last several months, I have continued to wonder what it is that makes station work feel different from traditional small-group work. After all, station work puts students in small groups, and many times in the past students worked through a series of activities in their small groups. With stations, however, students focus on activities one at a time within a set time limit and then move on. If a certain station doesn't "work" for them as a group—either they get stuck or disagree—they know that they'll move to the next activity soon. Physically moving from one location to the next refocuses their attention and their work; they become intent on what the next station asks them to do rather than on waiting for me to tell them what to do. The geography of the classroom shifts; the materials and tasks at each station become the focus, not the teacher. When working in stations, students spend the majority of a class meeting talking to each other in a setting where they can each be heard.

Of course, I don't use stations every class meeting; part of their value lies in breaking up classroom patterns and shifting students' work and attention during the class period. Nevertheless, stations are a valuable addition to the patterns of my classroom. They help me resist pontificating, resist the comfortable space allotted to me at the front of the classroom, resist a role as the disseminator of information, resist becoming the director of work and talk. This resistance is, I believe, healthy for my pedagogical perspective.

Appendix 20-A. Poetry Station Directions

Station 1

Remember Ralph Fletcher's advice to "write small"? Poets, too, write small; as poets we use the "observation door" (Heard, 1999) to look for everyday things for inspiration. Living like a poet means having a willingness to live life like a writer, but even more intensely. It means seeking out poems, looking for where they hide. It means, as well, living like a scientist—both observing and experiencing life.

Directions: Spend 10 minutes wandering the halls of the school. You'll want to be aware of the following:

- Colors that catch your eye
- Conversations you overhear
- Written language you see on the wall or on chalkboards
- Sounds you hear

Take notes in your writer's notebook. Don't worry about the poem yet; just take as many notes as possible. You may find one small thing and spend your time making notes on it. You may find bits and pieces anywhere. Try to have between half a page and a whole page of notes when you come back. Keep these notes with you and use them to start poems at other stations.

Station 2

A poem can have interior structures without rhyming—in fact, rhyming can often feel forced and awkward. At this station you'll work on using syllables for interior structure.

Using your observation notes from the previous station, arrange some of the images into lines. Then do *one* of the following:
- Write down the number of syllables you'd like to try in each line and work to craft your poem within that
- Write one line. Count the line's number of syllables; write the rest of the poem with this number of syllables per line.
- Write your poem in a pattern of syllables (for example, 8/6/8/6 or 5/3/7/3/ or 1/7/2/6/3/5). Choose one of these or make up your own pattern.
- Write the poem in a pattern of verses with increasingly bigger or smaller syllables per line, for example: 2/3/2, 3/4/3, 4/5/4, or 3/3/3, 6/6/6, 9/9/9.

Station 3

This station invites you to get your writer-poet mindset focused. Use it to play with concrete objects and how to describe them (from Heard, 1999 and Hewitt, 1998).

Choose an object from the box and follow these directions:
1. Divide a piece of paper in your writer's notebook into two columns. Title the left one "surface language" and title the right column "one step closer language."
2. Spend 2 minutes just describing the object using the first words that come to mind.
3. Review what you've written. For each "ordinary" word you've listed, describe it more closely in the second column by using metaphor, simile, or describing its exact details. Below is an example for safety pin.

Silver	thread of silver gleam
Metal	reminds me of mom sewing
Safety pin	a shiny dart
Holds clothes together	hugs a debuttoned shirt
Sharp	a shirt's arrow collar

Take your time: Find an object that speaks to you even in its ordinariness. If you have time, begin crafting it into a poem.

Station 4

At this station, you get to enjoy yourself by reading poetry. Choose a book of poetry to read or skim through several books. You may also look for one of your favorite "classic" poets in the anthologies. Spend most of the time just reading. About 10 minutes before the end of your time at this station, complete the assignments below:

1. Poetry needs to be savored; read it slowly. Reread poems that surprise you, interest you, speak to you. List several titles, and in one sentence for each title, describe how each poem surprised you, interested you, or spoke to you.
2. Read like a sponge—try to soak up everything you like about the poem.
3. In the last 10 minutes, review a poem or two that especially interested you and read it again—this time as a writer would do. Answer the following questions in your writer's notebook: (a) What is the pattern of the poem? (b) How does the writer use language? (c) What kind of language does the writer use? (d) How does the writer use metaphors, similes? (e) How does the writer use rhythm or rhyme?

Station 5

Inside each envelope is a published poem that's been cut into words and phrases. Two of you will have the same poem. For the first half of the time at this station, work independently and follow these directions:

1. Take one envelope. Consider the words a writer's gift to you; now see what you can make with the words. Experiment with line breaks, interior rhythm and rhyme, repetition. Challenge yourself to use only these words (but if you need to change word endings or add connecting words, that's fine).
2. Write your version in your writer's notebook.

Then (and only then!) compare your version, your partner's version, and the original. Discuss the following questions: (a) What did each of you do with the language of the poem? (b) What images and lines speak in different ways because of the different arrangement?

Note: The point here is not that your poems should be the same as the original writer's poem. Instead, be challenged by what you can do with a limited set of words, and be intrigued by the differences that spring from different poets.

Station 6

Sometimes we get caught up in imagining the serious, weighty matters that poems must work with—and we need to remember that poems can be light-hearted and funny as well. For some writers, form poems are overly restrictive; for many of us, they help to give us a structure to work from—they "let us in" on structures and free us to concentrate on matters of content and word choice.

Limericks are just one kind of fun, light-hearted poetry. Experiment with the rhythm and rhyme scheme (you'll likely have to mumble them out loud!) Traditionally, they follow a kind of pattern:

There once was a .... (a)	There once was a cowboy named Bill
Who .... (a)	Who carried his horse up a hill.
.... (b)	His friends were impressed;
.... (b)	His horse was not stressed,
.... (a)	But Bill's hernia bothers him still.

See also the posted examples.

Directions: Read the posted examples. You may want to read one aloud to a partner, and listen to one being read as well. Write an autobiographical limerick about some humorous incident in your life. (Or if you have another direction in which you want to go, go for it!)

Station 7

A concrete poem is a poem whose physical shape and arrangement echoes the subject of the poem itself (Dunning & Stafford, 1992). Please note the posted examples.

Directions: Sketch an object about which you'd like to write. Some possibilities are (but not limited to) pencil, pen, computer, leaf, acorn, firefly, face, hair, soccerball, volleyball, basketball, heart, finger.

Get the idea? It can be anything. The example may spark your imagination as well.

Now use the shape of the object to fill in poetic (concrete, specific, metaphoric terms) phrases and ideas. Have fun!

References

Ballenger, B. (1999). *Beyond notecards: Rethinking the freshman research paper*. Portsmouth, NH: Heinemann.

Cazden, C. (1988). *Classroom discourse: The language of teaching and learning*. Portsmouth, NH: Heinemann.

Dunning, S., & Stafford, W. (1992). *Getting the knack: 20 poetry writing exercises*. Urbana, IL: National Council of Teachers of English.

Elbow, P. (1998). *Writing without teachers*. (2nd ed.). New York: Oxford University Press.

Finkel, D. L. (2000). *Teaching with your mouth shut*. Portsmouth, NH: Heinemann.

Fletcher, R. (1993). *What a writer needs*. Portsmouth, NH: Heinemann.

Garnes, S., Humphries, D., Mortimer, V., Phegley, J., & Wallace, K. (Eds.). (1996). *Writing lives: Exploring literature and community*. New York: Bedford/St. Martin's Press.

Heard, G. (1999). *Awakening the heart: Exploring poetry in elementary and middleschool*. Portsmouth, NH: Heinemann.

Hewitt, G. (1998). *Today you are my favorite poet*. Portsmouth, NH: Heinemann.

Rose, M. (1990). *Lives on the boundary: A moving account of the struggles and achievements of America's educational underclass*. New York: Penguin.

Scribner, S. (1996). Literacy in three metaphors. In S. Garnes, D. Humphries, V. Mortimer, J. Phegley, & K.Wallace (Eds.), *Writing lives: Exploring literature and community*. New York: Bedford/St. Martin's Press.

Tchudi, S., Estrem, H., & Hanlon, P. (1997). Unsettling drafts: Helping students see new possibilities in their writing. *English Journal, 86* (6), 27–33.

Tchudi, S., & Tchudi, S. (1999). *The English language arts handbook: Classroom strategies for teachers* (2nd ed.). Portsmouth, NH: Boynton/Cook.

21

Using Technology to Handle the Paper Load

Christine A. Hult

It's nearing the end of an arduous school year and your desk is piled high with student papers. You sigh deeply as you contemplate the days of reading and grading that lie before you. Surely there must be a better way! You'll be happy to learn that recently developed technologies can help you to handle the paper load. Web course management systems (e.g., Blackboard, WebCT, Course Compass, or SyllaBase), initially designed for distance education courses, provide classroom teachers with excellent tools to help manage the deluge of papers and assignments they face each term. Word processing features such as "document comments" and "track changes" help to turn responding to student writing and grading papers from a chore to a pleasure (almost).

The Paradigm Shift in Writing Assessment: A Brief Overview

With the help of the National Writing Project (NWP) and other process-writing advocates, a "paradigm shift" in teaching writing has occurred over the past 2 decades, from product-based to process-based. In process-based writing classrooms, students freewrite and cluster ideas; they prewrite and invent; they draft, rewrite, and do peer review. What does all this process mean for the paper load, however? How do teachers grade all this *process*?

Writing teachers and researchers have responded with a variety of ideas. Weaver (1998) points out in "Grading in a Process-Based Classroom" that "process-based pedagogies, because of their attempt to decenter authority, are particularly vulnerable to being undermined by traditional grading schemes" (p. 141). He argues that we have to rethink our grading to somehow include evaluation of both the process and the product. Weaver describes his system of process grading—one in which students write reflective cover letters on their process, which are then graded by the teacher. He also describes Peter Elbow's (1993) idea for "evaluation-free zones" in which students are encouraged to experiment and explore without the fear of grading. I believe that the best writing teachers use some combination of evaluation-free zones and process grading, in addition to the traditional product grading.

Another suggestion comes from Freedman (1987) in her report of successful public school teachers' responses to student writing. Surveying in 106 NWP sites throughout the country, she notes that although successful writing teachers differed in the ways they teach, they all shared a similar philosophy about response to student writing:

1. Leave ownership of the writing in the hands of the students.
2. Communicate high expectations for all students.
3. Accompany high expectations with sufficient help during the writing process itself to foster improvement—that is, provide support that leads toward success (p. 161).

Portfolio Assessment Meets Computers

Portfolios are either an overall assessment of a collection of student writing or else they consist of an assessment of student-selected pieces that are representative of a larger body of writing. Many teachers have recently begun to combine process writing approaches with the evaluation-free zones found in portfolio assessment. As Smith and Dunstan (1998) point out, "Both holistic assessment (White) and portfolio grading (Belanoff and Elbow) were developed in order to replace assessment that seemed inconsistent with current composition pedagogy" (p. 166). Yancey and Weiser (1997) agree maintaining that portfolios have helped to shift assessment from "objectively based, empiricist methods of evaluating writing to ones more contextually situated, more rhetorically defined, more process oriented" (p.102).

Hawisher and Selfe (1997) discuss the combination of computers and portfolios into an electronic portfolio that contains writing "created and stored in a digitized form" (p. 308). This is the kind of portfolio that I use in my own classes, for both an electronic working portfolio—that is, a collection of works in progress, and an electronic presentational portfolio, that is, a portfolio of polished work. Yancey and Weiser (1997) describe the ways in which completed portfolios differ from those that are in process: "The content and structure of the *completed* portfolio, however, are typically more formal, more clearly defined, and more focused. The completed portfolio is no longer an archive, but a presentation, a performance" (p. 109).

Computers Help to Manage the Paper Load

Grading portfolios can be extremely time- and labor-intensive. Any system of process grading is a tall order for busy teachers with multiple classes and too many students. As Burke (1999) puts it, "It is easy to see how out of control [the paper load] can get when you start talking about essays and more formal writing instruction" (p. 112). Burke refers to the "tricks of the trade" for reducing the paper load (such as ungraded writing, journals, and peer editing groups) that can be learned from books like *How to Handle the Paper Load* (Stanford, 1979)). He also points out that the strategic use of student conferences can help teachers to manage the paper load. In addition to these time-tested strategies, I've found in my own teaching that computers can be used to good advantage to overcome this process-writing hurdle. I will describe the two main ways in which computers can help teachers to handle the paper load: course management systems and word processing systems.

Course Management Systems

Course management systems help teachers translate their classroom materials into Web-based documents that students can access through the Internet. These systems all provide a similar range of user-friendly course tools, from chat rooms to bulletin boards to grade books. Many regular classroom teachers have found that Web classrooms are a convenient way to provide information such as course schedules and class assignments to their students. They also may use a Web classroom to communicate with students between class periods through discussion forums, bulletin boards, e-mail lists, or chat rooms. Some schools even encourage the use of the Web as a way for teachers to communicate more directly with parents.

What many teachers don't realize, however, is that Web classrooms also provide excellent help for managing student assignments—including both on-line quizzes and written work. English teachers frequently use quizzes to check student comprehension of key ideas and concepts being covered in the course. Web classrooms provide teachers with quiz builders that will help to design and build not only multiple-choice questions but also short-answer and essay questions. Teachers can set their quizzes to self-grade and be automatically e-mailed to the teacher upon completion. They can also be set so that students can retake the quiz for mastery learning. The Web classroom's quiz program can automatically record scores in the on-line grade book—a huge time saver for teachers.

Another option is to have randomly generated question sets that ensure that students each get a different quiz with different questions. This feature can also be used if teachers want students to practice a skill or concept—such as a grammar concept—until they can show understanding and mastery. This kind of computer-generated quiz allows teachers to individualize for specific students with specific needs. For example, a student who is having trouble with subject-verb agreement can work a series of computer quizzes until he or she understands the concept. Then the teacher can follow up on correct applications of the concept in the student's written work.

Course management systems can help teachers to keep track of students' written work. Using the Web classroom's homework manager, the teacher lists assignments that are due, and the students upload their homework (often written essays) by the due date. The homework manager can be configured to allow students multiple submissions of their writing, for the times when teachers intend to read successive drafts of assignments as students work on them. The homework manager keeps track of when each draft is submitted by a student or returned by the teacher with comments. This system allows teachers to read drafts of student work in progress, at the point of need, and not just when it is turned in for final grading. We know from years of research in composition that such guided practice, providing focused feedback during the students' actual writing process, is what helps writers to improve the most (as in Freedman's response principle number 3, cited above: Accompany high expectations with sufficient help during the writing process itself).

On-line portfolios in the Web classroom can be used as the repository for polished student writing that has received responses (from both teachers and peers) and has been significantly revised by the students. As Hawisher and Selfe (1997) describe it:

> The electronic portfolio differs from its paper cousin primarily in that the portfolio materials are created and stored in a digitized form (e.g., on a floppy disk, on a compact disc, on a computer network), with students often collaborating electronically on projects and sharing their work with other students and the instructor during the course of a semester. (p. 308)

To this description I would add the online Web portfolio, which consists of student work in the form of Web pages published within the on-line classroom.

Course management systems vary in the types of tools they provide that can serve as sites for student portfolios. Teachers can make use of the discussion forum tool, the file-sharing tool, or a portfolio tool specifically designed for this purpose. The beauty of this system is that it provides students with a collaborative site for both their working portfolios and their presentational portfolios. Teachers and students all have access to each others' work for collaboration and peer review. Collaborative writing projects, such as group-produced Web sites, can be included as a portion of a student portfolio. Everyone in the class has easy access to the work-in-progress through the Web classroom. I've found in my own teaching that this possibility of multiple audiences for students' work dramatically increases their attention to its presentation. Once their work is published on the Web, whether it is within the confines of the class itself (and password protected) or on the Web for all to find and view, students become much more motivated to produce their best work. They know that others besides the teacher will read it.

How do on-line portfolios help teachers with the paper load? The same principle of multiple audiences can help with multiple evaluators: On-line portfolios can be evaluated by "the student authors themselves; peer readers; teachers; parents; administrators; evaluation experts; or mixed audiences" (Hawisher & Selfe, 1997, p. 308). To this list I would add topic experts (e.g., a local naturalist organization when students are producing an environmental Web site), other teachers and classes, and interested members of the community. By making the audiences and the evaluators real, students get a sense of the expectations from a real-world audience and the teacher is able to share the evaluation task in meaningful and productive ways—thus effectively lightening the paper load.

Word Processing Systems

As mentioned earlier, the best response to writing provides for guided practice, with teachers and peers commenting and responding to each other during the composing process. When work is exchanged electronically, comment and response can happen much more easily and more often, thus facilitating formative assessment and stimulating productive revision. Modern word processing programs have a terrific tool for responding to writing called "document comments." In a nutshell, document comments allows the reader of an electronic text to insert a comment within the text while they are reading it on screen. The comment will be identified by a highlighted word in the text, and when the mouse is held over the highlighting, the comment box will appear within the text. This kind of embedded commenting meets all three of the principles of effective response articulated by Freedman (1987):

1. It allows the student to retain ownership of his or her text (because the comments are embedded separately within the text and do not change the text itself).
2. It allows the teacher to communicate high standards and expectations (through comments that question, guide, praise, direct).
3. It provides tangible support for the student from a teacher coach or guide (in the form of the comments themselves).

Word processing programs have another tool which is helpful for seeing how students have made use of the comments when revising "track changes." Once a teacher or peer has commented on a piece of student writing, the student is expected to revise accordingly, either accepting or rejecting the comments and suggestions made by reviewers. Track changes is on the Tools menu in Microsoft Word. When selected, this feature will visually mark in the text (using a red line, a strike-out, an underline, or a colored font) any changes made to the text. With track changes, the student and teacher can both see at a glance the revisions that have been made. If the student forgets to turn on this feature, the changes can still be tracked by using the "document compare" feature, which compares two versions of a draft and highlights any changes that have been made.

I will discuss how I use both of these features in the sections below.

Handling the Paper Load: Course Management and Word Processing Systems

I use a course management system called SyllaBase (developed by the English department at Utah State University, www.3gb.com), and a comprehensive word processing program, Microsoft Word, in all of the courses that I teach to help me handle the paper load. You could adapt these procedures for your students and classes, using any course management and word processing systems available to you. Many such course management systems are now offered by publishers free of charge when you adopt a particular textbook (e.g., *Course Compass* from Pearson Education).

Prior to the start of the semester, I set up my Web classrooms using SyllaBase. I upload to the Web classroom my syllabus, course policies, and assignments, as well as a calendar that indicates when assignments are due. I designate a space in the classroom where students can save their work in the form of individualized, electronic writing portfolios. I also set up the "homework manager" that will automatically post to students' Web pages the course assignments as they are due. Since I primarily teach writing courses, most of the assignments are essays and written projects, although I do give a few quizzes on items of grammar and usage, using the Web classroom's quiz builder. Figure 21-1 shows the homework manager from a typical writing class using SyllaBase.

Figure 21-2 shows the quiz builder.

Figure 21-1. Homework Manager

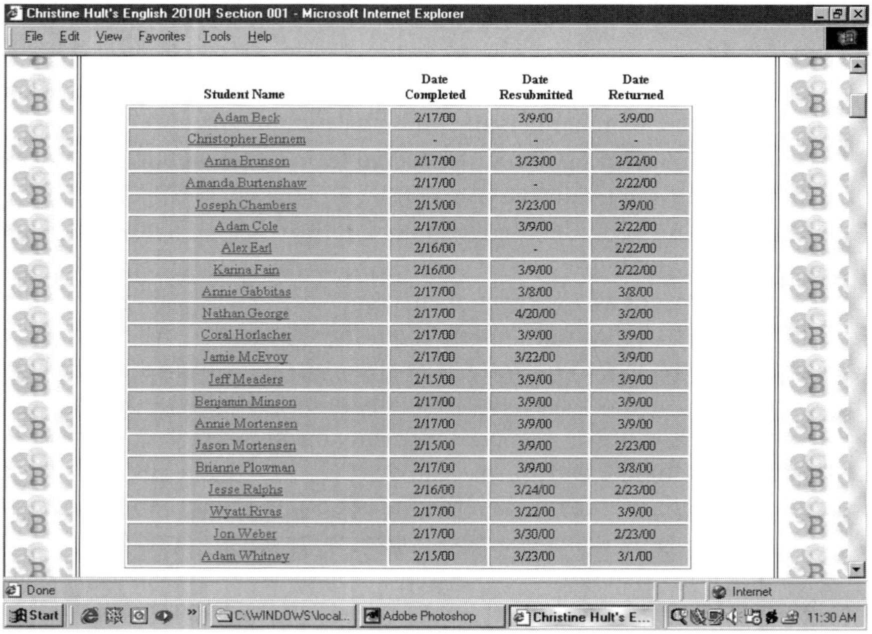
Christine Hult's English 2010H Section 001 - Microsoft Internet Explorer

File Edit View Favorites Tools Help

Student Name	Date Completed	Date Resubmitted	Date Returned
Adam Beck	2/17/00	3/9/00	3/9/00
Christopher Bennem	-	-	-
Anna Brunson	2/17/00	3/23/00	2/22/00
Amanda Burtenshaw	2/17/00	-	2/22/00
Joseph Chambers	2/15/00	3/23/00	3/9/00
Adam Cole	2/17/00	3/9/00	2/22/00
Alex Earl	2/16/00	-	2/22/00
Karina Fain	2/16/00	3/9/00	2/22/00
Annie Gabbitas	2/17/00	3/8/00	3/8/00
Nathan George	2/17/00	4/20/00	3/2/00
Coral Horlacher	2/17/00	3/9/00	3/9/00
Jamie McEvoy	2/17/00	3/22/00	3/9/00
Jeff Meaders	2/15/00	3/9/00	3/9/00
Benjamin Minson	2/17/00	3/9/00	3/9/00
Annie Mortensen	2/17/00	3/9/00	3/9/00
Jason Mortensen	2/15/00	3/9/00	2/23/00
Brianne Plowman	2/17/00	3/9/00	3/8/00
Jesse Ralphs	2/16/00	3/24/00	2/23/00
Wyatt Rivas	2/17/00	3/22/00	3/9/00
Jon Weber	2/17/00	3/30/00	2/23/00
Adam Whitney	2/15/00	3/23/00	3/1/00

Done Internet

Start C:\WINDOWS\local... Adobe Photoshop Christine Hult's E... 11:30 AM

Other Web classrooms will offer similar management programs to the ones shown here.

Figure 21-2. Quiz Builder

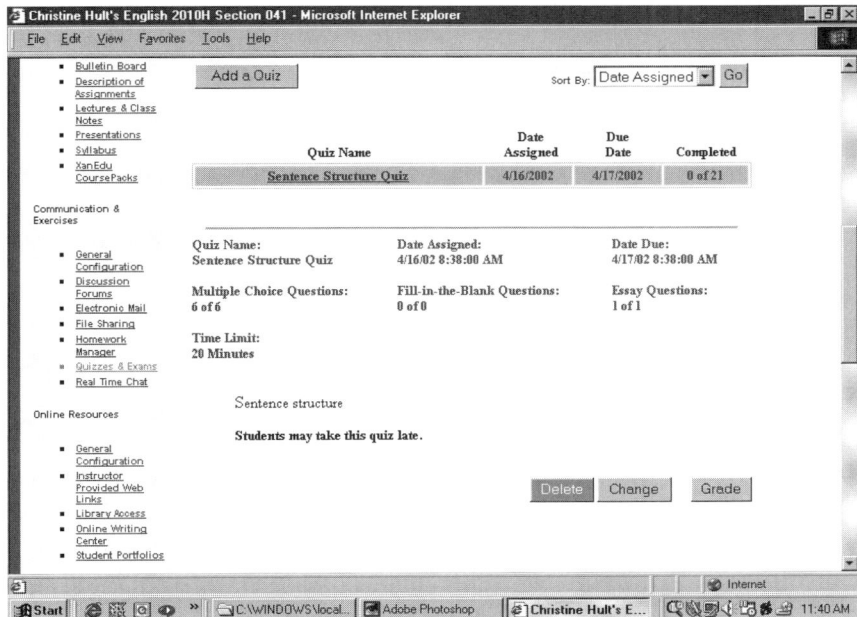

Electronic Homework Manager

By using a homework manager that logs assignments as they are turned in and keeps track of assignments for me, I no longer have that old paper shuffle—dragging papers around with me from home to work; spilling coffee on them while reading them in the lounge chair; leaving them at the dentist's office, and so forth. You'll also recall the times when you drag all the papers to class only to find that three students are absent. Their papers sit in your office, unclaimed, until either you or the students remember to retrieve them. If students are absent the day papers are returned, it doesn't matter, since they are all stored electronically in the Web classroom. I don't have to haul papers home with me either; I simply retrieve them from the Internet when I'm ready to read them, whether I'm at home, in the office, or even in a hotel room at a conference. What about those students who habitually turn in late work? You can set the homework manager to reject any papers that aren't uploaded by your deadline.

By using the quiz builder and on-line grade book, I can check the class's comprehension of key principles and ideas covered in the course, assign and grade essay test questions on readings, quiz individuals on points of grammar or usage they are having trouble with, provide guided practice for mastery learning, and have responses e-mailed to me and automatically recorded in my online grade book. As you can imagine, all of this electronic course management greatly reduces my paper load. It helps students, too, because they have their own individualized version of the grade book when they log into the class Web site, and so each student can easily keep track of his or her progress in the course.

No More Handwritten Comments

I don't know about you, but since I started writing at a keyboard, my handwriting has deteriorated to the point where it is indecipherable, even to me! Handwritten comments on student papers therefore become a problem of communication: If students are going to revise according to my comments, they need to be able to understand them first! Because I now respond to student writing electronically, I never have to worry about translating my illegible comments for students. Rather, I use the "insert/comment" feature of my word processing program to type the comments into the student papers at the relevant location in their documents (Figure 21-3).

This feature, now common in word processing programs, is one of the best technological innovations to help teachers handle the paper load. I find that I can download and respond to student drafts (using the homework manager and document comments) much more quickly than I could when my comments were handwritten. Besides, I can elaborate as much or as little as I like with document comments, which makes them seem much more as though they are coming from an interested, supportive reader, as in Freedman's principle number 3.

Figure 21-3. Document Comments

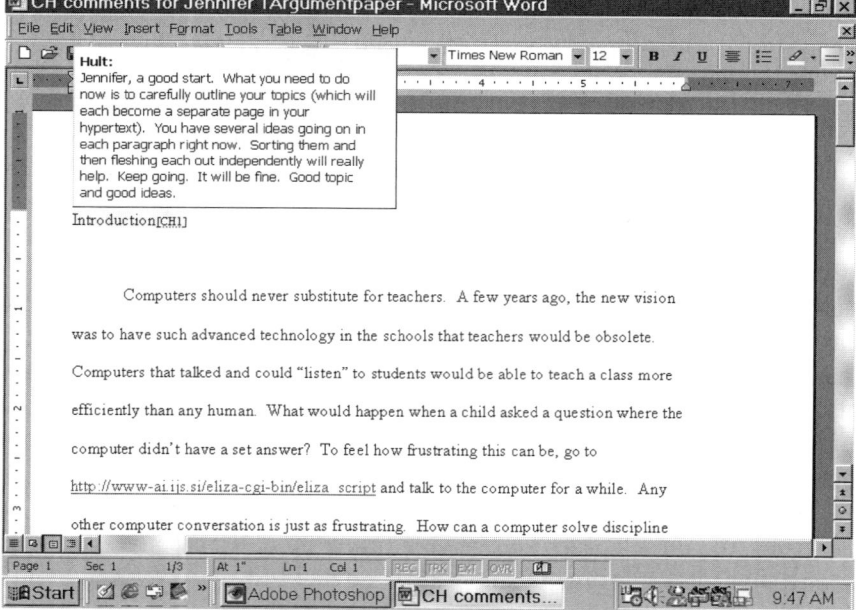

As you can see in Figure 21-3, the document comments are indicated by highlighting in the text. When the mouse is held over the highlighting, the comment box will appear. Students find this a much less obtrusive way of commenting on their papers; in other words, you are not "denigrating" their work by writing ("bleeding") all over it with your red pen. Rather, you are making constructive comments and suggestions that they, as writers, can consider and respond to—leaving the ownership of the work with the students (Freedman's principle number 1). When students revise their work, I have them revise and upload the commented copies through the homework manager so that there is a record of their work and of the ways in which they have followed up on my suggestions. This is also a terrific mental aid for me—often when I read subsequent drafts, I can't recall the advice I gave on the first round! With document comments, we are all operating from the same assumptions. In addition, they can comment back to me as well, asking specific questions and seeking guidance on their writing. Comments are identified in the text by the initials of the person making them.

I also frequently have students use the track changes feature when they begin to work on revising their drafts (Figure 21-4). In the Tools menu of Word, select "track changes/highlight changes" to turn on this feature (WordPerfect has a similar feature called "review document"). Once the "highlight changes" is activated, every change made to the document will be recorded visually, using color, strike-outs, or underlines. How changes are highlighted can be customized at the "tools/options/track changes" menu. I use this feature in a number of ways—when students are revising and resubmitting a draft through the homework manager, but also when I want to illustrate appropriate editing and revising in a brief section of a paper—that they can then emulate throughout the rest of the paper.

Figure 21-4. Track Changes

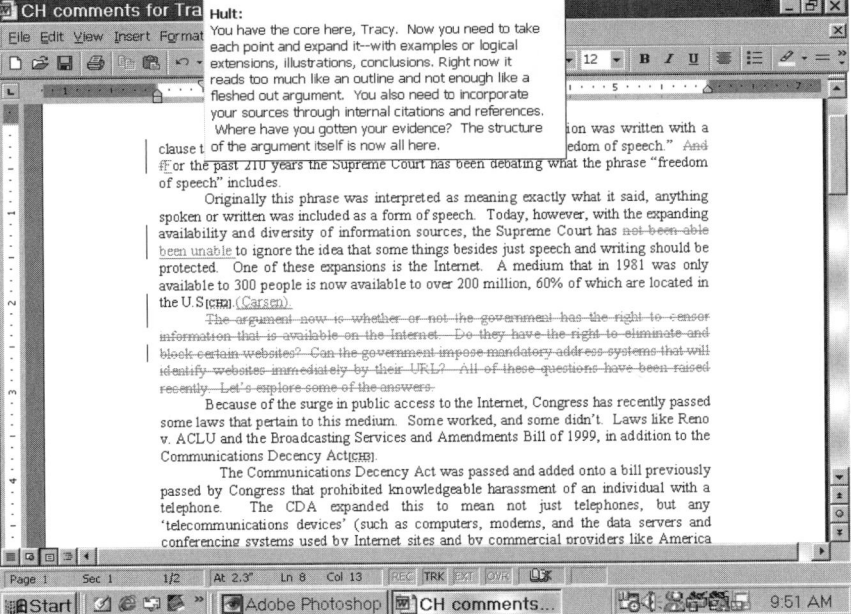

Often peers edit and comment on each others' papers, using both document comments and track changes; the writer can either accept or reject those suggestions at the track changes menu. The papers can be exchanged by students at a file-sharing space on the Web classroom, as attachments to a post in a discussion forum, or through e-mail attachments (Figure 21-5). There is no more endless photocopying for peer reviews of each other's essays. Students can learn how to read and respond to each others' work electronically while they are learning the importance of revision.

Figure 21-5. File Sharing

Student work for my classes is stored in electronic portfolios in the Web classroom. Each student's portfolio is available for everyone in the class as a work-in-progress until the end of the semester (Figure 21-6). Each piece within the portfolio may be revised throughout the term, to be graded by me (preliminarily) at midterm and for a final grade at the end of the course. I am very explicit about the criteria for grading each item within the on-line portfolio. Everything goes through a series of comments, responses, peer reviews, and revisions before their writing assignments ultimately become transformed from a working portfolio into a presentation portfolio. Figure 21-7 shows the listing of work from an online portfolio done by a student in a graduate class.

Figure 21-6. Portfolio Idea

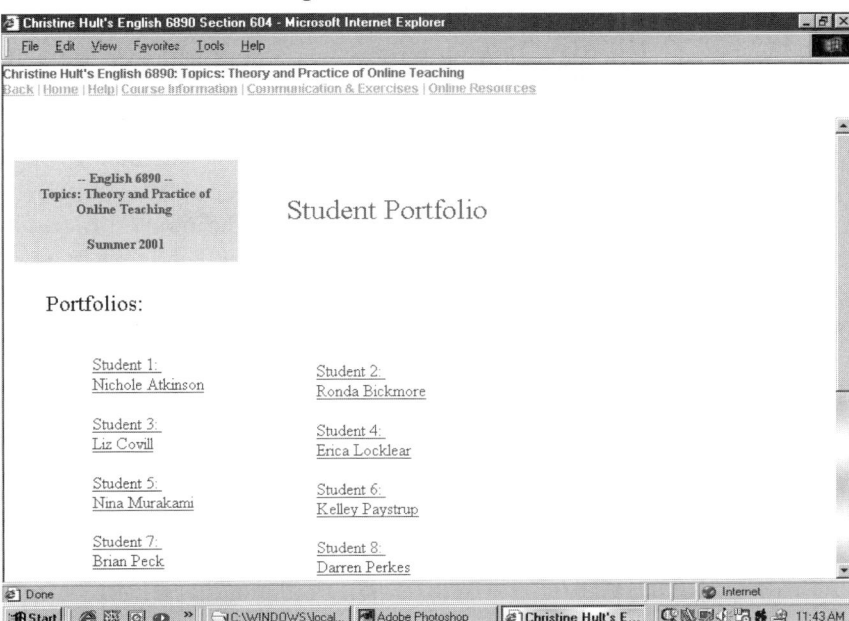

Figure 21-7. Student Portfolio

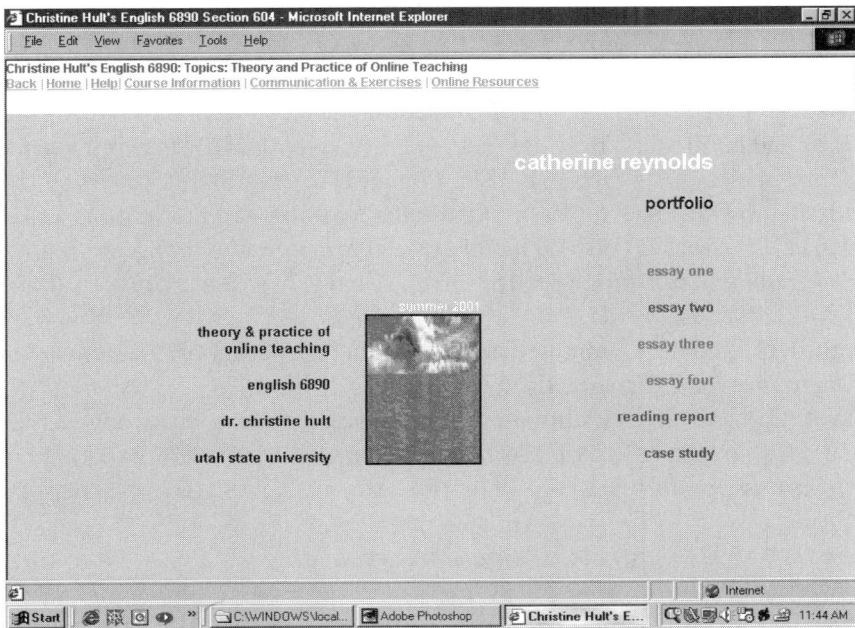

I have tried to show in my examples that not only onethe use of a Web classroom and a word processing program for electronic exchange of student work more pedagogically appropriate to a process-oriented writing classroom, but also that this computer-assisted pedagogy is more helpful to the teacher who often faces overwhelming obstacles from a burgeoning paper load. Yancey and Weiser (1997) sum up our goals well in the final reflections on their portfolio collection: "Whose needs are served by viewing writers in process and over time and as capable of helping us help them? Increasingly, the answer seems to be: this view serves us all" (p. 115).

If you are not yet convinced that technology can help you to handle the paper load, try one of the commenting techniques I have outlined with your next writing assignment, perhaps using e-mail attachments as the method of paper exchange. You don't need to do everything at once; start small and take incremental steps toward using more technology in your classes. It is a fact that students are all writing with computers now, so we teachers might as well capitalize on that fact. To do so will produce a double benefit: assisting not only our students but ourselves.

References

Belanoff, P., & Elbow, P. (1991). State university of New York and Stony Brook portfolio-based evaluation program. In P. Belanoff, & M. Dickson, (Eds.), *Portfolios: Process and product* (pp. 3–6). Portsmouth, NH: Boynton/Cook Heinemann.

Burke, J. (1999). *The English teacher's companion*. Portsmouth, NH: Boynton/Cook Heinemann.

Elbow, P. (1993). Ranking, evaluating, liking: Sorting out three forms of judgment. *College English, 55* (2), 135–55.

Freedman, S. W. (1987). *Responding to student writing*. Urbana, IL: NCTE.

Hawisher, G., & Selfe, C. L. (1997). Wedding the technologies of writing portfolios and computers. In K. B. Yancey & I. Weiser (Eds.), *Situating portfolios: Four perspectives* (pp. 305–321). Logan, UT: Utah State University.

Smith, C., & Dunstan, A. (1998). Grade the learning, not the writing. In F. Zak and C. C. Weaver (Eds.), *The theory and practice of grading writing: Problems and possibilities*. (pp. 163–170). Albany, NY: State University of New York.

Stanford, G., and the Committee on Classroom Practices. (1979). *How to handle the paper load*. Urbana, IL: NCTE.

Weaver, C. C. (1998). Grading in a process-based writing classroom. In F. Zak and C. C. Weaver (Eds.), *The theory and practice of grading writing: Problems and possibilities*. (pp. 141–150). Albany, NY: State University of New York.

White, E. (1992). *Assigning, responding, evaluating* (2nd ed.). New York: St. Martin's Press.

Yancey, K. B. (Ed). (1992). *Portfolios in the writing classroom: An introduction*. Urbana, IL: NCTE.

Yancey, K. B., & Weiser, I. (Eds.), (1997). *Situating portfolios: Four perspectives*. Logan, UT: Utah State University.

22

Carnival in the Classroom: Bakhtin and My Search for Democracy

Jonathan Segol

Classroom Democracy: Possibility or Failure?

How often have teachers and students been faced with a decision, and after making it a student exclaims jokingly (or not), "Majority rule"? The existence and extent of democracy in our classrooms has been an ongoing issue of classroom structure for both my students and me. Inasmuch as every class is a societal simulation, every teacher receives the challenge as to what type of society he or she wishes to create.

Most of my colleagues define their political sympathies as liberal democratic yet run their classrooms in a totalitarian manner. Despite the legitimate concerns and conditions most often used to justify this type of rule—efficiency, crowd control—many of my colleagues risk disenfranchising the people they most wish to empower. Many even risk reducing themselves to burned-out despots in a short matter of years. At the other extreme, I've seen teachers begin their careers committed to instituting democratic structures in their classroom, only to be overrun by chaos both in classroom management and in their learning standards.

Shortly before I began teaching, I was lucky enough to experience a disastrous experiment in democracy that tempered my radical democratic leanings as I continued to labor silently on the question of where democracy belongs in the classroom. It was a graduate course in which the professor announced at the beginning of the semester that he would abdicate his position of running the class. Instead, we graduate students could sign up for a day and teach class ourselves, ostensibly to further our own projects while sharing our discoveries with the entire class.

Pedagogically speaking, it was a fiasco, an insipid rotation of wretched facilitators subjecting us to private agendas of irrelevance. Nor was there any significant accumulation of learning, either in class material or in group discourse. If the professor had any knowledge to contribute, we were kept ignorant of it. His silence was palpable throughout the semester. Here at the graduate level I was allowed to see how a simple construct of "pure democracy"—abdication of authority accompanied by a sign-up sheet—proved as unsuitable for class structure as did the totalitarian models that had led our instructor to seek another method.

To be fair, I've seen totalitarian classrooms succeed, particularly in cultures with stable traditional hierarchies that place the teacher at the upper level of the given hierarchy. Our particular school in Brooklyn, however, was one of the approximately 100 schools in danger of being shut down by the state. Most of the students had been subjected to elementary and middle schools with demonstrably high levels of disorder and low levels of learning. To compensate for the disorder and large class sizes, far too many teachers turned to tyranny as a way to overcome large class size.

What I Wanted for My Students

Due in part to lingering anger toward the tyrants of my own secondary school English education, I chose to teach English. I wanted my students to experience the intellectual stimulation and the sense of enfranchisement that my subsequent studies had given me. I have since met other educators who empower the disempowered through music, math, and other subjects. Just the same, much of my direction has come from thinkers who have articulated the link between language and social control—George Orwell and Frederick Douglass, to name two. Their writings and others have given me a sense of purpose in fusing the ideals of an enlightened society with an effective English class.

Tools for Synthesis: Mikhail Bakhtin

Two particular thinkers in the field of language have given me the most tools in the synthesis noted above: Mikhail Bakhtin and Crazy Eddie. The former was a major literary theorist whose writings on Fyodor Dostoevsky, Francois Rabelais, and the novelistic genre itself continue to receive ample scholarly attention. The latter is currently serving time for tax fraud, though not without having produced and starred in some of my favorite television commercials of all time. With all due respect to Edward ("Crazy Eddie") Santar, this chapter focuses primarily on the ideas of Bakhtin as they pertain to the classroom rather than to the polyvocal aspects of fiction.

In two of Bakhtin's books, *The Dialogic Imagination* (1981) and *Problems of Dostoevsky's Poetics* (1984), Bakhtin discusses the novel as a genre mixing many voices, more than any previous literary genre. Dostoevsky is treated as a high point in this development, and one that exemplifies the free flow of ideas made possible in a rich cast of characters. Any one of Dostoevsky's major characters is imbued with more ideas and opinions than the average main character of most other novels. These novels are particularly democratic in the sense that despite the pervasive traffic of ideologies and philosophies, no one character's ideology proves the others wrong. Never do Dostoevsky's major novels work as a proof of a given ideology, but only as a traffic venue for the discussion of several.

Some of Bakhtin's key terms—*dialogism* and *dialogue*—have also been useful discourse for cultural critic Paolo Freire (1990). Freire, in fact, puts it most strongly: "Only dialogue, which requires critical thinking, is capable of generating critical thinking. Without dialogue, there can be no education, there can be no communication, and without communication there can be no true education" (1990, p. 81). In Freire's discourse on dialogue, education must be a multidirectional flow of information and skills if it is to succeed. This view addresses and confirms Bakhtin's positive value placed on multivocality, the presence of simultaneous multiple voices in language, and places it within the realm of education.

Another possible vehicle of democratization discussed by Bakhtin is that of festive culture in general and the carnival in particular. In his dissertation on Rabelais, Bakhtin speaks of the medieval carnival period as one capable of scrambling or inverting the local hierarchy of authority in such a way as to make bums into kings and vice versa. In addition to its provision of an outlet for mass society, this carnival time helped to stabilize the hierarchical order during the noncarnival time. It is these concepts of Bakhtin, dialogism and carnival, which have contributed most to my classroom's progress toward democracy.

The concept of multivocality and dialogism transfers quite readily to the classroom, in the form of discussions, small-group work, oral reports, and even guest speakers. It is the carnivalistic mode that took longer to locate and implement. It may appear odd to look for democratic models in medieval village society. Most of us think of looking elsewhere for democratic models, perhaps in the writings of Alexis de Tocqueville, Thomas Jefferson, Emma Goldman, or others. However, the classroom remains a place structured and choreographed by a monarch, the teacher, to whatever extent he or she believes is necessary. Consequently, the quest for a pure democracy identical to that which we envision in our ideal society may be ill-suited for the classroom. Paradoxically, classroom democracy must coexist with the monarchy of the teacher in order to make strides toward any actual democracy that does not sacrifice learning standards. In this respect, carnivalism suggests a democracy that can be turned on and off.

Despite the connotation of the word, my own carnivalism usually operates at a modest level. When considering activities and objectives for a given unit, I sometimes consider what hierarchy would best guide us through the activity. For example, here in New York state where I teach, a new set of academic standards emerged during the 1990s. I'm told that these new standards are now the hardest in the country, which may explain all the nervous administrators I have met during this time. One of the more perplexing demands we were issued during this time was to make the students fully understand the new state standards, the areas of evaluation for a piece of writing, and the descriptions of each level of quality for each aspect of writing. Although it may be in the students' best interests to know what New York now expects of them, I noticed it was hard enough to get the *teachers* to read the new state standards. It was considerably harder to bring the students to spend time reviewing these standards, especially because they saw the new standards as a structure with which their own writing would be attacked.

I only succeeded in bringing my students to study these new standards when I allowed them to assign me homework and to grade me the next day. As my homework for them, I wrote essays like the ones required on the statewide exams (Appendix 22-A). Armed with typed requirements from the New York State Department of Education, my students became my teachers. In a room full of 30 teachers and one student, they jabbed fingers at state-printed rubrics, exclaiming how the essay met a certain requirement in one way but not in another. They debated writing subtleties with a relish that rarely if ever occurred when revising their own work.

Critiquing the Teacher

It is also worth noting the predictable: Several of these students became drunk with power when critiquing the teacher's writing. They ranted against my typos and corrected grammar with bursts of triumph. I didn't discourage any of this, for these tyrants of grammar started a nice momentum for the class as they worked their way toward the subtler concepts of writing, as detailed in our state curriculum and others.

In some classes, I found myself doing this exercise five or six times a year—once for each section of the Regents exams and once for each long-term writing project I gave the class, whether a book journal, a term paper, or a book report. In this latter group of assignments—that is, those that do not come from the state—I found that this process could give the students a hand in establishing class standards for any given assignment. It was especially effective in eliciting responses from students who otherwise were too often disengaged about the writing process.

Students As Teachers

On other occasions students also got to be teachers one at a time. This may sound the same as oral reports. However, a subtle difference in framing the format made a world of difference in class environment, the confidence of the presenter, often the breadth of presentation, and the students' responses to being taught by their peers. This student-becomes-teacher metamorphosis was not my idea. The idea and its potential were suggested to me by one of my wildest students. One day at the beginning of class, he asked, half-jokingly, "Mr. Segol, why don't you let me teach class today?"

This student knew all my preferred approaches and formats for in-class reading and discussion. After all, he was taking my English 2 class for the third time.

True to my expectations, he got up, paced the reading, directed the questions, and guided discussion with a stage presence that riveted students' attention. Incidentally, he was also much stricter than I was. He asked difficult questions, using them to rein in daydreamers and focus those already listening. He even rearranged a few seats at the beginning of class, with the stated purpose of minimizing distractions.

This student-turned-teacher took great joy in pushing the students to discuss the text and to pay close attention to the reading. I found later that year that this process also works in the reverse direction: students who work their teacher hard toward similar ends. In my best class of teachers, the students each had selected a 20th century American poet whose life and poetry they would teach to the rest of the class. We kept it fairly straightforward: a lecture that included a close reading of one of the poet's poems, followed by a question-and-answer session, which the teacher could also use to facilitate a larger discussion of the poetry. The more lessons of this type that we had, the more the students worked at bringing up challenging questions. Granted, the motivation at work was to make their friends think on their feet. However, the effect was to raise the discussion level to one that I had rarely if ever seen at a high school.

Some preparations are certainly in order before most students can stand up, teach, facilitate, and successfully field questions from students who delight in playing stump-the-teacher. In this unit, I wrote a straightforward lesson outline for students to use: the lecture, reading passage, and question-and-answer session (Appendix 22-B). I gave two of these presentations before any of the students' teaching days so that they could see how such a format might look. Each student had a meeting with me a day or two before their day to teach. In that meeting we discussed what the student wanted to present. The student brought to our meeting the poem he or she would teach the class. To the extent we agreed necessary, we would outline the presentation much as a teacher would outline the order of events of a given class. More than anything, these meetings resembled my own meetings with my mentor or department head, both of whom were happy to brainstorm with me prior to their own observations of my classes.

I should also add that I have found it helpful to keep a low profile while my students teach. I simply take a seat with other students, keep my head low, and take notes—some things I might hope the other students would do. This has helped to diminish the oral report and perform-for-the-teacher aspect of the lesson. It can also go without saying that during this time I never speak without raising my hand and waiting to be called on.

To my own surprise I have also found it helpful to scramble the hierarchy during the first week of class. For many of my classes, I spend the second and/or the third day of class in contract negotiations with the students. This contract encompasses expectations regarding class work, homework, major projects, attendance, behavior, and calculation of grade. Ideally, this negotiations process causes the rules and requirements to be less an oppressive device of the teacher and more a mutual construct of both parties.

Further Tools for Synthesis: Crazy Eddie

It is in these contract sessions that I occasionally draw upon the wisdom of the fine public speaking of Crazy Eddie. Even as a young child with no disposable income for electronics or stereos, I felt a great desire to see this place where they were giving it all away, where their prices were insane. As an adult, I have made insane offers and agreed to insane demands if only to give long-disenfranchised students some sense of enfranchisement in the making of the ground rules of their English class. No surprise tests? Okay. No tests without seven days' notice? Okay. Three 100s averaged in for perfect attendance during the marking period? Okay. That last one was a class of truants, and the agreement served me as well as it did them. If you keep your educational goals safe, you can give in to wild demands on the grading process (the students' most pressing concern) without sacrificing any of your own standards.

Violating Contracts As Carnivalized Moments

At least once a year I attempt to violate the contract so that the students can assert their rights. I have found the legalistic tussle a valuable exercise in close reading of a text. Inevitably, several students have their contracts on hand. Inevitably, a few star lawyers emerge, ready to cite and explain lines that consequently save the class from the predatory test-multiplying tendencies of the teacher. Also inevitably, I have found this action to merge the best aspects of both cooperative and competitive activities. Students work together to score a victory over the teacher. This victory serves more than one long-term purpose in the English classroom. Students mine the texts for the purpose of upholding the rule of law in the classroom. I should caution that you may not wish to carry out this exercise until you are far enough along into the year to have established sufficient rapport with the students. By then, such an exercise results in respect for the law and not in disrespect for the teacher.

The contract violation activity is a carnivalized moment that carries weight past the carnival time. It is also a straightforward example of the carnivalized system stabilizing the uncarnivalized system, not necessarily through release of tension as much as through the exact type of role reversal taking place. It is centered on the rule of law. If the teacher has become the lawbreaker, then surely the students must be the law enforcers. It is in this spirit that during regular classes I have also awarded quality-control points to students who correct mistakes that should not exist (on exams or project instructions). Naturally, this incentive prevents even lectures from becoming a strictly univocal activity.

Positive Changes: Evaluating Student Outcomes

In the most successful applications, such activities have helped to foster a different relationship to law among my students—that is, knowledge of law and its texts as something empowering, not simply restricting. This process is of key importance in the case of my students, many of whom have their own difficulties with the law outside class. They have since brought this process to a higher level and formed the nation's only vocational school chapter of Amnesty International, in which they have closely followed and written about human rights in Colombia, Nigeria, Indonesia, and New York City in particular. In addition to the usual letter-writing campaigns, we created a human rights library, an enclave within the school library. Several students use this library, if only to check up on the New York City police force.

In our advanced cases of class carnivalization, our alternative hierarchical structure became more complex than simple role-reversal or student teachers. For instance, as the SAT approached, we desired to create a game-show activity that would help them to review. Together we created "Who Wants to Be a 1600?" I could facilitate, since I had access to all the appropriate vocabulary lists. However, the students possessed superior knowledge of the rules of the game. Their game ultimately resulted in more four-digit SAT scores than the school had seen in some time (Appendix 22-C).

Our game show developed in the spring, when my students had successfully blurred the line between carnival time and noncarnival time. This boundary blurring was additionally displayed when the students and I found ourselves jointly outlining lesson schedules for the week, considering aloud on what areas we wanted to focus our progress. In so doing, they played a role in planning their week, secure in the knowledge that they would be working just as hard as ever. Their motivations included ensuring themselves an SAT review and retaining momentum on literature they were enjoying. By the end of the year many of these students knew more about the Harlem Renaissance than did any of the teachers in the school, including me a year prior to using this method to teach that semester. Given my usual advocacy of an ever-expanding repertoire of carrots and sticks to motivate every class, I was gratified to note that toward the end of the year, most of these students had grown into a process of learning for learning's sake.

The above class remains the standard, the ideal of Bakhtinian democracy. Other classes that year progressed in that direction, though not to the same extent. Amid the student-teacher rotations, assigning of homework to the actual teacher, the contract negotiation, and game shows, one might ask if I am asserting that the path to true democracy is fake democracy. I won't deny it. A less absurd comparison might be seen in the more notable examples of decolonization in the 20th century—India, Israel, and several Caribbean islands, to name a few. In the best instances, the colonized peoples develop sufficient civic institutions of their own to constitute a shadow government or government-in-waiting. Through their not-yet-national institutions, they proceed with the exercises of governing and of democratic processes, enough to make the transition to independence without devouring themselves in military coups or other such convulsions. Given most of my students' education histories, left to schools unable to serve them properly, it is safe to consider what occurs in my classroom as a form of decolonization.

A strict Bakhtinian might not treat our classroom usage of carnivalization as a path toward democracy, but rather as a break in the monarchic action. It is also true that critics have questioned Bakhtin's discussion of hierarchical subversion and empowered common folk in the context of events—medieval carnivals, for instance—in which people were often drunken, beaten, or worse. In this light I consider the classroom a more realistic place to enact the positive aspects of carnival as described in Bakhtin's writings.

A significant condition that framed our experiments in democracy was our school's rank in the hierarchy of the school system. After viewing the condition of their high school, particularly with the awareness of well-maintained schools elsewhere in the city, my students have become keen about the school system's role in reflecting (one may even say perpetuating) the disparity between rich and poor. One of the most positive assessments of our own work in this context were several students who agreed, "He's teaching us like rich kids."

Most of my students look primarily at specific results, test or otherwise, in evaluating their own progress. For some it may be SAT scores. Others passed state exams a year earlier than scheduled. The top students received a visit from a *New York Times* reporter who informed us that we were the only vocational school in the country with an Amnesty International chapter. I saw a chapter that grew dramatically in numbers and activity in the wake of the Amadou Diallo shooting, a political discontent now expressing itself in writing campaigns and in research. The students for the most part told the reporter that we may be the only one, but "Mr. Segol asked us." Lewis Robinson, one of my best writers, once reflected in his paper that our work "has also made us livelier conversationalists." We have all found satisfaction in this approach.

Even the classes that have not achieved top democracy-wielder status have found English class a place in which they looked forward to participating. Along with correcting my papers, teaching class themselves, negotiating contracts, and whatever other roles they would play in class, many of these students developed a sense of enfranchisement in their classes, of helping to make these classes what they became. I would like to think that they will carry this enfranchisement and these dialogue skills on to their next classes, as well as to any other hierarchies they must navigate.

Appendix 22-A. Homework for the Teacher

The Task

Write a critical essay in which you discuss two works of literature you have read from the particular perspective of the statement that is provided for you in the Critical Lens below. In your essay, provide a valid interpretation of the statement, agree *or* disagree with the statement as you have interpreted it, and support your opinion with specific references to appropriate literary elements from the two works.

Critical Lens: "All art is quite useless."—Oscar Wilde

Guidelines

Be sure to do the following:
- Provide a valid interpretation of the critical lens that clearly establishes the criteria for analysis.
- Indicate whether you agree or disagree with the statement as you have interpreted it.
- Choose two works you have read that you believe best support your opinion.
- Use the criterion suggested by the critical lens to analyze the works you have chosen.
- Avoid plot summary. Instead, use specific references to appropriate literary elements (e.g., theme, characterization, setting, point of view) to develop your analysis.
- Organize your ideas in a unified and coherent manner.
- Specify the titles and authors of the literature you wish to choose.
- Follow the conventions of standard written English.

Homework for English 11

Critical Lens: "All art is quite useless" —Oscar Wilde

Beyond this quote lies this question: What is it that we want our art to do? Do we want it to change the world? Certainly some books have had such an effect on society. *The Jungle* by Upton Sinclair exposed the wretched conditions of the workers in the meat-packing industry and led to their improvement. However, if this is an expectation we put on our literature, we can expect to be disappointed 99% of the time. I agree with the novelist Milan Kundera, who once said that the goal of the novel is questioning answers, rather than answering questions. In this manner of opening discussions rather than closing them, art is useful in helping to prevent the simplemindedness that many societal institutions would impose on our language and thinking.

In *Shame*, by Salman Rushdie, there are no main characters; there is no single thread of plot that one can follow from beginning to end. The only main character is shame itself. Shame makes its mischief in the fictionalized land of Pakistan. What can such a strange novel do for us? Of course it answers nothing. It does, however, open up a great number of questions about the effects that shame can have on a culture as a whole, as characters pursue twisted journeys to cover up their shame.

Franz Kafka's *The Trial*, covers the plight of someone who has been arrested for no reason that is revealed to him. He is then led through a mysterious prison bureaucracy that provides him with no insight into his situation but only confuses him further. Moreover, he remains in prison. The tale holds back from any deep characterization so as to focus our attention on this absurd situation. Did this book do anything for the world? It didn't even do anything for Kafka. He died a depressed man before he could see his books published. However, his books do discuss an eerie modern theme: the insanity that can result when the system is working properly. Consequently, when a friend refers to a Kafkaesque visit with the Department of Motor Vehicles or the Board of Education, I sit ready for an irony-filled story that would be funny if it weren't real.

In both of these novels, no questions are answered. Instead, discussions are initiated. One concerns the role of shame in the culture at large and the other concerns the effects of bureaucracy in the modern age. Both novels leave us with deeper understandings from their questions than we might receive from a thousand answers.

Appendix 22-B. The Day You Teach Class

You will give a presentation of roughly 10 minutes on a poet and his or her work.

Three days prior to the day you teach, you will meet with me to discuss what you plan to teach. Please bring with you (a) the poem you plan to read with the class (photocopy it *now*) and (b) at least one or two of the books you have used in your research.

After our meeting and before the day you teach, you will prepare a page that you will hand me at the conclusion of your lesson. This page will include (a) a brief biography of the poet (either a paragraph or a list of facts), (b) notes for your presentation, and (c) a properly prepared bibliography.

The day you teach, you will briefly summarize the poet's life, the poet's work, and any major work worth mentioning. Read one poem with the class, discuss your observations on the poem and its meaning, and answer any questions from the class.

Appendix 22-C. Who Wants to Be a 1600?

(Note: I have found this game to be successful with classes of students who enjoy listening to the questions much as one would enjoy listening to a game show. It encourages auditory intelligence and skill.)

The Questions

Each question is a definition, with a choice of four words to match that definition (or vice versa—four definitions for each word). The four choices are written on easel paper so that the entire class may view the choices.

Options

Each contestant can use each of the two options below once during each of the first two rounds.

50-50: Two of the incorrect choices are immediately eliminated.

Lifeline: The contestant can ask any one person the question that is being posed to them. Of course, a contestant is free to take or disregard this advice. On the show, the contestant has a telephone and is free to call anyone in the world. You may choose to restrict the lifeline option to the classroom. We also experimented with allowing contestants 30 seconds to find anyone nearby to ask.

The Rounds

Round 1: Open to all students. Each contestant has a turn in which he or she is asked five questions. Those who answer all five questions correctly go on to the second round.

Round 2: Same as Round 1, except each contestant is faced with three questions instead of five. Those who answer all three correctly proceed to Round 3.

Round 3: A spelling-bee-style "sudden death" round, in which a wrong answer eliminates you, provided someone else answers that round correctly. (I have a round like this only for those classes that require a "winner." To my surprise, this was not always the case.) Since our school does not possess the means of rewarding contestants in a manner comparable to that of game shows, we managed with extra credit points.

References

Bakhtin, M. (1981). *The dialogic imagination*. (M. Holquist, Ed., & C. Emerson, Trans.). Austin, TX: University of Texas Press, Austin.

Bakhtin, M. (1984). *Problems of Dostoevsky's poetics*. (C. Emerson, Ed. & Trans.). Minneapolis, MN: University of Minnesota Press.

Emerson, C. (1997). *The first hundred years of Mikhail Bakhtin*. Princeton, NJ: Princeton University Press.

Freire, P. (1990). *Pedagogy of the oppressed*. New York: Continuum.

Hirschkop, K. (1999). *Mikhail Bakhtin: An aesthetic for democracy*. Oxford, UK: Oxford University Press.

Index

Adventures of Huckleberry Finn, The, 37, 166
Aesthetics, 108–109, 110–111
Age of Innocence, 9, 10
Albers, Randall, 96
Allen, Janet, 35
Assessment,
    authentic, 208
    formative, 54–55
    portfolio, 240
    summative, 55–56
    writing, 95, 239–240
Atwell, Nancie, 32, 121
Auden, W. H., 136
Austen, Jane, 17

Bakhtin, Mikhail, 252–254
Ballenger, Bruce, 230
Baxter, Charles, 46
Bean Trees, The, 51–57
Beat movement, 150, 166, 199
Bloom, Benjamin, 146, 148
Book clubs, 38
Books,
    audio, 33, 34, 35–36
    covers of, 1–12
    selecting, 39–40
Boredom, avoiding, 33
Britton, James, 197–198
Brooks, David, 46
Brooks, Gwendolyn, 108–110
Brooks, Terry, 101
Brown, Hazel, 100

Call It Courage, 15
Call of the Wild, The, 39
Cambourne, Brian, 100
Civil Rights Movement, 213–223
Classroom
    arrangement of space in, 225–237
    democracy in, 251–261

Collard, Sneed, 38
Comparison-and-contrast activity, 214
Conrad, Joseph, 9, 10–11
Coover, Robert, 45
Course management systems, 241–243
Cruz, Victor Hernandez, 113
Cultural issues, 12, 110, 121, 124

Daniels, Harvey, 37
Deduction, 6–7
Drama, 197–202

Elbow, Peter, 230, 239
Electronic homework manager, 245
Elkins, Marilyn, 124
English as a Second Language, 3

Fences, 122, 123, 124, 125
Films and documentaries, 215
Finkel, Donald, 226, 230
Fitzgerald, F. Scott, 145, 146
Flash fiction, 45–49
Forced-choice activity, 214
Frankenstein, 21
Freedom's Children, 213–223
Freire, Paolo, 253
French, Larry, 47, 48
Frontloading, 21
Frost, Robert, 186

Gardner, Howard, 146–147, 147–148
Gonzales, Kyle, 35
Grading, 119–120, 201–202
Graves, Donald, 39, 96
Great Gatsby, The, 4. 145–156

Hamlet, 59–72
Harper, Michael, 108, 109, 110
Hatchet, 100
Hazuka, Tom, 45
Heart of Darkness, 9, 10–11

Henry V, 83–93
Hugo, Victor, 37

Interviewing, 215–216

Jackson, Shirley, 136
Journals, 52–55

Kaywell, Joan E., 124
King, Martin Luther, 93, 214, 217, 218
Kingsolver, Barbara, 51, 55

Lane, Barry, 97, 99, 102
Lee, Harper, 15
Les Miserables, 37
Letter From a Birmingham Jail, 93
Levine, Ellen, 213
Literacy,
  definitions of, 108
  gaps, 111
Literary analysis, 131–141
Literature
  circles, 37–38
  partners, 37
London, Jack, 39
Lourie, Dick, 74

Macbeth, 15, 16
McPherson, Sandra, 112–113
Modeling, 38–39
Moyers, Bill, 113
Murray, Donald, 95, 97
Museum project, 163–176

National Writing Project, 239
Native Son, 1–2, 3, 7
Nonfiction, 213–223

O'Connor, Philip F., 45
Opinionnaires, 19–20, 27

Paulsen, Gary, 100, 101
Piano Lesson, The, 122, 123, 124, 125
Pigs in Heaven, 55
Poe, Edgar Allan, 48, 199

Poetry, 73–81, 102–104, 107–120, 197–202, 205–211, 230
Portfolios, 185–196, 240–243, 248–250
PowerPoint presentation, 205–211
Prereading strategies, 15–27
  importance of, 16
  journals, 52–53
  two kinds of, 17–19
Prewriting, 228–230
Pride and Prejudice, 17
Prior knowledge, 17
Prown, Jules, 5–7

Randall, Dudley, 216
Randle, Kristen D., 38
Read-alouds, 33, 34
Reading,
  resistance to, 185–186
  strategies, 31–40
  tests, 35
Reflection, 194
Reports, 61
Rhetoric, Aristotelian, 83–84
Rico, Gabriele Lusser, 73
Rief, Linda, 34
Rocha, Mark William, 124
Roll of Thunder, Hear My Cry, 99
Romano, Tom, 99
Romeo and Juliet, 19, 39
Rubrics, 63–64, 117–119, 188–189

Scenarios, 21
  courage, 24
  science and nature, 22–24
Self-censorship, by teachers, 125
Shakespeare, William, 37, 39, 59, 83, 84, 93, 156–160
Shannon, Sandra, 124
Shapard, Robert, 45
Shaughnessy, Mina, 47, 48
Small-group work, 19, 234
Smith, Frank, 97
Sperry, Armstrong, 15
Stations, 227–237
Stevick, Philip, 46

Sustained silent reading, 32–34
Sword of Shannara, 101

Talk shows, 55–56, 222–223
Tannen, Deborah, 140
Taylor, Mildred, 99
Tchudi, Susan, 230
Tchudi, Stephen, 230
Teachers,
   critiquing, 254
   students as, 254–255
Team teaching, 205–211
Technology, 239–250
Television show, class project modeled
   on, 177–183
Thomas, Denise, 45
Thomas, James, 45
To Kill a Mockingbird, 15, 16, 19
Twain, Mark, 37
Twice-Told Tales, 48

Wharton, Edith, 9, 10
Williams, Carol Lynch, 38
Williams, William Carlos, 19
Wilson, August, 121–128
Word processing systems, 243–244
Wright, Richard, 1
Writing; see also Journals; Poetry
   autobiographical, 17–19, 25–27
   letters, 101–102
   multigenre research papers, 99–100
   reading as a model for, 100–101
   revision of, 231–233, 246–248
   tributes, 98–99
   voice in, 95–105
Wuthering Heights, 8–9

Author Biographies

Editors

Patricia M. Gantt has taught middle school and high school for more than 20 years and has served as K–12 Language Arts/Social Studies coordinator in North Carolina. She is presently an associate professor in Utah State University's English Department, Logan, Utah, and co-director of the Women and Gender Studies Program. Dr. Gantt teaches English Education, American literature, and Women's Studies courses, and is chair of the English Education program. In addition to supervising student teachers, she continues her work with secondary teachers as an Advanced Placement literature trainer and table leader and as a writing consultant for the SAT II. Dr. Gantt has won numerous awards for high school and university teaching, including Star Teacher, NC Region 8 Teacher of the Year, First Union Teacher of the Year, Red Lobster Teacher of the Year, the Doris Betts Award for Teaching Composition, multiple Mortar Board Professor Awards, and the Utah State University President's Diversity Award. She is a nominee for Carnigie Professor of the Year.

Lynn Langer Meeks taught high school in Stoughton, Massachusetts, and Scottsdale, Arizona, for 15 years before joining the faculty at Utah State University. She was also the English Language Arts coordinator for the State of Idaho Department of Education. Currently Dr. Meeks is a professor of English and director of the Writing Program at Utah State University, Logan, Utah. In addition to mentoring first-year graduate instructors, she teaches English Education courses to preservice and inservice teachers. She recently co-authored *Literacy in the Secondary English Classroom: Teaching the Way Kids Learn* (Allyn Bacon Longman, 2003) with Carol Austin, the English Department chair at Mountain Crest High School, Hyrum, Utah. She has won the Utah State University English Department Mentor of the Year Award for 3 years beginning in 2000 and was a finalist for the Utah State University Mentor of the Year Award in 2001.

Contributors

Carol F. Bender was a teacher of grades 7–12 in Davenport, Iowa, and Midland, Michigan for 7 years. She is currently a professor of English at Alma College, Alma, Michigan, where she teaches Modern American Literature, English Education, and Composition. Dr. Bender has won several awards for teaching, including the Sears-Roebuck Foundation Award for Teaching Excellence and Campus Leadership, the American Association for Higher Education Outstanding Teacher Award, the Barlow Award, and the Lee Posey Award.

Agnes A. Cardoni is a member of the English Department of Wilkes University in Wilkes-Barre, Pennsylvania. Before she joined the Wilkes University English Department in 2002, Dr. Cardoni was a public school teacher for 33 years. She taught college preparatory and Advanced Placement courses in high school, as well as English methods and literature courses at the college level. In addition, Dr. Cardoni has been a university associate in rhetoric at the University of Illinois at Urbana-Champaign. She received fellowships and scholarships from Lehigh University, Bethlehem, Pennsylvania, for her doctoral work. She also received the Johanna Mertz Award from Delta Kappa Gamma for her research on the papers of Margaret Atwood. A former member of Phi Delta Kappa, Dr. Cardoni was also awarded the Alumni Achievement Award from her undergraduate alma mater, College Misericordia, Dallas, Pennsylvania.

Danette DiMarco is an associate professor of English at Slippery Rock University of Pennsylvania. She teaches basic and advanced courses in composition and literature, including World and Latino Literature. Dr. DiMarco has published articles on literature in *Mosaic* and *Willa* and has a forthcoming collaborative article on new media in the anthology *Eloquent Images* (MIT Press). Her conference work includes presentations at National Council of Teachers of English and Modern Language Association. She is a past recipient of the Slippery Rock University President's Award for Excellence in Teaching.

Ginny Dochety, a keyboarding applications teacher at West Greene High School, Mosheim, Tennessee, collaborated with author Annette McGrew to guide their students in creating successful PowerPoint presentations for "Powerful Poetry: Team Teaching Across the Disciplines." Ms. Dochety has taught in Mississippi, Michigan, Florida, Texas, Tennessee, and California.

Heidi Estrem has been a reading and writing volunteer for almost 2 years in an alternative school for pregnant teenagers and has spent extensive time in high school classrooms as a mentor, a volunteer, or a participant-observer. As part of her research agenda, Dr. Estrem spent a semester in a classroom for recently paroled teenagers. Currently, Dr. Estrem is an assistant professor of English at Eastern Michigan University, Ypsilanti, Michigan. She teaches a wide range of courses, from first-year writing to upper-level courses for future teachers, and she also assists in administering the first-year writing program. Dr. Estrem won the Outstanding Teaching Assistant Award and the Scott Douglas Excellence in Teaching Award at the University of Nevada, Reno, in 1999.

Lynda Hamblin is currently in her 13th year at Preston Junior High School in Preston, Idaho, where she teaches seventh- and eighth-grade English. Ms. Hamblin received her master's degree in Theory and Practice of Writing from Utah State University in 1999. She was awarded the Paul and Kate Farmer Award for Outstanding Article in *The English Journal* for 2000. Because of Ms. Hamblin's excellent classroom teaching, she has been selected to serve as a coordinator and facilitator for the Utah Writing Project for the past 8 years. For the past 3 years, she has taught a memoir writing class for teachers in her school district.

Jeff House, a teacher of 24 years, is currently employed at Presentation High School in San Jose, California. He teaches AP World Literature, newspaper, and composition courses. The recipient of several National Endowment for the Humanities grants, he has garnered many teaching awards, including the Dorothy M. Wright Award for Excellence in Teaching, and he has been twice been presented with awards for excellence in teaching by his students. An AP reader, Mr. House lectures for the College Board and has addressed state and national National Council of Teachers of English conventions. He has published in *English Journal* and recently produced a CD-ROM and book (Christopher-Gordon Publishers, in press) on composition entitled *Writing Is Dialogue: A Conceptual Approach*.

Christine A. Hult was a high school teacher for 3 years before returning to graduate school at the University of Michigan, where she received her Ph.D. in English and education. Currently, Dr. Hult is professor of English and associate department head at Utah State University, Logan, Utah. Her research interests include computers in writing as well as program and teacher evaluation, as reflected in recent publications, including the second edition of *The New Century Handbook* (with Tom Huckin, Longman, 2002) and *Evaluating Teachers of Writing* (NCTE, 1994). Her teaching awards include the 2002 Innovative Excellence in Teaching, Learning and Technology from Utah State University and the 13th International Conference on College Teaching and Learning, 2002. She has also been selected as Outstanding Faculty Member, Utah State University for 2000 and Humanist of the Year, Department of English, in 1999.

Annette McGrew is presently an English teacher at West Greene High School in Mosheim, Tennessee. She has been named Star teacher, an award given by the West Greene High School valedictorian to his or her most influential teacher, and she has been included in *Who's Who Among America's Teachers*. Ms. McGrew collaborated with Ginny Dochety, a keyboarding applications teacher at West Greene High School, to develop the strategies described in their chapter.

Brett C. McInelly is an assistant professor of English at Brigham Young University, Provo, Utah, where he teaches composition and literature courses. As a graduate student, Dr. McInelly led weekly instructors' meetings for less experienced teachers, observed their classroom teaching, and provided a formal review of their teaching. As an M.A. student at BYU, Dr. McInelly was selected from among 70 teachers as one of five finalists for the Edward M. and Minnie Berry Rowe Teaching Award, which recognizes teaching excellence in first-year composition courses taught by graduate instructors.  Dr. McInelly was also recognized for his outstanding teaching at the University of Cincinnati, where he earned his Ph. D. As a course coordinator for first-year composition, Dr. McInelly devotes considerable time to teacher training and development.

 **Scott Minar** has assisted in the preparation of hundreds of high school and middle school teachers in the United States and Canada for 20 years. Currently, Dr. Minar is an assistant professor of English and the coordinator of tutoring activities for Ohio University, Lancaster. His teaching awards include Phi Eta Sigma Honor Society's Outstanding Teacher Award, the Josef Stein Award, and the Faculty Appreciation Award from the Elmira College Student Association. He has taught at universities in the United States and Canada and has also won a number of awards for his poetry. Dr. Minar teaches courses in composition, creative writing, and literature. Dr. Minar continues to present creative writing workshops and practicums to a wide variety of students, from teenagers to the retired.

Kimberly R. Myers taught grades 9–12 for 6 years and has taught college-level courses for English education majors for 5^1/$_2$ years. Currently Dr. Myers is an associate professor of English at Montana State University, Bozeman, Montana, where she teaches 19th- and 20th-century British literature, Irish literature, pedagogy, and specialty courses that she designs, including a course called Literature and Medicine. Dr. Myers has won several awards for university teaching, including the 2002 President's Award for Excellence in Teaching, four MSU Alumni Association/ Bozeman Chamber of Commerce Awards for Excellence, and Teacher of the Year from the Montana Alpha Chapter of Pi Beta Phi.  A member of Phi Kappa Phi, Dr. Myers was also awarded the honorary title of Teaching Improvement Fellow for MSU. She won the Earl Hartsell Award for Excellence in Teaching Composition at the University of North Carolina at Chapel Hill. Dr. Meyers was recently named the Distinguished Educator for 2002–2003 by the Montana Association of Teachers of English Language Arts.

Darren Perkes is in his fourth year at Sky View High School, Smithfield, Utah, where he teaches AP English, concurrent enrollment first-year English, and first-year literature for Utah State University. Mr. Perkes also taught eighth- and ninth-grade English and French at Box Elder Middle School, Utah. Mr. Perkes is the acting president for the school's on-site committee, the Multicultural Club advisor, and the school's literary journal advisor. He was awarded Sky View High School's Teachers Making a Difference award, nominated for Student Teacher of the Year, and was a recipient of the Terrel H. Bell Scholarship.

Terri Rodriguez is in her seventh year of teaching English at the secondary level. She currently lives in Puerto Rico with her husband and three children, where she is studying Spanish Language and Literature at the University of Puerto Rico in Myaguez. Ms. Rodriguez has taught secondary English, English as a Second Language, and Spanish in both public and private schools in the United States. She holds a B.A. in English from the University of Maryland, European Division, and an M.Ed. in secondary English education from Columbus State University in Columbus, Georgia. She was recognized as an outstanding educator and has provided professional development training to fellow teachers. In the fall of 2000, Ms. Rodriguez won the "Ideas From Our Teachers" contest sponsored by A&E Television Networks.

Johnathan Segol is currently a teacher at Ithaca High School, New York. He has taught English at various schools in Brooklyn, Queens, and Manhattan. In Brooklyn he was nominated for Disney's national award for innovative teaching. He is now running the In-School Suspension program in Ithaca.

Author Biographies

Lu Ann Brobst Staheli has 24 years experience teaching English in grades 7–12: 5 years in Rockville, Indiana, and most recently at Payson Junior High School in Payson, Utah. She has also supervised student teachers and was recognized as a master teacher by Payson Junior High School. Ms. Staheli was selected as the Utah English Language Arts Teacher of the Year for 2000 and Utah Christa McAuliffe Fellow for her project *Contemporary Adolescent Literature: A Teacher and Parent Guide*. In 2001 she won the Utah Arts Council Original Writing Competition for the Juvenile Novel division for her young adult book, *Just like Elizabeth Taylor*. Staheli is a former President of the League of Utah Writers and currently serves as the President of the Utah Council of Teachers of English/Language Arts and chair of the English Department at Payson Junior High School.

Paul Stein is in his 28th year of teaching at the grade 7–12 level. Since becoming an administrator 5 years ago, he has continued to teach two courses every year. Mr. Stein is the director of studies at St. Gregory School in Tucson, Arizona, where he supervises faculty development through inservice education and oversees the mentoring program for new teachers. Mr. Stein has received grants for independent and group study from the Council for Basic Education, Summer Seminar and Summer Institute grants from the National Endowment for the Humanities, and wrote and directed a grant program for the public funded by the Arizona Humanities Council. In the spring of 2002, he was an American Schoolteachers Fellow at the University of St. Andrews, Scotland.

Elizabeth Teare taught for 10 years in grades 7–12, 9 at Westlake School for Girls and Harvard-Westlake in Los Angeles. During 2002–2003 she taught at the Latin School in Chicago while on leave from the University of Dayton, Dayton, Ohio, where she is currently an assistant professor of English. Dr. Teare teaches British and children's literature. She has received a summer Klingenstein Fellowship from Columbia Teachers College and a Bing Faculty Recognition Award from the Westlake School for Girls in Los Angeles.

Dr. Teare would like to thank the University of Dayton students who enthusiastically tell her what they think of lesson plans, good and bad. She sends a special thanks to the students in English 302 (Survey of Later English Literature) who allowed her to quote from their responses: Patrick Carr, Katie Martens, Carrie Miller, Michael Rasey, and Jill Triplett.

Trysh Travis is a former high school teacher, having taught for 4 years at Trinity School in New York City. She is now an assistant professor of English at Southern Methodist University in Dallas, Texas. Her research in 20th-century American literary and book history has appeared in the *Journal of Modern Literature, American Literature History*, and the *Chronicle of Higher Education*. Her teaching awards include a National Endowment for the Humanities Summer Seminar for School Teachers, the Yale University Teaching Fellowship prize, and SMU's Golden Mustang Award for Outstanding Junior Faculty.

Brian White taught English in grades 7–12 before completing his Ph.D. in Curriculum and Instruction at the University of Wisconsin–Madison. His classroom experience includes grade levels 9–12, over a 4-year period. Recently he spent a good portion of his sabbatical from Grand Valley State University, Allendale, Michigan, as a full-time teacher of grades 10 and 11. In his usual position he teaches preservice teacher preparation courses and graduate courses for secondary school English teachers in addition to supervising student teachers. Dr. White has published in *Middle School Journal, English Education*, the *Journal of Educational Research*, the *National Association of Secondary School Principals Bulletin*, and  *Clearing House*. His interests include democratic role models for teachers of English, the role of friendship in teaching, and strategies for helping students to view literary characters as people. Dr. White received the Grand Valley State University's Outstanding Educator Award in 1998.

Albert E. Wilhelm is a professor of English at Tennessee Technological University, Cookeville, Tennessee, where he received the Outstanding Faculty Award for Teaching. Dr. Wilhelm has been a Senior Fulbright Lecturer in American Literature on two occasions: once at Marie Curie-Sklodowska University in Lublin, Poland, and most recently at Seoul National University, Seoul, Korea. He has also received fellowships from the National Endowment for the Humanities for research at Yale and Columbia Universities. Earlier in his career, Dr. Wilhelm taught at Morehouse College and Duke University. Dr. Wilhelm currently serves as a consultant with the Educational Testing Service for the Graduate Management Admissions Test, the SAT II Writing Test, the Test of Written English, and the Advanced Placement Examination in English. He reviews texts for Prentice-Hall and Simon and Schuster, in addition to reviewing books for *Publishers Weekly*, *Library Journal* and *American Reference Books Annual*. He received his Ph.D. and M.A. in English from the University of North Carolina, Chapel Hill.

Rebecca Woosley taught high school language arts in grades 9–12 for 15 years and part time for 7 years. Currently Ms. Woosley is the writing consultant for Scott County High School in Georgetown, Kentucky, where she advises all teachers—but especially new teachers—on ways to include reading and writing strategies in their classrooms. As the grade 12 regional writing coordinator for the Central Kentucky region, she also serves on the State Writing Advisory Committee. Ms. Woosley received the Air Force Association's Chapter Teacher of the Year Award in 1999 for excellence in education, in the spirit of Christa McAuliffe and in recognition of sustained, outstanding performance as an educator. She describes her daughter, Kimberly Woosley, as "the wind beneath my wings" for encouraging Ms. Woosley to submit a chapter for this collection.

```
LB 1631 .T42 2004

Teaching Ideas for 7-12
   English Language Arts : b
```

CALLAHAN LIBRARY
ST. JOSEPH'S COLLEGE
25 Audubon Avenue
Patchogue, NY 11772-2327